Transfer Pricing Developments Around the World 2024

Transfer Pricing Developments Around the World 2024

Edited by

Michael Lang
Raffaele Petruzzi

Wolters Kluwer

Published by:
Kluwer Law International B.V.
PO Box 316
2400 AH Alphen aan den Rijn
The Netherlands
E-mail: lrs-sales@wolterskluwer.com
Website: www.wolterskluwer.com/en/solutions/kluwerlawinternational

Sold and distributed by:
Wolters Kluwer Legal & Regulatory U.S.
920 Links Avenue
Landisville, PA 17538
United States of America
E-mail: customer.service@wolterskluwer.com

ISBN 978-94-035-2628-7

e-Book: ISBN 978-94-035-2638-6
web-PDF: ISBN 978-94-035-2648-5

Printed in the Netherlands.

Editors

Prof. Dr DDr hc Michael Lang is head of the Institute for Austrian and International Tax Law of WU (Vienna University of Economics and Business) and Academic Director of both the LLM Programme in International Tax Law and the doctoral programme in International Business Taxation (DIBT) of this university. He is president of the Austrian Branch of the International Fiscal Association (IFA). He has been a visiting professor at Georgetown University, New York University, Sorbonne, Bocconi, Peking University (PKU), University of New South Wales (Sydney) and other universities.

Dr Raffaele Petruzzi, LLM, is the Managing Director of the WU Transfer Pricing Center at the Institute for Austrian and International Tax Law at WU (Vienna University of Economics and Business), the Founder and CEO of PETRUZZI Advisory, and an independent advisor on international tax and transfer pricing matters. He is also a member of the United Nations Subcommittee on Transfer Pricing.

Raffaele gained extensive experience by working for many years within big four firms, international law firms, and in-house positions. He is a frequent speaker in international conferences and lecturer of numerous courses all over the world, as well as author of many publications. Among others, he is an editor of Linde Transfer Pricing International Journal and a member of the International Fiscal Association (IFA) and Transfer Pricing Economists for Development (TPED). Raffaele holds a PhD in International Business Taxation from WU, an LLM in International Tax Law from WU, and an MSc in Business Administration and Law from Bocconi University.

Assistant Editors

Bence Péter Komár holds a Master's in business law from the Vienna University of Economics and Business (WU). He is a teaching and research associate at the Institute for Austrian and International Tax Law and is pursuing his doctoral studies in business law. Before joining the Institute, he was employed in the tax practice group of an international law firm. Bence Péter contributed to Chapter 1 of this book.

Abhishek Padwalkar is a research and teaching associate at the WU Transfer Pricing Center at the Institute for Austrian and International Tax Law at WU (Vienna University of Economics and Business, Austria). He has worked as a tax counsel in Mumbai (India), where he advised clients on matters related to international tax, transfer pricing, arbitration, and company and constitutional law. He has also litigated before various fora, including the Bombay High Court and the Income Tax Appellate Tribunal. Abhishek holds an advanced LLM in International Tax Law from the University of Amsterdam (IBFD), the Netherlands, and another LLM in Constitutional and Administrative Law from the University of Mumbai, India. Abhishek is also a Doctoral Candidate in Business Law at the WU (Vienna University of Economics and Business, Austria). Abhishek contributed to Chapter 1 of this book.

Contributors

Mukesh Butani is the founder and managing partner of BMR Legal Advocates, a Tier 1 law firm. He served as co-founder and chairman of BMR Advisors, among India's leading professional services firms in the areas of Tax, Risk & M&A, which was featured in the Harvard Business Review case study, BMR Advisors – 'Competitive on Quality'. Additionally, Mukesh held leadership positions in two of the Big 4 firms. With specialization in corporate international tax and transfer pricing, he has experience in advising multinationals and Indian conglomerates on a range of matters concerning business reorganizations, cross-border structuring, and tax controversy. He is an acknowledged expert in the area of international tax policy, controversy, and advocacy and has to his credit several landmark judicial pronouncements and depositions before expert committees. He is an expert in issuing opinions, witness statements, examinations, and cross-examinations before appellate/arbitration forums. He has also been deposed as an expert witness on contentious cross-border tax treaties and TP matters in foreign jurisdictions.

Mukesh served as vice-chair of the ICC Paris Tax Commission and as a member of the Permanent Scientific Committee of the International Fiscal Association and OECD BIAC. Mukesh engages with Indian Government agencies and thinktanks, NITI Aayog, Prime Minister's Economic Advisory Council & Invest India on public policy aspects. As a fellow chartered accountant, he holds a double Bachelor's in Accounting and Financial Management and a degree in Law, practising before Indian tribunals and courts. He serves as an independent board member in leading Indian and multinational corporations. He is a visiting faculty at the University of Vienna and the University of Lausanne. He shall be defending his thesis on 'Allocation of Taxing Rights' from the University of Lausanne Faculty of Law Justice and Public Administration. He has consistently been featured in the India Business Law Journal's 'A-List' among India's top 100 lawyers and in the FORBES India Legal Power list. He has to his credit several authorships. Mukesh contributed to Chapter 5 of this book.

Stefaan De Baets has been a senior counsel in the transfer pricing team of PwC Belgium since 1 January 2016, where he is responsible for avoiding and settlement of transfer pricing controversy, further developing the transfer pricing market, and promoting the key presence of PwC on that market as well as delivering contributions to the development of transfer pricing policies. From 1 April 2011 to 31 December 2015, he was a transfer pricing advisor at the OECD in Paris, France. Until he joined the OECD, Stefaan worked for the Federal Public Service of Finances in Belgium, mostly on transfer pricing and international tax, for more than twenty years. He was a delegate for Belgium to OECD Working Party 6 (transfer pricing) from March 1996 to March 2011 and to the Joint Transfer Pricing Forum from March 2003 to March 2011.

Stefaan is an arbitrator under the EU Arbitration Convention. He is a guest lecturer on international taxation at the University of Lausanne, Switzerland, the Ecole des Mines (France) and the Catholic University of Leuven, Belgium. He is a regular guest speaker or panellist at international tax events. Stefaan contributed to Chapter 3 of this book.

Prof. Dr Xaver Ditz studied Economics in Mannheim and Hamburg (1999 Diplom-Kaufmann, 2003 Dr rer. pol.). He has been a partner with Flick Gocke Schaumburg in Bonn since 2005. Xaver is a professor at Trier University, lectures at the universities of Zurich (LLM programme) and Lausanne (Executive Programs in Transfer Pricing), and at the Federal Financial Academy of the German Finance Ministry. He co-edits a commentary on double tax treaty law and the German Foreign Tax Act, handbooks on transfer pricing and permanent establishment taxation, and journals such as 'Internationale Steuerrundschau' and 'International Transfer Pricing Journal'. Xaver is the president of the German branch of the International Fiscal Association, chairman of the German Institute of Tax Advisors, a board member of TAXAND, and he is also a member of the Foreign Tax Law Committee of the Institute of Public Auditors in Germany. Xaver contributed to Chapter 4 of this book.

Alexandra Jaszczuk is a seasoned expert in the fields of transfer pricing (ca. fifteen years) and artificial intelligence (AI). With a strong background in finance and technology, she brings a unique perspective to the intersection of these two domains. Throughout her career, Aleksandra has demonstrated a deep understanding of transfer pricing regulations and methodologies, helping organizations navigate complex international tax landscapes. Aleksandra is passionate about leveraging AI and advanced analytics to optimize transfer pricing strategies and mitigate risks. Her innovative approaches have led to significant cost savings and improved compliance for multinational corporations. As a thought leader in the industry, Aleksandra frequently shares her insights through publications, speaking engagements, and advisory roles. With a commitment to excellence and continuous learning, Aleksandra is dedicated to pushing the boundaries of transfer pricing practices in the era of AI. She holds a proven track record of driving business success through strategic planning, technology adoption, and interdisciplinary collaboration. Alexandra contributed to Chapter 7 of this book.

Seema Kejriwal has a Master's in Law from Golden Gate University in the United States. She is also a chartered accountant from the Institute of Chartered Accountants of India and a commerce graduate from Mumbai University, India. She has nearly twenty-five years of experience in advising Fortune 500 multinationals on corporate international tax and transfer pricing matters; apart from this, Seema advises clients on tax policy matters. She has co-authored several publications, regularly speaks at global seminars, and contributes to research papers and columns on tax and transfer pricing policy that find mention in leading academic publications such as IBFD, Kluwers, Bloomberg, Tax Notes, etc. Seema contributed to Chapter 5 of this book.

Paolo Ludovici has been a partner of GPBL since 2021 following the merger with L&P - Ludovici Piccone & Partners, a firm he founded in 2014. Previously, he worked for twenty-three years at Maisto e Associati since its establishment, becoming a partner in 2000. He advises on all areas of tax law. His expertise includes domestic and international corporate reorganizations, M&A and structured finance transactions, and tax planning for high net-worth individuals and trusts. He often acts as an expert in criminal and tax proceedings. Since 2021, he has been awarded 'Tax Star Status' by Chambers & Partners Europe with the support of overwhelming praise from clients. He is a recognized 'Leading Individual' by Legal500 EMEA and recommended 'Band 1' in Chambers HNW Guide and has furthermore been identified among the leading experts by Who's Who Legal in Private Client and Corporate Tax practice. He has been awarded 'Professional of the Year' at Legalcommunity Tax Awards 2023, 2022, 2020, and 2019, the prize 'Professional of the Year Tax Consultancy' at TopLegal Awards 2021, and 'Professional of the Year International Tax' at the TopLegal Awards 2022. He regularly writes for leading Italian financial newspapers as well as for other major tax reviews and magazines. He regularly speaks at tax conferences and lectures in post-graduate specialization courses. He has recently been appointed vice president of the Tax & Legal & Compliance Commission in AIPB (Italian Private Banking Association), and he is a member of the Tax and Legal Commission in AIFI (Italian Private Equity and Venture Capital Association). He is a member of the STEP Society of Trust and Estate Practitioners at Bocconi University. He was admitted to the Italian Chartered Accountant Association in Milan. Paolo contributed to Chapter 6 of this book.

Kirsty Rockall leads the Transfer Pricing team in the United Kingdom. She joined Grant Thornton after almost twenty-two years with KPMG, where she was a partner in their Global Transfer Pricing Practice. Two of those years were spent on secondment to Canada. She brings to the team her significant experience in designing and implementing transfer pricing policies for businesses as they grow, expand, develop, and maintain their operations and international presence. Kirsty routinely works on projects that involve implementing transfer pricing strategies that take into consideration the number of stakeholders affected (tax authorities, investors, boards, etc.). As such, she understands how to develop practical solutions that mitigate the risk of transfer pricing adjustments/ challenges. Kirsty contributed to Chapter 2 of this book.

Niklas Schwemin is a partner at Greenfield Steuerberatungsgesellschaft and is responsible for the transfer pricing services. He is a German-certified tax advisor and has multiple years of experience in in-house tax positions and in the consulting business. In his current role, he focuses on solutions to simplify operational tasks of transfer pricing professionals and to improve transfer pricing compliance. Niklas contributed to Chapter 7 of this book.

Luca Tortorella has been working at Gatti Pavesi Bianchi Ludovici (GPBL) in Milan since 2021. He has fifteen years of experience in the transfer pricing and international tax arena. He gained significant experience with major multinational entities, both domestic and foreign investors, in cross-border business restructurings and negotiation of APAs, patent box, and rulings with the tax authorities. He also regularly assists multinationals in international procedures aimed at eliminating double taxation and in complex tax dispute resolutions through settlements and tax litigations in front of the tax courts. He is the author of various articles on transfer pricing matters in leading Italian financial newspapers and tax magazines. He is also a speaker at national and international conferences.

Before joining GPBL, he worked in the Italian transfer pricing team at EY for eight years, where he became senior manager in 2019, commuting between London and Milan. He also worked for two years as a tax and transfer pricing manager in the London office of GlaxoSmithKline and began his career with PwC Tax and Legal Service.

He graduated in Business Administration, and he was admitted to the Italian Association of Chartered Accountants. Luca contributed to Chapter 6 of this book.

Brendan Van Kets: Brendan Van Kets has been an associate in the transfer pricing team of PwC Belgium since 1 June 2022 where he focuses on value chain transformation and economic value creation. He holds a Master's in Law from KU Leuven University (2018-2020) and an LLM in Asian Economic Integration and Law from Waseda University in Tokyo in March 2022. Next to transfer pricing, Brendan's research is primarily dedicated to comparative law research of estate planning with a specific focus on trusts and foundations. He contributed to Chapter 3 of this book.

Isabel Verlinden is a Corporate Strategy Partner helping the world's most successful and admired companies navigate through the current plethora of (draft) rules destined to transform the international tax architecture. As a strategic priority, building and maintaining resilient value chains encompasses a fiscal dimension that is rooted in a deep technical approach to transfer pricing, which Isabel has at her fingertips thanks to over thirty years of mileage within PwC (in Brussels and Washington DC). It is of paramount importance to ensure that tax policy initiatives that are often inspired by political and (social) media sentiment are turned into actionable priorities to marry value chain and corporate tax sustainability. Pivotal in Isabel's work is clients' unfettered access to a global market without being overly hampered by an avalanche of derogating domestic interpretations and codifications.

Isabel is an arbitrator under the EU Arbitration Convention. She holds a Master's in Applied Economics, Financial Economics, and Commercial and Financial Sciences. Isabel is an active writer for international tax and business periodicals. She has co-authored over 125 articles and books to date. She teaches at various academic institutions, is an active IFA Member and is also a regular speaker at conferences and seminars. She is listed in Euromoney's 'Best of the Best Transfer Pricing Advisors'. Isabel contributed to Chapter 3 of this book.

Summary of Contents

Preface

Transfer pricing is currently one of the most relevant and challenging topics in the international tax environment. It is under constant development around the globe, and the year 2023 was certainly no different in this regard. The intense work of international organizations has provided new guidance on transfer pricing topics with several projects, while the world around transfer pricing did not cease to be challenging on many different levels.

One of the notable areas of progress included advancements in implementing the OECD/G20 Inclusive Framework on BEPS, particularly through the continued work on Pillar One's Amount B, which aims to simplify transfer pricing rules for baseline marketing and distribution activities. Additionally, the United Nations, through its Sub-Committee on Transfer Pricing, has produced detailed reports addressing the implications of recent global events, such as the COVID-19 pandemic, on transfer pricing practices. These reports cover a wide range of topics, from green certificates to pricing special commodities, and reflect a holistic approach to the economic consequences of the pandemic and environmental considerations in transfer pricing. Concurrently, the European Union has actively worked towards new directives on transfer pricing and BEFIT, which suggests a growing alignment within the Union to standardize and perhaps tighten the transfer pricing norms in response to global trends.

The above guidance and reports aim to complement the guidelines that have come into force as part of the legislative changes in several countries. The work of international organizations and the European Union also provided further clarity and support to tax administrations and multinational enterprises to help them understand the evolution of transfer pricing provisions at the local and global levels. The proposals of the OECD, the UN, and the EU will significantly affect the future comprehension of the international transfer pricing environment. Consequently, an in-depth understanding of the proposed concepts and their implications for multinationals, governments, advisors, and academia is crucial.

The WU Transfer Pricing Center at the Institute for Austrian and International Tax Law has conducted research projects to analyse the transfer pricing topics mentioned above and their global impacts. The current research is based on seven topic-based papers that have been drafted by international experts on transfer pricing. The results of this work were presented and discussed at the yearly 'Global Transfer Pricing Conference: Transfer Pricing Developments around the World' in February 2024, organized by the Transfer Pricing Center at WU Vienna University of Economics and Business. This book is aimed at academics and practitioners, including the business community and advisory firms, international organizations, and government officials who are tax and transfer pricing experts, as well as CEOs and CFOs who are interested in this topic. It provides a detailed analysis of the topics described above as well as the global impacts and suggestions for future solutions to any issues that are raised.

The first chapter on Global Transfer Pricing Developments provides not only a general overview of the Transfer Pricing World in 2023, covering the work of international organizations such as the OECD, the UN, and the EU, but also critically analyses developments at a country level. As in previous years, it elucidates the most important cases and legislative changes in the transfer pricing world.

The second chapter presents a comprehensive analysis of the current Amount B framework, exploring the significant challenges that multinationals and tax administrations face in its practical adoption. The third and fourth chapters dive into the two directive proposals by the European Union – BEFIT and Transfer Pricing. BEFIT aims to establish a unified corporate tax rulebook for the EU, introducing crucial components such as a common tax base and profit allocation among Member States based on a formula. This cross-border application could significantly alter the existing transfer pricing framework and may require a new system for companies with cross-border activities within the EU. Meanwhile, the Transfer Pricing Directive seeks to harmonize transfer pricing legislation across the EU. The fifth chapter evaluates the attribution of profits to new-age permanent establishments arising out of remote work, digital gaming, artificial intelligence, metaverse, etc. The sixth chapter deals with the ESG considerations and how the transition towards more sustainable business practices affects the transfer pricing analysis within a multinational. Finally, the seventh chapter focuses on adopting new technologies in managing and implementing transfer pricing solutions that could benefit both multinationals and governments.

The editors would like to express their sincere thanks to the authors who made it possible to provide this ambitious work. Many thanks are forwarded to Kluwer Law International for supporting and cooperating with this publication project. Last, but not least, the editors would like to thank Abhishek Padwalkar and Bence Péter Komár for their precious support and Jenny Hill for providing linguistic support to the authors during the publishing process.

Prof. Dr DDr hc Michael Lang
Dr Raffaele Petruzzi, LLM

CHAPTER 1

Global Transfer Pricing Developments

Abhishek Padwalkar & Bence Péter Komár

1 INTRODUCTION

In the trajectory of the past years, transfer pricing (TP) developments maintained their prominence throughout 2023 and shared prominence with the widely discussed Pillar Two initiatives. Despite not immediately apparent, the TP issues identified during the year align with ongoing trends rather than representing a groundbreaking shift.

At the level of the Organisation for Economic Co-operation and Development (OECD), the Pillar One project progressed significantly, especially in working groups handling Amounts A and B. While the outcomes for the former may be deemed complex and controversial and potentially achieve finality with the release of the Multilateral Convention (MLC), ongoing work on the latter by the OECD's Working Party 6 (WP6) grapples with finding a balance between accuracy and simplicity. The public consultation that garnered over seventy responses from stakeholders depicts the complexity that is involved in this ongoing endeavour. The (almost) final version of the document was published in February 2024; thus, it remains uncertain how countries will respond to and adopt this new framework.

The European Union (EU) also continued to initiate measures for ensuring tax transparency, harmonization, and simplification among its Member States. On 12 September 2023, the European Commission adopted a key package of initiatives to reduce tax compliance costs for large, cross-border businesses in the EU. Two proposals are proposed in that package. The first is the Transfer Pricing Directive (TP Directive), which focuses on harmonizing the arm's length principle (ALP) within the EU. It provides a comprehensive definition of the ALP along with normative prescriptions concerning associated enterprises, arm's length range, adjustments, methodologies, comparability analysis, and more. The second is the Business in Europe: Framework for Income Taxation (BEFIT) proposal that outlines details for a common corporate tax system in the EU. Additionally, 2023 also witnessed progress in the cases dealing with TP and state aid. Advocate General Pitrtuzella's Opinion in *Commission v.*

Ireland and Others ('the *Apple* case')[1] was published on 9 November 2023. The Advocate General proposes that the Court of Justice of the European Union (CJEU) set aside the judgment of the General Court of the European Union (GCEU) on 'tax rulings' adopted by Ireland in relation to Apple and refer the case back to it for a new decision on the merits. The CJEU handed down a decision in *Commission v. Luxembourg* ('the *Amazon* case')[2] on 14 December 2023, in which it rejected the European Commission's appeal of the judgment of the GCEU in Amazon's TP dispute.

At the level of the United Nations (UN), the Committee of Experts on International Tax Matters (UN Tax Committee) held sessions in March and October. The Subcommittee on TP prepared and published reports on five of its six workstreams: (a) TP during the COVID-19 economic downturn; (b) TP compliance assurance; (c) TP of carbon offsets and credits; (d) industry/sector guidance for primary products; and (e) industry/sector guidance for the pharmaceutical industry.[3] Furthermore, the UN General Assembly approved a resolution towards the end of 2023 on promoting inclusive and effective tax cooperation.

On a jurisdictional level, a multitude of new rules were embraced to enhance and refine TP frameworks. A particularly notable evolution occurred within the Brazilian legislative landscape, where a comprehensive adoption of TP rules based on the ALP was the primary focus. This marked a pivotal shift in Brazil's approach to regulating intercompany transactions to adhere to its practices more cohesively with international standards. Numerous other countries joined the wave of regulatory adjustments by either implementing or proposing changes to their existing TP rules. This global trend signifies a collective effort to modernize and align TP practices with the evolving dynamics of international business transactions. The common thread among these modifications is their harmonization with the guidance delineated in the OECD Transfer Pricing Guidelines (TPG).

Examining the case law of 2023 reveals a noteworthy shift in the TP disputes landscape. There was a substantial increase in transactions involving intra-group goods and services that signals departing from the emphasis on financial transactions observed in previous years. Courts placed a greater amount of emphasis on the issue of selection and application of TP methods rather than accurately delineating a transaction. The outcomes of these cases offer insights into the trajectory of TP audits and potential areas of focus. Notably, a majority of the cases under scrutiny came from the lower judiciary thereby indicating a surge in newly emerging TP disputes. As assessments during the COVID-19 period are awaited, it is conceivable that the landscape might witness a shift, with tax authorities potentially redirecting their attention from traditional TP cases to those involving business restructuring, intangibles, and intragroup financing.

1. AG Pitruzella 9 November 2023, *Commission v. Ireland and Others*, C-465/20 P.
2. CJEU 14 December 2023, *Commission v. Luxembourg, Amazon.com Inc., and Amazon EU Sàrl*, C-457/21 P.
3. Committee of Experts on International Cooperation in Tax Matters, Twenty-sixth session, New York, 27-30 March 2023, Transfer Pricing, Co-Coordinator's Report, E/C.18/2023/CRP.7, 10 March 2023; Committee of Experts on International Cooperation in Tax Matters, 17-20 October 2023, Transfer Pricing, Co-Coordinator's Report, E/C.18/2023/CRP.26, 2 October 2023.

Within this context, this chapter accentuates a number of the developments in the TP area in 2023. Section 2 of the chapter addresses policy and developments within international organizations. Section 3 provides an overview of the developments at jurisdictional levels, including legislative changes and relevant case laws. Section 4 provides concluding thoughts.

2 RECENT DEVELOPMENTS IN THE WORK OF INTERNATIONAL ORGANIZATIONS

2.1 TP Developments at the OECD

2.1.1 Administrative Guidance on the Global Anti-Base Erosion Model Rules (Pillar Two)

The Global Anti-Base Erosion Model Rules of Pillar Two (GloBE Rules)[4] have fundamentally transformed the way businesses are taxed by introducing a global minimum tax of 15% and the incorporation of tax accounting concepts into tax law for the purposes of considering effective tax rates.[5] Countries are implementing the GloBE Rules into domestic legislation, and the Income Inclusion Rule (IIR) and Undertaxed Payments Rule (UTPR), as well as qualified domestic minimum top-up tax rules (QDMTT), are coming into effect for accounting periods beginning on or after 31 December 2023.[6] The GloBE Rules' complete implementation is intended by 1 January 2025.[7] As far as TP is concerned, they stipulate that transactions between constituent entities must be recorded at the ALP (cf., Article 3.2.3. GloBE Rules).[8] They were approved and released by the Inclusive Framework (IF) on 20 December 2021.[9] Its

4. OECD (2021), *Tax Challenges Arising from the Digitalisation of the Economy: Global Anti-Base Erosion Model Rules (Pillar Two) – Inclusive Framework on BEPS*, OECD Publishing, Paris, https://doi.org/10.1787/782bac33-en (GloBE Rules).
5. T. van den Berg, M. Kriek & Y. Than, *Tax Challenges Arising from the Digitalization of the Economy: The Calculation of the Effective Tax Rate – Pillar Two versus Financial Accounting*, 29 Intl. Transfer Pricing J. 7 (2022), Journal Articles & Opinion Pieces IBFD (accessed 12 March 2024) https://doi.org/10.59403/2xxwtr6.
6. OECD, *Statement on a Two-Pillar Solution to Address the Tax Challenges Arising from the Digitalisation of the Economy* (8 October 2021), https://www.oecd.org/en/about/news/announcements/2021/10/statement-on-a-two-pillar-solution-to-address-the-tax-challenges-arising-from-the-digitalisation-of-the-economy-october-2021.html (accessed 12 March 2024); OECD (2023), *Outcome Statement on the Two-Pillar Solution to Address the Tax Challenges Arising from the Digitalisation of the Economy* (11 July 2023), OECD/G20 Base Erosion and Profit Shifting Project, available at www.oecd.org/tax/beps/outcome-statement-on-the-two-pillar-solution-to-address-the-tax-challenges-arising-from-the-digitalisation-of-the-economy-july-2023.htm (accessed 12 March 2024).
7. F.S. Scandone, L. Scordo & L. Marino, *Pillar One, Pillar Two and BEFIT: The End of an Unexpected Journey?*, 31 Intl. Transfer Pricing J. 1 (2024), Journal Articles & Opinion Pieces IBFD (accessed 12 March 2024) https://doi.org/10.59403/2z2kyr1; cf., s. 3.3.
8. Cf., R. Petruzzi & A. Padwalkar, *Pillar One, Pillar Two, Transfer Pricing and the Arm's Length Principle: A Tangled Web of New and Old Taxing Rules*, 77 Bull. Intl. Taxn. 10 (2023), Journal Articles & Opinion Pieces IBFD (accessed 12 March 2024) https://doi.org/10.59403/1v4xcrm.
9. A.W. Oguttu, *Preventing International Tax Competition and the Race to the Bottom: A Critique of the OECD Pillar Two Model Rules for Taxing the Digital Economy – A Developing Country*

members have agreed, under Article 8.3 of the GloBE Rules, that national jurisdictions will apply them consistent with 'Agreed Administrative Guidance' that is subject to any requirements of domestic law. This guidance is defined in Article 10.1 as being issued by the IF on either 'the interpretation or administration of the GloBE Rules'. Therefore, it will play an important role in promoting legal certainty under those rules. This is achieved by clarifying their interpretation and providing guidance to tax administrations on how to apply them. As 'Agreed Administrative Guidance' will also reflect the IF's common understanding of how the GloBE Rules should be interpreted and applied, it will also be significantly relevant in ensuring coordinated outcomes under the rules and providing a state of equality for multinational enterprise (MNE) groups.[10]

In 2023, the OECD published two administrative guidance documents on the GloBE Rules.[11] Administrative guidance on Tax Challenges Arising from the Digitalisation of the Economy – Administrative Guidance on the Global Anti-Base Erosion Model Rules (Pillar Two) of February 2023[12] focuses on the GloBE Rules' scope of application, income and taxes, their application to insurance companies, transition rules, and the QDMTT.[13] Another administrative guidance was released in July 2023: Tax Challenges Arising from the Digitalisation of the Economy – Administrative Guidance on the Global Anti-Base Erosion Model Rules (Pillar Two). It entails general currency conversion rules for the GloBE Rules, guidance on tax credits, information on substance-based income exclusion, the QDMTT, and safe harbours.[14]

Perspective, 76 Bull. Intl. Taxn. 11 (2022), Journal Articles & Opinion Pieces IBFD (accessed 12 March 2024) https://doi.org/10.59403/zzqmwy; B.J. Arnold, *An Investigation into the Interaction of CFC Rules and the OECD Pillar Two Global Minimum Tax*, 76 Bull. Intl. Taxn. 6 (2022), Journal Articles & Opinion Pieces IBFD (accessed 12 March 2024) https://doi.org/10.59403/exqfjd.

10. OECD (2023), *Tax Challenges Arising from the Digitalisation of the Economy: Administrative Guidance on the Global Anti-Base Erosion Model Rules (Pillar Two)*, OECD/G20 Inclusive Framework on BEPS, OECD, Paris, https://www.oecd.org/tax/beps/agreed-administrative-guidance-for-the-pillar-two-globe-rules.pdf and OECD (2023), *Tax Challenges Arising from the Digitalisation of the Economy: Administrative Guidance on the Global Anti-Base Erosion Model Rules (Pillar Two)* (July 2023), OECD/G20 Inclusive Framework on BEPS, OECD, Paris, www.oecd.org/tax/beps/administrative-guidance-global-anti-base-erosion-rules-pillar-two-july-2023.pdf.
11. *Ibid.*
12. OECD (2023), *Tax Challenges Arising from the Digitalisation of the Economy: Administrative Guidance on the Global Anti-Base Erosion Model Rules (Pillar Two)*, OECD/G20 Inclusive Framework on BEPS,OECD, Paris, www.oecd.org/tax/beps/administrative-guidance-global-anti-base-erosion-rules-pillartwo.pdf.
13. M.F. de Wilde & Y. Than, *Pillar Two and the Transitional Rule for Intra-Group Asset Transfers*, 77 Bull. Intl. Taxn. 8 (2023), Journal Articles & Opinion Pieces IBFD (accessed 12 March 2024) https://doi.org/10.59403/2h2dbhe.
14. OECD (2023), *Tax Challenges Arising from the Digitalisation of the Economy: Administrative Guidance on the Global Anti-Base Erosion Model Rules (Pillar Two)* (July 2023), OECD/G20 Inclusive Framework on BEPS, OECD, Paris, www.oecd.org/tax/beps/administrative-guidance-global-anti-base-erosion-rules-pillar-two-july-2023.pdf; V. Chand & K. Romanovska, *The Impact of Pillar Two on Corporate Tax Incentives and Incentives Post Pillar Two: The Potential Rise of Tax Credits and Subsidies*, 6 Intl. Tax Stud. 9 (2023), Journal Articles & Opinion Pieces IBFD (accessed 12 March 2024) https://doi.org/10.59403/1tywms8.

2.1.2 *Outcome Statement on the Two-Pillar Solution to Address the Tax Challenges Arising from the Digitalisation of the Economy: Pillar Two*

The OECD released an Outcome Statement on 11 July 2023 that considers both Pillar One and Pillar Two.[15] Concerning the latter (Part III of the Outcome Statement), the OECD focuses on the subject-to-tax rule (STTR) under Pillar Two. It is an integral part of the consensus on Pillar Two for developing country members of the IF. Those that apply nominal corporate tax rates below 9% to intra-group interest, royalties, and a limited number of other payments will implement the STTR in their treaties with developing IF Members upon request.[16]

2.1.3 *MLC to Facilitate the Implementation of the Pillar Two Subject to Tax Rule*

After releasing the detailed Model Treaty Provisions for the STTR (the STTR Model Rule and Commentary)[17] in July 2023, the MLC to Facilitate the Implementation of the Pillar Two Subject to Tax Rule (STTR MLC)[18] was adopted on 15 September 2023 by the OECD/G20 IF on Base Erosion and Profit Shifting (BEPS) and published in October 2023.[19] Concurrently with the STTR MLC, the OECD released an explanatory statement to the STTR MLC that is a summary overview including a roadmap towards signature and a frequently asked questions document.[20] The OECD stated that 'the STTR is

15. OECD (2023), *Outcome Statement on the Two-Pillar Solution to Address the Tax Challenges Arising from the Digitalisation of the Economy* (July 2023), www.oecd.org/tax/beps/outcome-statement-on-the-two-pillar-solution-to-address-the-tax-challenges-arising-from-the-digitalisation-of-the-economy-july-2023.pdf; F.S. Scandone, L. Scordo & L. Marino, *Pillar One, Pillar Two and BEFIT: The End of an Unexpected Journey?*, 31 Intl. Transfer Pricing J. 1 (2024), Journal Articles & Opinion Pieces IBFD (accessed 12 March 2024) https://doi.org/10.59403/2z2kyr1.
16. B.J. Arnold, *Earth to OECD: You Must Be Joking – The Subject to Tax Rule of Pillar Two*, 78 Bull. Intl. Taxn. 2 (2024), Journal Articles & Opinion Pieces IBFD (accessed 13 March 2024) https://doi.org/10.59403/3j8ntgs; OECD (2023), *Tax Challenges Arising from the Digitalisation of the Economy: Subject to Tax Rule (Pillar Two) – Inclusive Framework on BEPS*, OECD/G20 Base Erosion and Profit Shifting Project, OECD Publishing, Paris, https://doi.org/10.1787/9afd6856-en (accessed 13 March 2024); OECD (2023), *Explanatory Statement to the Multilateral Convention to Facilitate the Implementation of the Pillar Two Subject to Tax Rule*, https://www.oecd.org/en/topics/sub-issues/subject-to-tax-rule/multilateral-convention-to-facilitate-the-implementation-of-the-pillar-two-subject-to-tax-rule.html (accessed 13 March 2024).
17. OECD (2023), *Tax Challenges Arising from the Digitalisation of the Economy: Subject to Tax Rule (Pillar Two) – Inclusive Framework on BEPS*, OECD/G20 Base Erosion and Profit Shifting Project, OECD Publishing, Paris, https://doi.org/10.1787/9afd6856-en (accessed 13 March 2024).
18. OECD, *Multilateral Convention to Facilitate the Implementation of the Pillar Two Subject to Tax Rule* (2 October 2023), Treaties & Models IBFD, also available at www.oecd.org/tax/beps/multilateral-convention-to-facilitate-the-implementation-of-the-pillar-two-subject-to-tax-rule.htm (accessed 13 March 2024).
19. B.J. Arnold, *Earth to OECD: You Must Be Joking – The Subject to Tax Rule of Pillar Two*, 78 Bull. Intl. Taxn. 2 (2024), Journal Articles & Opinion Pieces IBFD (accessed 13 March 2024) https://doi.org/10.59403/3j8ntgs.
20. OECD, *International Community Adopts Multilateral Convention to Facilitate Implementation of the Global Minimum Tax Subject to Tax Rule*, https://www.oecd.org/tax/international-community-adopts-multilateral-convention-to-facilitate-implementation-of-the-global-minimu

designed to help developing countries – notably those with lower administrative capacities – to protect their tax base'.[21] Other public documents by the IF also frequently reiterate that the underlying rationale of the STTR is to restore some of the taxing rights that developing countries surrender under the provisions of their tax treaties with regard to the covered payments when the other contracting state does not tax those at a reasonable rate.[22] The STTR was the last part of the Pillar Two package to be finalized.[23]

2.1.4 Outcome Statement on the Two-Pillar Solution to Address the Tax Challenges Arising from the Digitalisation of the Economy: Pillar One

The above-mentioned Outcome Statement also considers Pillar One and focuses on the MLC on Amount A and Amount B.[24] The former will establish a taxing right for market jurisdictions for a defined portion of the residual profits of the largest and most profitable MNEs operating in their markets, prevent the proliferation of digital service taxes (DSTs) and relevant similar measures, avoid double taxation and excessive compliance burdens, and enhance stability and certainty in the international tax system.[25] This statement summarizes the package of deliverables developed by the IF to address the remaining elements of the Two-Pillar Solution. It comprises four parts: MLC and Amount A of Pillar One, Amount B of Pillar One, the STTR under Pillar Two, and Implementation Support.[26]

m-tax-subject-to-tax-rule.htm; OECD (2023), *Multilateral Convention to Facilitate the Implementation of the Pillar Two Subject to Tax Rule*; OECD (2023), *Explanatory Statement to the Multilateral Convention to Facilitate the Implementation of the Pillar Two Subject to Tax Rule.*

21. B.J. Arnold, *Earth to OECD: You Must Be Joking – The Subject to Tax Rule of Pillar Two*, 78 Bull. Intl. Taxn. 2 (2024), Journal Articles & Opinion Pieces IBFD (accessed 13 March 2024) https://doi.org/10.59403/3j8ntgs.
22. Cf., OECD (2023), *Tax Challenges Arising from the Digitalisation of the Economy: Subject to Tax Rule (Pillar Two) – Inclusive Framework on BEPS*, OECD/G20 Base Erosion and Profit Shifting Project, OECD Publishing, Paris, https://doi.org/10.1787/9afd6856-en (accessed 13 March 2024); OECD (2023), *Explanatory Statement to the Multilateral Convention to Facilitate the Implementation of the Pillar Two Subject to Tax Rule* (accessed 13 March 2024).
23. B.J. Arnold, *Earth to OECD: You Must Be Joking – The Subject to Tax Rule of Pillar Two*, 78 Bull. Intl. Taxn. 2 (2024), Journal Articles & Opinion Pieces IBFD (accessed 13 March 2024) https://doi.org/10.59403/3j8ntgs.
24. S. Kale & M. Shi, *Maximizing Amount B of the OECD's Pillar One for Developing Countries*, 78 Bull. Intl. Taxn. 1 (2024), Journal Articles & Opinion Pieces IBFD (accessed 12 March 2024) https://doi.org/10.59403/3z4z8t7.
25. R. Petruzzi & A. Padwalkar, *Pillar One, Pillar Two, Transfer Pricing and the Arm's Length Principle: A Tangled Web of New and Old Taxing Rules*, 77 Bull. Intl. Taxn. 10 (2023), Journal Articles & Opinion Pieces IBFD (accessed 12 March 2024) https://doi.org/10.59403/1v4xcrm; M.H. Barbosa Moura & A. Padwalkar, *Amount A and Its Design So Far: Feasibility in Sight?*, 30 Intl. Transfer Pricing J. 2 (2023), Journal Articles & Opinion Pieces IBFD (accessed 13 March 2024) https://doi.org/10.59403/ntq2z3.
26. OECD (2023), *Outcome Statement on the Two-Pillar Solution to Address the Tax Challenges Arising from the Digitalisation of the Economy* (July 2023), www.oecd.org/tax/beps/outcome-statement-on-the-two-pillar-solution-to-address-the-tax-challenges-arising-from-the-digitalisation-of-the-economy-july-2023.pdf; concerning Amount cf., S. Kale & M. Shi, *Maximizing*

2.1.4.1 *The MLC to Implement Amount A of Pillar One*

In October 2023, the IF delivered a text of an MLC that will allow the parties to the MLC to exercise a domestic taxing right (Amount A) for a defined portion of MNEs' residual profits that meet certain revenue and profitability thresholds and that have a defined nexus to the markets of these parties.[27] The MLC specifies the substantive features necessary to prepare it for signature, including the scope of application and operation of the permissible taxing right, the mechanisms for eliminating double taxation, a process for ensuring tax certainty, the conditions for abolishing existing DSTs, and relevant similar measures upon its entry into force.[28] Furthermore, it stipulates a commitment not to introduce new DSTs and relevant similar measures. The MLC also contains several provisions designed to take into account the special circumstances of the developing countries that are IF members. It was accompanied by an Explanatory Statement[29] setting out the common understanding of the MLC.

2.1.4.2 *Public Consultation Document Pillar One: Amount B*

In the above-mentioned Outcome Statement, the IF also recognized that Amount B is a critical component of the broader agreement on Pillar One and, as such, has achieved consensus on many aspects of that framework. To ensure the appropriateness of the scope and pricing framework, it was announced in the Outcome Statement that further work would be undertaken on specific aspects. At the completion of the public consultation, the IF would approve and publish a final Amount B report, and its content would be incorporated into the OECD TPG by January 2024.[30]

In accordance with that announcement, the OECD released a public consultation document on Amount B under Pillar One on 13 July 2023.[31] Amount B provides for a simplified and streamlined approach to applying the ALP to in-country baseline

---

Amount B of the OECD's Pillar One for Developing Countries, 78 Bull. Intl. Taxn. 1 (2024), Journal Articles & Opinion Pieces IBFD (accessed 12 March 2024) https://doi.org/10.59403/3z4z8t7.

27. OECD (2023), *The Multilateral Convention to Implement Amount A of Pillar One: Two-Pillar Solution to Address the Tax Challenges of the Digitalisation of the Economy*, available at https://www.oecd.org/en/topics/sub-issues/reallocation-of-taxing-rights-to-market-jurisdictions/multilateral-convention-to-implement-amount-a-of-pillar-one.html (accessed 12 March 2024); Moura & Padwalkar, *The Transfer Pricing World in 2023*, TPI 194 (2023).
28. Moura & Padwalkar, *The Transfer Pricing World in 2023*, TPI 194 (2023).
29. OECD (2023), *Explanatory Statement to the Multilateral Convention to Implement Amount A of Pillar One* (October 2023), https://www.oecd.org/tax/beps/explanatory-statement-multilateral-convention-to-implement-amount-a-of-pillar-one.pdf (accessed 13 March 2024).
30. OECD (2023), *Outcome Statement on the Two-Pillar Solution to Address the Tax Challenges Arising from the Digitalisation of the Economy* (July 2023), www.oecd.org/tax/beps/outcome-statement-on-the-two-pillar-solution-to-address-the-tax-challenges-arising-from-the-digitalisation-of-the-economy-july-2023.pdf (accessed 13 March 2024); S. Kale & M. Shi, *Maximizing Amount B of the OECD's Pillar One for Developing Countries*, 78 Bull. Intl. Taxn. 1 (2024), Journal Articles & Opinion Pieces IBFD (accessed 13 March 2024) https://doi.org/10.59403/3z4z8t7.
31. OECD (2023), *Public Consultation Document: Pillar One – Amount B*, www.oecd.org/tax/beps/public-consultation-document-pillar-one-amount-b-2023.pdf (accessed 13 March 2024).

marketing and distribution activities (BMDA) with a particular focus on the needs of low-capacity countries.[32]

The public consultation document outlines the design elements of Amount B and has been released in order to obtain inputs from stakeholders on its technical aspects.[33] The scope of Amount B is focused on a set of baseline wholesale distributors that can be reliably priced under a one-sided TP method by applying the pricing framework in Section 4. In-scope distributors, for instance, should not own unique and valuable intangibles, nor should they assume certain economically significant risks. The scope of Amount B allows distributors to perform non-distribution transactions when they can be adequately evaluated and reliably priced on a separate basis under the general principles of the OECD TPG.[34,35] The Amount B scoping framework also permits undertaking *de minimis* retail sales while excluding the distribution of services and commodities from its scope.[36] As highlighted in the Outcome Statement, further work will be undertaken on the following aspects:

- ensuring an appropriate balance between a quantitative and qualitative approach in identifying baseline distribution activities; and
- the appropriateness of:
  - the pricing framework, including in light of the final agreement on scope;
  - the application of the framework to the wholesale distribution of digital goods;
  - country uplifts within geographic markets; and
  - the criteria to apply Amount B utilizing a local database in certain jurisdictions.[37]

The current Consultation Document on Amount B represents an ongoing exercise and extends the progress made from the one of December 2022 that aimed at

32. S. Zucchetti, G. Lishi & M. Erb, *Pillar One, Amount B: Current Implications and Future Perspectives*, 30 Intl. Transfer Pricing J. 5 (2023), Journal Articles & Opinion Pieces IBFD (accessed 13 March 2024) https://doi.org/10.59403/1q2y51x; cf., also OECD (2020), *Tax Challenges Arising from Digitalisation: Report on Pillar One Blueprint – Inclusive Framework on BEPS*, OECD/G20 Base Erosion and Profit Shifting Project, OECD Publishing, Paris, https://doi.org/10.1787/beba0634-en (accessed 13 March 2024).
33. OECD (2023), *Public Consultation Document: Pillar One – Amount B*, www.oecd.org/tax/beps/public-consultation-document-pillar-one-amount-b-2023.pdf (accessed 13 March 2024).
34. OECD, *Transfer Pricing Guidelines for Multinational Enterprises and Tax Administrations* (January 2022).
35. S. Zucchetti, G. Lishi & M. Erb, *Pillar One, Amount B: Current Implications and Future Perspectives*, 30 Intl. Transfer Pricing J. 5 (2023), Journal Articles & Opinion Pieces IBFD (accessed 13 March 2024) https://doi.org/10.59403/1q2y51x; F.S. Scandone, *Let It (Amount) B*, 30 Intl. Transfer Pricing J. 2 (2023), Journal Articles & Opinion Pieces IBFD (accessed 13 March 2024) https://doi.org/10.59403/sb1en2.
36. S. Zucchetti, G. Lishi & M. Erb, *Pillar One, Amount B: Current Implications and Future Perspectives*, 30 Intl. Transfer Pricing J. 5 (2023), Journal Articles & Opinion Pieces IBFD (accessed 13 March 2024) https://doi.org/10.59403/1q2y51x.
37. OECD (2023), *Outcome Statement on the Two-Pillar Solution to Address the Tax Challenges Arising from the Digitalisation of the Economy* (July 2023), www.oecd.org/tax/beps/outcome-statement-on-the-two-pillar-solution-to-address-the-tax-challenges-arising-from-the-digitalisation-of-the-economy-july-2023.pdf.

simplifying the application of the ALP to BMDA. While it outlines several elements of the ongoing work on Amount B and shows promising advancements from the previous document, it appears to fail to represent the consensus views of the IF, which leaves numerous open-ended issues.[38]

2.1.4.3 Pillar One: Amount B – IF on BEPS (Final Report)

On 19 February 2024, the IF released its final report[39] on Amount B of Pillar One. The approach set out in this report answers the call of low-capacity countries for what the African Tax Administration Forum (ATAF) has described as '*vital*' changes to the OECD TPG, providing what 'could be a game changer for the African transfer pricing landscape'. Content from the report has now been incorporated into the OECD TPG.[40] The new report provides a simplified approach and guidance for applying the ALP at the jurisdiction level. The new approach is expected to reduce TP pricing disputes and compliance costs as well as enhance tax certainty both for tax administrations and taxpayers, particularly across what is known as low-capacity jurisdictions. For a detailed demonstration of Amount B, the authors direct the reader to Chapter 2.

2.2 TP Developments at the UN

2.2.1 26th and 27th Sessions of the UN Tax Committee

The UN Tax Committee[41] held its 26th and 27th sessions at the UN Headquarters in Geneva, Switzerland, from 27 to 30 March 2023 and from 17 to 20 October 2023. Its primary focus was directed at further advancing its work to meet the ambitious work plan it has adopted for the 2021-2025 period. Issues on the agenda include matters such as taxing the digitalized and globalized economy, tax treaties, environmental taxes, health taxes, wealth taxes, extractive industries taxation, and TP, among others. The timed agenda will be available in due course.

On the 26th session's agenda were three main TP issues concerning the economic downturn due to the COVID-19 pandemic, TP of carbon offsets and carbon credits, and assurance of TP compliance (cf., End-to-End Toolkit). The 27th session focused on those issues discussed at the 26th session and on industry/sector guidance for primary products (agricultural products) and industry/sector guidance for the pharmaceutical industry.

---

38. WU TPC Comments Amount B.
39. OECD (2024), *Pillar One: Amount B – Inclusive Framework on BEPS*, OECD/G20 Base Erosion and Profit Shifting Project, OECD Publishing, Paris, https://doi.org/10.1787/21ea168b-en (accessed 13 March 2024).
40. OECD, *Tax Challenges Arising from Digitalisation: Release of Amount B Report to Simplify Transfer Pricing Rules and Conforming Changes to the Commentary of the OECD Model Tax Convention* (19 February 2024), https://www.oecd.org/tax/beps/release-of-report-on-amount-b-relating-to-the-simplification-of-transfer-pricing-rules-and-conforming-changes-to-the-commentary-of-the-oecd-model-tax-convention.htm (accessed 13 March 2024).
41. Committee of Experts on International Cooperation in Tax Matters.

The economic downturn caused by the COVID-19 pandemic has created unique challenges in applying the ALP as guided by the United Nations Practical Manual on Transfer Pricing for Developing Countries (Manual). Taxpayers and tax administrations were and are facing uncertainties during the years impacted by COVID-19 and the post-pandemic phase of economic recovery. Since there is only minimal detailed guidance on practical solutions by tax administrations and taxpayers, the TP Subcommittee published a guidance document at the 26th session that focused on the fundamental application of the ALP within the scope of the manual. It provides practical examples focusing on: (a) accurately delineating and recognizing the actual controlled transaction between associated enterprises, (b) selecting and applying the most appropriate TP methods, including the comparability analysis, (c) effective approaches in applying existing dispute avoidance and resolution tools to enhance tax certainty, and (d) potential approaches to improve standardization and simplification during the years impacted by the COVID-19 economic downturn.[42]

The TP Subcommittee has further published a document concerning what is referred to as an End-to-End Toolkit[43] that is intended to provide tools and examples of good practices to support efficient and effective TP compliance. It emphasizes the priorities and needs of developing and capacity-constrained countries. The toolkit is primarily aimed at tax administrations of developing countries that have TP rules in place. It assumes that the country's corporate income tax system is predominantly based on self-assessment, with audits and assessments carried out by the tax administration only in certain circumstances. This toolkit discusses the development of an end-to-end TP compliance assurance programme encompassing population and individual taxpayer-level risk assessment through comprehensive audits or examinations. It puts the practicalities of undertaking TP risk assessments and audits into the context of a holistic, end-to-end process. The objective is to help ensure a systematic review of the tax environment, minimize potential deficiencies in both information and revenues and reinforce an overall goal of optimizing compliance and sound tax administration.[44]

A third document was published at the 26th session of the UN Tax Committee with regard to TP carbon offsets and carbon credits.[45] The purpose of this workstream is to elaborate on the value chain of carbon emission abatement activities that serve to generate carbon credits (or carbon offsets).[46]

The (high-level) overview presented in this paper aims to provide some insights as to:

42. Transfer Pricing Subcommittee, Transfer Pricing during the COVID-19 Economic Downturn, Annex A to E/C.18/2023/CRP.7; cf., also Annex A to E/C.18/2023/CRP.26 from the 27th session; a seemingly identical document to the one from the 26th session.
43. Cf., Paper for Approval from the Transfer Pricing Subcommittee, Transfer Pricing Compliance Assurance - An End-to-End Toolkit, Annex B to E/C.18/2023/CRP.7 and ANNEX B to E/C.18/2023/CRP.26.
44. Cf., Annex B to E/C.18/2023/CRP.7 and Annex B to E/C.18/2023/CRP.26.
45. Cf., Paper for Approval from the Transfer Pricing Subcommittee, Transfer Pricing of Carbon Offsets and Carbon Credits, Annex C to E/C.18/2023/CRP.7; cf., also Annex C to E/C.18/2023/CRP.26.
46. Annex C to E/C.18/2023/CRP.7; cf., also Annex C to E/C.18/2023/CRP.26.

- different ways in which carbon credits may be generated;
- the (still evolving) regulatory system that allows for creating, using, and trading these credits (including a mention of the monitoring, reporting, and verification systems material for the functioning of the relevant systems) that may serve to improve the understanding of what steps and actions are required to comply; and
- the (intercompany) transfer of carbon credit.[47]

At the 27th session, the paper Transfer Pricing and Agricultural Products[48] was prepared by the UN Subcommittee on TP in response to the need often expressed by developing countries for practical guidance in applying the ALP to agricultural products. Agriculture is of immense importance to all countries, both developed and developing and has an enormous impact on the global economy, with MNEs active in agricultural production and along agricultural global value chains. It also intersects with many other industries including producing chemicals, engaging in logistics, and machinery.[49]

A report was prepared to also react to developing countries' repeatedly communicated need for practical guidance in applying the ALP to the pharmaceutical industry. The UN TP Subcommittee prepared the report Transfer Pricing and the Pharmaceutical Industry[50] for the 27th session. Tax administrations, particularly from developing countries, face resource and capacity constraints in a specialized area such as TP. Thus, it is important to ensure that limited resources are targeted as efficiently and effectively as possible. Given the importance of the pharmaceutical industry to both developed and developing countries, this report intends to provide practical guidance for this industry.[51]

2.2.2 A New UN Tax Convention?

On 22 November 2023, the UN General Assembly approved a resolution proposed by Nigeria on behalf of the Group of African States on the Promotion of inclusive and effective international tax cooperation at the UN by a large majority (125 for, 48 against, 9 abstentions). With that resolution, an ad hoc intergovernmental committee was established that shall elaborate the draft terms of reference for a framework convention. Until August 2024, the focus will be on developing those terms of reference for a new UN Framework Convention on International Tax Cooperation. Based on these, governments will then proceed to negotiate the new UN Tax Convention.[52]

47. Annex C to E/C.18/2023/CRP.7; cf., also Annex C to E/C.18/2023/CRP.26.
48. Annex D to E/C.18/2023/CRP.26.
49. *Ibid.*
50. Annex E to E/C.18/2023/CRP.26.
51. *Ibid.*
52. Resolution 78/230 adopted by the General Assembly on 22 December 2023, Promotion of inclusive and effective international tax cooperation at the UN.

2.3 TP Developments at the EU

2.3.1 Directive Business in Europe: Framework for Income Taxation

As the second part of the BEFIT package, the European Commission adopted a proposal for the BEFIT directive on 12 September 2023.[53] It is a new, single set of rules to determine the tax base of groups of companies and can be used to reduce tax compliance costs for large, cross-border businesses in the EU.[54]

Dealing with twenty-seven different national tax systems makes tax compliance difficult and expensive for companies. This puts European businesses at a competitive disadvantage compared to businesses outside of the EU. Hence, simplification is crucial to growth and competitiveness in the EU. BEFIT seeks to reduce tax compliance costs for large businesses, primarily those that operate in more than one Member State. At the same time, its aim is to make it easier for national authorities to determine which taxes are rightly due.[55] This proposal pursues a way forward that reconciles all of those aspects by introducing a common framework for corporate income taxation in the EU. It will simplify the tax environment in the internal market by replacing the current twenty-seven different ways for determining the taxable base for groups of companies that have annual combined revenues exceeding EUR 750 million.[56] Consequently, the common framework will create equal opportunities, enhance legal certainty, reduce compliance costs, encourage businesses to operate cross-border and stimulate investments and growth in the Union.[57]

The proposal builds on the OECD/G20 international tax agreement on a global minimum level of taxation and the Pillar Two EU Directive.[58] It defines a hybrid scope for applying the rules under BEFIT. The 'mandatory scope' comprises the same groups as Pillar Two (i.e., groups with annual combined revenues of at least EUR 750 million) but is limited to the Union sub-set of entities that meet the 75% ownership threshold (cf., Articles 5 and 6). The BEFIT proposal would also apply to non-EU-headquartered

53. European Commission, *Proposal for a Council Directive on Business in Europe: Framework for Income Taxation (BEFIT)*, Strasbourg, 12.9.2023, COM(2023) 532 final.
54. J. Provencher, A. Mulky Dange & S. Kuijper, *The BEFIT Directive: A Game Changer for Transfer Pricing or an Irrelevant Buzz?*, 31 Intl. Transfer Pricing J. 1 (2024), Journal Articles & Opinion Pieces IBFD (accessed 15 March 2024) https://doi.org/10.59403/zf1zf5.
55. Cf., European Commission, *Proposal for a Council Directive on Business in Europe: Framework for Income Taxation (BEFIT)*, Strasbourg, 12.9.2023, COM(2023) 532 final, 2023/0321 (CNS), Explanatory Memorandum, 1; A. Xygka, *BEFIT: A Blast From the Past or a Modernized Approach to Tax Simplification?*, 64 Eur. Taxn. 1 (2024), Journal Articles & Opinion Pieces IBFD (accessed 15 March 2024) https://doi.org/10.59403/3f130y8.
56. J. Provencher, A. Mulky Dange & S. Kuijper, *The BEFIT Directive: A Game Changer for Transfer Pricing or an Irrelevant Buzz?*, 31 Intl. Transfer Pricing J. 1 (2024), Journal Articles & Opinion Pieces IBFD (accessed 15 March 2024) https://doi.org/10.59403/zf1zf5.
57. Cf., European Commission, *Proposal for a Council Directive on Business in Europe: Framework for Income Taxation (BEFIT)*, Strasbourg, 12.9.2023, COM(2023) 532 final, 2023/0321 (CNS), Explanatory Memorandum, 2.
58. Cf., European Commission, *Proposal for a Council Directive on Business in Europe: Framework for Income Taxation (BEFIT)*, Strasbourg, 12.9.2023, COM(2023) 532 final, 2023/0321 (CNS), Explanatory Memorandum, 4.

groups exceeding specific thresholds.[59] There is also a 'voluntary scope' for smaller groups that can opt in if they so wish, provided they prepare consolidated financial statements. Normally, smaller groups that operate cross-border have limited resources to dedicate to compliance with multiple national corporate tax systems; therefore, this 'voluntary scope' could particularly be of interest to them.[60]

All companies that are members of the same BEFIT group will calculate their tax base in accordance with a common set of tax adjustments to their financial accounting statements.[61] The tax bases of all group members will be aggregated into one single tax base. This will entail cross-border loss relief because losses will automatically be offset against profits across borders. Consequently, there will also be increased tax certainty in TP compliance.[62] By using a transitional allocation rule, each member of the BEFIT group will have a percentage of the aggregated tax base calculated based on the average of the taxable results in the previous three fiscal years.[63]

BEFIT aims to facilitate compliance regarding transactions with associated enterprises outside the BEFIT group. Those are entities of the group that are not in the Union or that do not meet the 75% ownership threshold. For transactions with such associated enterprises, BEFIT provides a risk assessment tool ('traffic light system') with benchmarks. This feature only focuses on simplifying compliance with TP and

59. Cf., European Commission, *Proposal for a Council Directive on Business in Europe: Framework for Income Taxation (BEFIT)*, Strasbourg, 12.9.2023, COM(2023) 532 final, 2023/0321 (CNS), Explanatory Memorandum, 12; J.J.A.M. Korving, *'BEFIT and HOT: FASTER and SAFE!' EU Law or Slogan for Slimming Pills?*, 63 Eur. Taxn. 12 (2023), Journal Articles & Opinion Pieces IBFD (accessed 15 March 2024) https://doi.org/10.59403/2jy6hxp; J. Provencher, A. Mulky Dange & S. Kuijper, *The BEFIT Directive: A Game Changer for Transfer Pricing or an Irrelevant Buzz?*, 31 Intl. Transfer Pricing J. 1 (2024), Journal Articles & Opinion Pieces IBFD (accessed 15 March 2024) https://doi.org/10.59403/zf1zf5.
60. Cf., European Commission, *Proposal for a Council Directive on Business in Europe: Framework for Income Taxation (BEFIT)*, Strasbourg, 12.9.2023, COM(2023) 532 final, 2023/0321 (CNS), Explanatory Memorandum, 12; A. Xygka, *BEFIT: A Blast From the Past or a Modernized Approach to Tax Simplification?*, 64 Eur. Taxn. 1 (2024), Journal Articles & Opinion Pieces IBFD (accessed 15 March 2024) https://doi.org/10.59403/3f130y8.
61. Cf., European Commission, *Proposal for a Council Directive on Business in Europe: Framework for Income Taxation (BEFIT)*, Strasbourg, 12.9.2023, COM(2023) 532 final, 2023/0321 (CNS), Explanatory Memorandum, 13 et seq.; J. Provencher, A. Mulky Dange & S. Kuijper, *The BEFIT Directive: A Game Changer for Transfer Pricing or an Irrelevant Buzz?*, 31 Intl. Transfer Pricing J. 1 (2024), Journal Articles & Opinion Pieces IBFD (accessed 15 March 2024) https://doi.org/10.59403/zf1zf5.
62. Cf., European Commission, *Proposal for a Council Directive on Business in Europe: Framework for Income Taxation (BEFIT)*, Strasbourg, 12.9.2023, COM(2023) 532 final, 2023/0321 (CNS), Explanatory Memorandum, 14 et seq.
63. Cf., Impact assessment, Version 3 – BEFIT 'Composite', European Commission, *Proposal for a Council Directive on Business in Europe: Framework for Income Taxation (BEFIT)*, Strasbourg, 12.9.2023, COM(2023) 532 final, 2023/0321 (CNS), Explanatory Memorandum, 9; A. Xygka, *BEFIT: A Blast From the Past or a Modernized Approach to Tax Simplification?*, 64 Eur. Taxn. 1 (2024), Journal Articles & Opinion Pieces IBFD (accessed 15 March 2024) https://doi.org/10.59403/3f130y8.

does not interfere with the substantive rules that determine whether a certain transaction has been priced at arm's length.[64]

The proposed BEFIT Directive shall be transposed by Member States by 1 January 2028 and applied by 1 July 2028.[65] For a more detailed presentation of it, the authors refer the reader to Chapter 3.

2.3.2 *Transfer Pricing Directive*

On 12 September 2023, the European Commission proposed a Council Directive on Transfer Pricing (TP Directive) to harmonize key TP principles across the EU. This proposal is part of the package known as 'BEFIT' (for the BEFIT directive itself cf., paragraph below) that includes two separate proposals: the above-mentioned BEFIT proposal (as a separate legal act) and the proposal for a TP Directive at issue. Besides the proposed TP Directive, there is another for a BEFIT directive. The TP proposal integrates key TP principles into EU law with the objective of proposing certain common approaches for Member States.[66]

The TP Directive's stated goal is to increase tax certainty, reduce compliance costs, and mitigate the risk of double taxation and litigation for cross-border intra-group transactions within the EU.[67] It would apply as of 1 January 2026,[68] however, it needs to be adopted unanimously in the EU Council. The OECD TPG were incorporated by the TP Directive as of 20 January 2022 as the binding standard for the interpretation and application of the ALP within the EU.[69] In its Article 5, the TP Directive also defines an 'associated enterprise' as a person (natural person or legal entity) who is related to another person in any of the following ways:

- significant influence on their management;
- a holding of over 25% of their voting rights;

64. Cf., European Commission, *Proposal for a Council Directive on Business in Europe: Framework for Income Taxation (BEFIT)*, Strasbourg, 12.9.2023, COM(2023) 532 final, 2023/0321 (CNS), Explanatory Memorandum, 16; J. Provencher, A. Mulky Dange & S. Kuijper, *The BEFIT Directive: A Game Changer for Transfer Pricing or an Irrelevant Buzz?*, 31 Intl. Transfer Pricing J. 1 (2024), Journal Articles & Opinion Pieces IBFD (accessed 15 March 2024) https://doi.org/10.59403/zf1zf5.
65. Cf., Article 78 BEFIT.
66. Cf., *European Commission, Proposal for a Council Directive on Transfer Pricing*, Strasbourg, 12.9.2023, COM(2023) 529 final, 2023/0322(CNS), Explanatory Memorandum, 1 et seq.; R. Petruzzi & A. Myzithra, *The EC's Proposal for a Directive on Transfer Pricing: Paving the Road for a Common Application of the Arm's Length Principle*, 31 Intl. Transfer Pricing J. 1 (2024), Journal Articles & Opinion Pieces IBFD (accessed 15 March 2024) https://doi.org/10.59403/6cd7v7.
67. Cf., European Commission, *Proposal for a Council Directive on Transfer Pricing*, Strasbourg, 12.9.2023, COM(2023) 529 final, 2023/0322(CNS), Explanatory Memorandum, 1 et seq.
68. Cf., Art. 20, para. 1 of the proposed Directive.
69. Cf., European Commission, *Proposal for a Council Directive on Transfer Pricing*, Strasbourg, 12.9.2023, COM(2023) 529 final, 2023/0322(CNS), Explanatory Memorandum, 4; R. Petruzzi & A. Myzithra, *The EC's Proposal for a Directive on Transfer Pricing: Paving the Road for a Common Application of the Arm's Length Principle*, 31 Intl. Transfer Pricing J. 1 (2024), Journal Articles & Opinion Pieces IBFD (accessed 15 March 2024) https://doi.org/10.59403/6cd7v7.

- a direct or indirect ownership of over 25% of their capital; or
- a right to over 25% of their profits.[70]

On the one hand, the definition of 'associated enterprise' allows for a certain harmonization. As of now, there is no uniform definition of the term across Member States.[71] On the other hand, the 25% threshold is a different way of defining a group compared to the criteria stipulated in the BEFIT and Pillar Two directives. This could create difficulties in coordinating the various regulations.[72] Finally, the TP Directive clarifies that a permanent establishment is an 'associated enterprise', which might not necessarily be the case under the national tax laws of Member States.[73]

Furthermore, the TP Directive provides mechanisms to enable what is referred to as the corresponding and compensating adjustments.[74] To avoid double taxation when a primary adjustment is made by a tax authority during an audit, the other Member State concerned shall make a corresponding adjustment (subject to identified circumstances).[75] Just as before, double taxation can furthermore be relieved through a Mutual Agreement Procedure (MAP). The TP Directive would also introduce an additional, new fast-track procedure whereby any double taxation that follows from TP adjustments made by an EU Member State will be resolved within 180 days.[76] In the long term, more frequent interactions between tax authorities should result in the ALP being applied more consistently across the Member States. Thus, a fast-track procedure could make a significant difference.[77] The Commission has also proposed to introduce '*corresponding adjustments*'. When associated enterprises set a price for their intra-group transactions that is different from the market price, they may need to perform a year-end adjustment to avoid double taxation. Currently, such practice is not allowed in some EU countries; however, introducing these adjustments' will allow for such

70. Q. Mulder et al., *A Closer Look at the European Commission Proposal for Harmonized Rules for Transfer Pricing*, 31 Intl. Transfer Pricing J. 1 (2023), Journal Articles & Opinion Pieces IBFD (accessed 15 March 2024) https://doi.org/10.59403/32kfnyx.
71. Cf., European Commission, *Proposal for a Council Directive on Transfer Pricing*, Strasbourg, 12.9.2023, COM(2023) 529 final, 2023/0322(CNS), Explanatory Memorandum, 2.
72. Cf., Art. 3, para. 3 Pillar Two and Art. 3, para. 1 and Art. 5 BEFIT Proposal.
73. Cf., European Commission, *Proposal for a Council Directive on Transfer Pricing*, Strasbourg, 12.9.2023, COM(2023) 529 final, 2023/0322(CNS), Explanatory Memorandum, 10; Art. 4, para. 7 of the proposed Directive.
74. Cf., European Commission, *Proposal for a Council Directive on Transfer Pricing*, Strasbourg, 12.9.2023, COM(2023) 529 final, 2023/0322(CNS), Explanatory Memorandum, 10 et seq.
75. Cf., Art. 6 of the proposed Directive; Q. Mulder et al., *A Closer Look at the European Commission Proposal for Harmonized Rules for Transfer Pricing*, 31 Intl. Transfer Pricing J. 1 (2023), Journal Articles & Opinion Pieces IBFD (accessed 15 March 2024) https://doi.org/10.59403/kyqk54; R. Petruzzi & A. Myzithra, *The EC's Proposal for a Directive on Transfer Pricing: Paving the Road for a Common Application of the Arm's Length Principle*, 31 Intl. Transfer Pricing J. 1 (2024), Journal Articles & Opinion Pieces IBFD (accessed 15 March 2024) https://doi.org/10.59403/6cd7v7.
76. Q. Mulder et al., *A Closer Look at the European Commission Proposal for Harmonized Rules for Transfer Pricing*, 31 Intl. Transfer Pricing J. 1 (2023), Journal Articles & Opinion Pieces IBFD (accessed 15 March 2024) https://doi.org/10.59403/kyqk54.
77. Recital No. 6 of the proposed Directive.

practice in the future. In that respect, the TP Directive stipulates clear rules for when Member States should accept an adjustment of this kind in their Article 7.[78]

According to the proposal, the five common TP methods in the OECD TPG must be used to determine the arm's length price. It is only if none of these methods can be reasonably applied that other valuation methods or techniques are permitted, but they must produce a result that is consistent with what third parties would achieve, and this has to be demonstrated by the taxpayers.[79] This is a stricter requirement than under the OECD TPG. Article 9 of the TP Directive refers to those main TP methods.[80] To establish the arm's length range, the interquartile range is relevant, and the TP Directive does not allow for any flexibility in that respect (for instance, the full range).[81] Tax authorities are generally not allowed to adjust a result that is within the interquartile range - unless a specific different positioning in the range can be justified. Pricing outside the interquartile range must be adjusted to the median by tax authorities. However, either the taxpayer or the tax authority can argue that a different result in the range is more suitable based on the specific facts and circumstances.[82]

Taxpayers should have sufficient information and analyses in place to prove that their intra-group transactions have been carried out on an arm's length basis. The Commission will later clarify the requirements in relation to the TP documentation in compliance with the provisions stipulated in Article 13. Elements such as standard templates setting the type and content of TP information, time frames to be covered, linguistic requirements and taxpayers in the scope of the documentation obligation may possibly be added.[83]

For a more detailed discussion on the proposed TP Directive, the authors refer the reader to Chapter 4.

78. Cf., European Commission, *Proposal for a Council Directive on Transfer Pricing*, Strasbourg, 12.9.2023, COM(2023) 529 final, 2023/0322(CNS), Explanatory Memorandum, 11.
79. Q. Mulder et al., *A Closer Look at the European Commission Proposal for Harmonized Rules for Transfer Pricing*, 31 Intl. Transfer Pricing J. 1 (2023), Journal Articles & Opinion Pieces IBFD (accessed 15 March 2024) https://doi.org/10.59403/32kfnyx.
80. Cf., European Commission, *Proposal for a Council Directive on Transfer Pricing*, Strasbourg, 12.9.2023, COM(2023) 529 final, 2023/0322(CNS), Explanatory Memorandum, 11 et seq.; This provision is inspired and should be interpreted in conjunction with the report JTPF/009/FINAL/2013/EN on compensating adjustments approved by the Joint Transfer Pricing Forum in 2013; cf., also EU Joint Transfer Pricing Forum Report on compensating adjustments (JTPF/009/FINAL/2013/EN): https://taxation-customs.ec.europa.eu/system/files/2016-09/jtpf_009_final_2013_en.pdf.
81. Q. Mulder et al., *A Closer Look at the European Commission Proposal for Harmonized Rules for Transfer Pricing*, 31 Intl. Transfer Pricing J. 1 (2023), Journal Articles & Opinion Pieces IBFD (accessed 15 March 2024) https://doi.org/10.59403/kyqk54; R. Petruzzi & A. Myzithra, *The EC's Proposal for a Directive on Transfer Pricing: Paving the Road for a Common Application of the Arm's Length Principle*, 31 Intl. Transfer Pricing J. 1 (2024), Journal Articles & Opinion Pieces IBFD (accessed 15 March 2024) https://doi.org/10.59403/6cd7v7.
82. Cf., European Commission, *Proposal for a Council Directive on Transfer Pricing*, Strasbourg, 12.9.2023, COM(2023) 529 final, 2023/0322(CNS), Explanatory Memorandum, 16.
83. *Ibid.*

2.3.3 *Unshell*

On 17 January 2023, the European Parliament voted on the European Commission's proposal for a directive on preventing shell companies from misusing their structure for tax purposes (Unshell) and approved it with amendments.[84] Following consultation with the European Parliament, the Unshell Directive requires unanimity in the Council for its adoption.[85] The negotiations in the Council are ongoing.[86] The European Commission presented a directive in December 2021 to prevent shell companies from exploiting their structure for tax purposes (Unshell).[87] Although company entities with no or minimal economic activity (shell companies) can serve useful commercial and business functions, they are sometimes abused by companies or individuals for aggressive tax planning or tax evasion. The Unshell Directive was proposed by the European Commission to ensure sustainable public finances under the exceptional circumstances imposed by the COVID-19 pandemic. The proposal introduces what is known as a 'filtering' system for EU company entities that have to pass a series of gateways relating to income, staff, and premises to ensure that the entity has sufficient 'substance'. Entities that are deemed to be lacking this are presumed to be 'shell companies';[88] however, this presumption is rebuttable.[89] Nevertheless, if companies cannot do this with additional evidence regarding the commercial, non-tax rationale of the entity, they will forfeit any tax advantages granted through bilateral tax treaties or EU directives.[90] When an undertaking is presumed to be a shell, the taxpayer has two possible ways to rebut the presumption by producing:

- additional concrete evidence that it is not a shell, such as by evidencing that the entity conducts a genuine economic activity and has a sufficient nexus with the Member State in which it claims to be a tax resident; or

84. European Parliament legislative resolution of 17 January 2023 on the proposal for a Council directive laying down rules to prevent the misuse of shell entities for tax purposes and amending Directive 2011/16/EU (COM(2021)0565 – C9-0041/2022 – 2021/0434(CNS)).
85. Baert Pieter, *'Unshell': Rules to Prevent the Misuse of Shell Entities for Tax Purposes, Think Tank European Parliament Briefing* (12 January 2023), https://www.europarl.europa.eu/thinktank/en/document/EPRS_BRI(2022)733648 (accessed 7 November 2023).
86. *Ibid.*
87. O. Popa, *Proposal for an EU Directive Laying Down Rules to Prevent the Misuse of Shell Entities for Tax Purposes (Unshell): Seven Steps Towards Disgrace or Redemption*, 62 Eur. Taxn. 4 (2022), Journal Articles & Opinion Pieces IBFD (accessed 15 March 2024) https://doi.org/10.59403/3jnp69c.
88. *Ibid.*
89. *Ibid.*
90. Baert Pieter, *'Unshell': Rules to Prevent the Misuse of Shell Entities for Tax Purposes, Think Tank European Parliament Briefing* (12 January 2023), https://www.europarl.europa.eu/thinktank/en/document/EPRS_BRI(2022)733648 (accessed 7 November 2023); O. Popa, *Proposal for an EU Directive Laying Down Rules to Prevent the Misuse of Shell Entities for Tax Purposes (Unshell): Seven Steps Towards Disgrace or Redemption*, 62 Eur. Taxn. 4 (2022), Journal Articles & Opinion Pieces IBFD (accessed 15 March 2024) https://doi.org/10.59403/3jnp69c.

- evidence of receiving no tax benefit when comparing the tax liability of the structure in the group to which it belongs with and without the interposition of the presumed shell.[91]

In this context, TP documentation could serve as a beneficial mechanism for proving that the undertaking has performed and continuously had control over as well as bearing the risks of the business activities that generated the relevant income or assets.

2.3.4 *The* Apple *and* Amazon *Cases*

In the *Apple* case, Ireland issued two tax rulings for two companies in the Apple group (Apple Sales International (ASI) and Apple Operations Europe (AOE)) that were incorporated under Irish law but were not resident for tax purposes in Ireland. The rulings approved a method proposed by ASI and AOE to determine their chargeable profits in Ireland arising from the activities of their Irish branches. In 2016, the commission considered that the tax rulings, by excluding profits derived from using intellectual property licences held by ASI and AOE from the tax base, granted state aid to those companies that were unlawful and incompatible with the single market and from which the entire Apple group had benefited. The European Commission ordered Ireland to recover that aid. In 2020, the GCEU annulled that decision following an action brought by Ireland, ASI and AOE, holding that the European Commission had failed to prove that there was an advantage resulting from adopting the tax rulings.[92]

The AG and GCEU both rejected the Commission's argument that an autonomous arm's length standard exists as part of the state aid rules in Article 107(1) of the Treaty on the Functioning of the European Union (TFEU).[93] However, according to the Advocate General, the GCEU committed several errors in law. The court held that the Commission had not established the requisite legal standard that the intellectual property licences held by ASI and AOE and the related profits generated by the sale of Apple products outside the United States should be attributed for tax purposes to the Irish branches. The Advocate General also considered that the GCEU failed to correctly assess the nature and consequences of certain methodological errors, which, according to the Commission's decision, vitiated the tax rulings. Therefore, the Advocate General proposed that the CJEU set aside the GCEU's judgment and refer the case back to it for a new decision on the merits.[94]

---

91. Proposal for a Council Directive laying down rules to prevent the misuse of shell entities for tax purposes and amending Directive 2011/16/EU.
92. GC 15 July 2020, *Ireland v. Apple*, T-778/16 and T-892/16; C. Garavan, *The Apple Case: Reviewing the Advocate General's Opinion in Light of Irish Law*, 64 Eur. Taxn. 2/3 (2024), Journal Articles & Opinion Pieces IBFD (accessed 15 March 2024) https://doi.org/10.59403/cbz1jb.
93. C. Garavan, *The Apple Case: Reviewing the Advocate General's Opinion in Light of Irish Law*, 64 Eur. Taxn. 2/3 (2024), Journal Articles & Opinion Pieces IBFD (accessed 15 March 2024) https://doi.org/10.59403/cbz1jb.
94. Opinion of Advocate General Pitruzzella, 9 November 2023, Case C-465/20, *Commission v. Ireland*; C. Garavan, *The Apple Case: Reviewing the Advocate General's Opinion in Light of Irish*

The *Amazon* case concerns royalties paid by Amazon's Luxembourg operating company, Amazon EU Sàrl (LuxOpCo), to its parent company, Amazon Europe Holding Technologies SCS (LuxSCS). Following a reorganization in 2006, LuxOpCo assumed primary responsibility for regional strategy and treasury management in Europe, and it recorded the revenues generated by orders placed on Amazon's EU websites. To perform these functions, LuxOpCo sublicensed from LuxSCS the European rights to exploit the Amazon group's technology, trademarks, and European customer lists. LuxSCS had acquired these rights through its participation in a cost-sharing arrangement with Amazon's US parent company. Before setting up this structure, Amazon successfully applied to Luxembourg for an advanced pricing agreement (APA), confirming the validity of the TP policy applicable to the new entity. The transactional net margin method (TNMM) formula in the APA allocated a fixed markup to LuxOpCo on its operating costs, while any residual profit earned by Amazon in the EU market was divided by total sales in the EU market to produce a royalty rate payable to LuxSCS. Subject to a minimum of 0.45% and a maximum of 0.55%, LuxOpCo paid the royalty calculated in this way to LuxSCS for the sublicensed intangibles. The Commission concluded in 2017 that the formula approved in the APA conferred a selective tax benefit in violation of TFEU Article 107.[95]

In its judgment, the CJEU principally adhered to Advocate General Kokott's opinion and dismissed the Commission's appeal of the GCEU's decision that Luxembourg did not grant state aid to the Amazon group.[96] In particular, the CJEU rejected the Commission's use of an autonomous EU arm's length standard and stipulated definitive limits on referencing the OECD TPG[97] to identify a selective advantage under EU state aid law.

3 RECENT DEVELOPMENTS IN COUNTRY-SPECIFIC TP LEGISLATION, GUIDELINES, JURISPRUDENCE, AND CASE LAWS

3.1 ALP and TP Methods

The year 2023 witnessed numerous countries either introducing or adapting changes to the ALP and TP rules. A significant development occurred in Brazil where deliberations on adopting new TP measures had been ongoing for an extended period. Through Law No. 14,596 of 14 June 2023,[98] Brazil adopted the TP framework aligning with OECD

Law, 64 Eur. Taxn. 2/3 (2024), Journal Articles & Opinion Pieces IBFD (accessed 15 March 2024) https://doi.org/10.59403/cbz1jb.

95. CJEU 14 December 2023, *Commission v. Luxembourg*, C-457/21 P; Alexander F. Peter, *Luxembourg Didn't Grant State Aid to Amazon Group, CJEU Holds*, 112 Tax Notes International (18 December 2023); Leopoldo Parada, *Amazon and the Future of State Aid Law in Direct Tax Matters*, Tax Notes International 595 (2024).
96. Alexander F. Peter, *Luxembourg Didn't Grant State Aid to Amazon Group, CJEU Holds*, 112 Tax Notes International (18 December 2023); cf., also CJEU 14 December 2023, *Commission v. Luxembourg, Amazon.com Inc., and Amazon EU Sàrl*, C-457/21 P.
97. OECD (2022), *Transfer Pricing Guidelines for Multinational Enterprises and Tax Administrations*.
98. Brazil, *Law No. 14,596* (14 June 2023).

TPG. Subsequent to that, the Brazilian Federal Revenue published Normative Instruction on 19 September 2023[99] that contains regulations related to the new TP rules. The erstwhile Brazilian TP rules diverged from international practices and followed a system with fixed margins. However, the current rules, in force since 1 January 2024, are based on comparability tests, thereby adopting the ALP. The new rules align with the OECD TPG and contain definitions of controlled transactions (Article 3) and associated enterprises (Article 4), as well as guidance on accurate delineation, comparability analysis, TP methods, documentation, etc. Specific guidance on transactions involving intangibles, business restructuring, and intra-group services, including safe harbour rules for low-value-adding services (LVAS) in accordance with Chapter VII of the OECD TPG and royalty transactions, is also provided.[100] In addition to the substantive rules on the ALP's applicability, the new rules allow for disregarding and recharacterizing a transaction when it is concluded that unrelated parties would not have entered into the controlled transaction as established. Three types of adjustments are introduced: spontaneous adjustments made by the taxpayer on the corporate income tax basis, compensatory adjustments made by the parties involved in the controlled transaction to adjust the intercompany transaction, and primary adjustments made by the tax authority to increase corporate income tax. The rules also provide detailed documentation requirements, the APA process, and penalties. Even after introducing the new system, the old regime was optional until the end of 2023, and taxpayers had until 31 December 2023 to choose the irrevocable election effective from 1 January 2023. However, from 1 January 2024, the new regime is mandatory for all related party transactions.

In June 2023, the Canadian Government released a consultation document to refine the TP rules.[101] This consultation was first announced following the Crown's defeat in the *Cameco* case.[102] Finally, after two years, the public consultation was released 'with a view to protecting the integrity of the tax system while preserving Canada's attractiveness as a destination for new investment and business activity'.[103] The language and concepts provided in the document are heavily influenced by the OECD TPG. The proposed changes focus on three types of guidance: general guidance on applying the ALP, guidance on administration, and detailed guidance on applying the ALP in specific situations. The measures proposed as part of the proposal include amendments to incorporate steps requiring the delineation of transactions and comparison of conditions into section 247 of the Income Tax Act and the existing TP adjustment rule. The delineation of the transaction is a new concept inspired by the OECD TPG and is defined to include factors that emphasize the 'actual conduct' of the

99. Brazilian Federal Revenue Service (RFB), *Normative Instruction 2,161/23* (19 September 2023).
100. *See* OECD, *OECD Transfer Pricing Guidelines for Multinational Enterprises and Tax Administrations 2022*, Ch. VII (OECD Transfer Pricing Guidelines for Multinational Enterprises and Tax Administrations, OECD 20 January 2022), available at https://doi.org/10.1787/0e655865-en Part D.
101. Department of Finance, Canada, *Consultation on Reforming and Modernizing Canada's Transfer Pricing Rules* (6 June 2023), available at https://www.canada.ca/content/dam/fin/consultations/2023/tp-pt-eng.pdf.
102. CA: Federal Court, 26 June 2020, *Cameco Corporation v. Her Majesty the Queen*.
103. Department of Finance, Canada, *supra* n. 101, at p. 4.

parties in priority to the contractual terms of transactions. Once the delineated transaction or series has been established, its 'conditions' are to be scrutinized and adjusted to arm's length conditions. When these differ from those that would have been agreed by unrelated parties, the taxpayer's reported income or expense amount should be adjusted to the quantum or nature that would have been determined if arm's length conditions had applied. The second proposed amendment includes repealing sections 247(2)(b) and (d) that currently comprise the recharacterization rule and substituting it with a non-recognition and replacement rule. The former would apply when the transaction or series differs from that which would have been entered into by arm's length parties dealing in a commercially rational manner in comparable circumstances. The delineated transaction or series would have to prevent the determination of a transfer price that would have been acceptable to the entities if they had been acting at arm's length. This amendment eliminates the 'tax benefit' requirement in the existing rules, which was one of the primary issues in the *Cameco* case. Finally, the consultation document also includes a 'consistency rule' requiring section 247 to be applied to achieve consistency with the OECD TPG unless the context otherwise requires. However, whether the application of the OECD TPG is to be done using a static or ambulatory approach to future guidance is unclear. If the proposed changes are adopted, it would represent the first substantial rewrite of the TP rules in section 247 since it was first enacted in 1997.

Similarly, in 2022, the UAE Ministry of Finance (MoF) introduced the new corporate tax regime introducing TP rules based on the ALP aligned with the OECD TPG. These rules were implemented from 1 June 2023. Moreover, on 23 October 2023, the Federal Tax Authority (FTA) released a 140-page Transfer Pricing Guide (Guide) providing detailed guidance on the practical application of the rules with numerous examples.[104] The FTA encourages taxpayers to refer to the OECD TPG if an issue is not specifically addressed in the Guide. However, it does not constitute a legally binding document even though it provides comprehensive guidance on how to apply the TP regulations.[105]

Even in Saudi Arabia, the Zakat, Tax and Customs Authority (ZATCA) approved amendments to the TP regulations as proposed in the public consultation document issued on 4 July 2022. This is a significant change in the Saudi Arabian tax landscape as, contrary to Saudi income taxpayers, Zakat payers were previously not subject to TP regulations. On 26 November 2023, ZATCA also issued detailed guidelines on related party transactions.[106] These amendments were effective from 1 January 2024.

Similarly, Malta also introduced formal TP rules effective from 1 January 2024.[107] However, those provide for a *de minimis* threshold for total related party cross-border transactions of EUR 6 million and EUR 20 million in revenue and capital, respectively,

104. Federal Tax Authority, UAE, *Transfer Pricing Guide, CTGTP1* (23 October 2023).
105. *Ibid.*, at s. 2.6.
106. *Guidelines on Related Party Transactions for Zakat Purposes* (Zakat, Tax and Customs Authority (ZATCA), Saudi Arabia).
107. MT: Ministry for Finance and Employment, Malta, *Transfer Pricing Rules, (S.L. 123.207)*.

measured in the preceding financial year. They also contain a carve-out for securitization transactions.

Even Kenya introduced Draft Income Tax (Transfer Pricing) Rules 2023 for public comments in order to revamp its TP rules introduced in 2006.[108] These rules are modelled based on the OECD TPG. Adding to the previously listed transactions subject to TP rules, the draft rules also include transactions pertaining to insurance and reinsurance; derivatives; cost-contribution arrangements; business restructuring or reorganization irrespective of whether it has a bearing on the financial position of the entity involved; financial transactions, including guarantees; the sale or purchase of marketable securities; any type of advances, and deferred payments or receivable. Specific guidance regarding the application of methods for commodity transactions has also been prescribed.

The Polish Income Tax Department at the MoF published guidance on 28 September 2023 for applying the cost-plus method. It addresses issues such as its proper application comparability criteria, errors in using it, comparison with other methods, and examples of its practical application.

Recently, on 26 January 2024, His Majesty's Revenue and Customs (HMRC) released detailed guidance on the TP risk framework.[109] The aim of this guidance is to convey the proper application of the six-step risk framework.

Apart from the developments at the country levels, even the court cases observed in 2023 focused mainly on the issues of selecting and applying TP methods. This is in accordance with the trends observed in the previous years. A complete list of these cases is provided in section 3.9 of this chapter.

3.2 The Blocked Income Conundrum

Foreign legal restrictions on cross-border payments and receipts have always been a point of controversy. A 'legal restriction to block income' is a law preventing a controlled tax-paying entity from establishing transfer prices at the market rate thus 'blocking' the entity from reporting income as a company involved in an arm's length transaction would.[110] Such restrictions exist when a country sets a minimum (or maximum) price for transferring certain goods and services.

The issue of blocked income has been particularly in the limelight due to two landmark cases decided by the US Tax Court – *3M*[111] and *Coca-Cola*.[112] In the *3M* case,

108. Cabinet Secretary for National Treasury, Kenya, *Draft Income Tax (Transfer Pricing) Rules, 2023* (4 September 2023).
109. HMRC, *INTM485025: Transfer Pricing Operational Guidance: Accurate Delineation of the Actual Transaction – Risk* (26 January 2023), available at https://www.gov.uk/hmrc-internal-manuals/international-manual/intm485025#Relevant%20profits.
110. J. Davlin, *The Uncertainty of Foreign Blocked Income: Trying to Reconcile the 1994 §482 Regulations with Procter & Gamble*, 5 Duke Journal of Comparative & International Law 117-144 (1994).
111. US: US Tax Court, 9 February 2023, *3M Company And Subsidiaries v. Commissioner of Internal Revenue*.
112. US: US Tax Court, 8 November 2023, *The Coca-Cola Company and Subsidiaries v. Commissioner of Internal Revenue*.

the issue arose due to a licensing arrangement that the 3M Co. had with its Brazilian subsidiary beginning in 2006 that allowed 3M's Brazilian subsidiary to use certain trademarks. Brazilian domestic law capped the royalty permitted at 1% as the maximum amount allowable for the Brazilian subsidiary to remit to its related party licensor, 3M. The blocked income issue was governed by a 1994 regulation that set the standards for when the taxpayer could rely on a foreign ban on payments in order to avoid current taxation. Even though the taxpayer admitted that it did not meet the regulation's procedural requirements, it challenged the regulation to be invalid. The taxpayer relied on various case laws, particularly *First Security Bank of Utah,*[113] *Proctor and Gamble,*[114] and *Exxon Corp.*[115] Distinguishing these precedents, the tax court rejected this administrative challenge with a narrow margin of 9-8.

This issue was also a point of contention in the *Coca-Cola* case decided on 8 November 2023 on the issue of blocked income. Even in this case, the Brazilian rules limiting the payment of royalties were at issue. Following the decision in *3M,* the tax court ruled in favour of the internal revenue service (IRS). It noted that, even though the Brazilian law restricted the royalty payment, it did not place any limitations on the 'amount'. The court held that the remaining amount could have been paid as a dividend from the Brazilian subsidiary.

Both of these cases have resulted from the restrictions placed under Brazilian law. However, these issues are likely to be mitigated in the future, given that Brazil has adopted the TP rules based on the ALP. However, the issue of blocked income is not just limited to Brazilian restrictions. Many countries place similar limitations on certain payments or receipts. Moreover, the restrictive measures by way of sanctions would also need to be examined from the perspective of the ALP. The OECD TPG recognizes the issue of blocked income and the difficulty in applying TP rules when such restrictions are placed by countries.[116] Additional guidance on these issues by world organizations and domestic legislation would be welcomed.

3.3 Taxation of Digital Economy

The principal aim of the BEPS 2.0 initiative by the OECD/G20 IF was to address issues arising from the digitalization of the economy and introduce the two-pillar solution. Over the years, the OECD has made considerable progress under both Pillars. Concerning Pillar Two, many countries have already passed legislation in accordance with the model rules, while others have made commitments to adopt these rules in the near future.

113. US: US Supreme Court, 21 March 1972, *Commissioner v. First Security Bank of Utah.*
114. US: US Sixth Circuit Court, 20 April 1992, *Procter & Gamble Co. v. Commissioner.*
115. US: US Fifth Circuit Court, 17 October 1996, *Exxon Corp. & Affiliated Cos. v. Commissioner.*
116. OECD (2022), *OECD Transfer Pricing Guidelines for Multinational Enterprises and Tax Administrations 2022,* OECD Publishing, Paris, https://doi.org/10.1787/0e655865-en, at para. 1.154.

Following is the list of countries which have passed legislation with respect to Pillar Two:[117]

Country	*Effective Date*	*Rules*
Austria	1 January 2024 1 January 2025 1 January 2024	IIR UTPR QDMTT
Belgium	1 January 2024 1 January 2025 1 January 2024	IIR UTPR QDMTT
Bulgaria	1 January 2024 1 January 2025 1 January 2024	IIR UTPR QDMTT
Canada	31 December 2023 31 December 2024 1 January 2024	IIR UTPR QDMTT
Cyprus	31 December 2023 31 December 2024 31 December 2023	IIR UTPR QDMTT
Czech Republic	31 December 2023 31 December 2024 31 December 2023	IIR UTPR QDMTT
Denmark	31 December 2023 31 December 2024 31 December 2023	IIR UTPR QDMTT
Finland	1 January 2024 1 January 2025 1 January 2024	IIR UTPR QDMTT
France	31 December 2023 31 December 2024 31 December 2023	IIR UTPR QDMTT
Germany	1 January 2024 1 January 2025 1 January 2024	IIR UTPR QDMTT
Hungary	31 December 2023 31 December 2024 31 December 2023	IIR UTPR QDMTT
Ireland	1 January 2024 1 January 2025 1 January 2024	IIR UTPR QDMTT
Italy	1 January 2024 1 January 2025 1 January 2024	IIR UTPR QDMTT
Japan	1 April 2024	IIR

117. As of January 2024.

Country	*Effective Date*	*Rules*
South Korea	1 January 2024 1 January 2024	IIR UTPR
Liechtenstein	1 January 2024 1 January 2025 1 January 2024	IIR UTPR QDMTT
Luxembourg	31 December 2023 31 December 2024 31 December 2023	IIR UTPR QDMTT
Malaysia	1 January 2025 1 January 2025	IIR QDMTT
Netherlands	31 December 2023 31 December 2024 31 December 2023	IIR UTPR QDMTT
New Zealand	1 January 2024 1 January 2025 1 January 2024	IIR UTPR QDMTT
Norway	1 January 2024 1 January 2025 1 January 2024	IIR UTPR QDMTT
Romania	31 December 2023 31 December 2024 31 December 2023	IIR UTPR QDMTT
Slovak Republic	31 December 2023	QDMTT
Slovenia	31 December 2023 31 December 2024 31 December 2023	IIR UTPR QDMTT
Sweden	1 January 2024 1 January 2025 1 January 2024	IIR UTPR QDMTT
Switzerland	1 January 2024 1 January 2025 1 January 2024	IIR UTPR QDMTT
United Kingdom	31 December 2023 31 December 2023 31 December 2023	IIR UTPR QDMTT
Vietnam	1 January 2024 1 January 2024	IIR QDMTT

Even though many other countries have also committed to implementing the Pillar Two rules, no formal legislation has been adopted.

In addition to the developments and implementation of Pillar Two, many countries have also taken unilateral measures to address tax issues arising from digitalization. It should be noted that one of the requirements of the two-pillar solution was abolishing DSTs and similar measures. Adopting such measures in certain jurisdictions indicates that they still prefer to tax these digital activities through other simplified means as adopting and implementing Pillar One in the domestic jurisdiction would be an administrative burden.[118]

The Colombian Government issued an executive decree on 28 November 2023 providing a regulatory framework for applying the significant economic presence rule for digital services.[119] This rule, applicable from 1 January 2024, establishes a new nexus criterion for tax liability in Colombia for non-resident companies engaged in selling goods to Colombian clients and/or providing 'qualified digital services' to Colombian clients/users. Non-residents falling within the scope of these rules may elect one of two mechanisms: a 10% withholding tax on gross income or a 3% rate over the gross income declared on a tax return. Similarly, Uganda implemented a DST in July 2023 that is applicable to digital services delivered via the Internet, an electronic network, or an online platform. Covered digital services include online advertising, data services, services delivered through an online marketplace or intermediation platforms, digital content, online gaming, cloud computing, data warehousing, and any other digital service prescribed by the Minister of Finance. The applicable tax rate is 5% on the gross payment.

In Kenya, the Finance Act 2023 enacted a withholding tax on income earned by residents and non-residents from digital content monetization. This tax applies to individuals and business owners generating income from online content creation including sponsorship, content monetization, advertising revenue, subscription services, licensing content, including photographs and music, and other related digital services and content creation. The withholding tax rate is 5% for residents and 20% for non-residents.

Even New Zealand introduced the Digital Services Tax bill in Parliament on 31 August 2023.[120] The bill allows the government to impose a tax of 3% on the gross revenues of large multinational entities with highly digitalized business models earning income from New Zealand. Taxable digital services revenues include those related to intermediation platforms, social media and content-sharing platforms, internet search engines, digital advertising, and user-generated data. The bill is likely to come into force on 1 January 2025 or at a later date fixed by the order.

The proliferation of DSTs and similar measures even after the finalization of Pillars One and Two indicates that some countries prefer simplified solutions, such as withholding taxes on these services, rather than the detailed rules under the two-pillar solutions as many of these countries lack the capacity to administer complicated rules.

Even at the EU level, Member States transposed and enacted the Directive on Administrative Cooperation (2021/514) (DAC7) as of 1 January 2023. Accordingly, operators of digital platforms that are resident, incorporated, managed, or have a permanent establishment in a Member State, as well as non-EU platform operators

118. It is to be noted that the OECD released a package of guidance in relation to Pillar One Amount A on 11 October 2023, including Multilateral Convention (MLC) which reflects the current consensus achieved among members of the IF. However, the MLC is not yet open for signature.
119. CO: Ministry of Finance Colombia, *Regulatory Decree 2039* (27 November 2023).
120. NZ: Inland Revenue, New Zealand, *Digital Services Tax Bill (DST BILL)* (31 August 2023), available at https://www.legislation.govt.nz/bill/government/2023/0288/latest/whole.html (accessed 12 March 2024).

performing certain activities in the EU, must report cross-border and non-cross-border transactions of their registered sellers to tax authorities. Platform operators must report information regarding their own identification and information regarding sellers, including identification, financial account identifier, and the respective holder, Member States of residence, payments to sellers, and fees or taxes charged or withheld.

3.4 Services

Intra-group services constitute a substantial portion of transactions among related parties. To streamline the application of TP rules to intra-group services, various jurisdictions have proposed or implemented changes concerning these transactions. The new Canadian draft legislation has suggested introducing safe harbour rules for certain LVAS. Aligned with the OECD TPG on LVAS, these establish a deemed arm's length return of 5% for the covered services.[121] Additionally, in accordance with the OECD's Amount B framework, modifications have also been suggested for arm's length remuneration for distributors engaged in relatively routine activities.[122] These changes are intended to reduce compliance and administrative burdens. Similar changes for the LVAS have also been enacted in Brazil and the UAE.

3.5 Financing

MNEs routinely engage in intercompany financial transactions to facilitate their global operations. These transactions encompass loans for capital investments or acquisitions, short-term working capital loans, factoring to release cash at a subsidiary, and cash pooling to optimize the group's internal cash utilization while minimizing external interest expenses. Consequently, financial transactions constitute a crucial element of MNE functionality. In the 2020 OECD Chapter X, financial transactions were incorporated into the guidance and offered a framework for taxpayers and tax authorities to address TP challenges arising from such transactions. Numerous jurisdictions have adopted rules over the past few years governing intra-group financial arrangements, aligning with the 2020 OECD guidance on financial transactions.

While enacting its TP legislation, Brazil also introduced rules for financial transactions aligned with Chapter X of the OECD TPG.[123] Historically, financial transactions were not subject to a TP analysis in Brazil. The new rules require a specific economic analysis for any intercompany transaction involving financial resources that are considered debt transactions. Their scope also includes transactions related to guarantees, cash pooling, and captive insurance.

121. *See* Department of Finance, Canada, *supra* n. 101, at s. D.1.
122. *See ibid.*, at s. D.2.
123. *Supra* n. 98, at s. VI. Law No. 14,596 provides a broad framework for how the ALP would apply to financial transactions. However, Normative Instruction 1,161/23 does not yet provide detailed rules on the topic.

In Germany, the Administrative Principles Transfer Pricing (AP TP 2023)[124] released on 6 June 2023 has excluded the contentious MoF viewpoint on interest deductions, aligning with the OECD TPG and recent German jurisprudence in which the Bundesfinanzhof (BFH; Federal Fiscal Court) contradicted the position of the MoF in a ruling published on 21 October 2021.[125] According to the ruling, the interest rate should be based on the borrower's (not the lender's) economic circumstances. However, with borrowers' increasing economic importance, the impact of their economic circumstances on the interest rate may be influenced by the group's economic circumstances due to implicit group support. It abandons the concept that lenders lacking control functions should earn a risk-free rate, thereby acknowledging the lender's economic circumstances. The AP TP 2023 also clarifies loan collateralization and states that it can be at arm's length contingent on third-party behaviours and economic benefits. According to the AP TP 2023, a specific informational advantage (*Wissensvorsprung*) resulting from the possibilities of influence and control under company law would be taken into account in setting the price between unrelated third parties if it was based on a contractually agreed position. The extent and impact of the informational advantage due to company affiliations have to be considered appropriately for the respective case at hand. Additionally, the AP TP 2023 maintains the stance that synergies in cash pools cannot follow a causation principle and emphasizes a case-by-case assessment. Although aligned with the OECD TPG on cash pool leaders earning routine profits, the AP TP 2023 eliminates the opportunity for interest rate spreads. The MoF maintains its stance that long-term debit and credit positions in cash pools indicate a loan arrangement and not a cash pool, emphasizing appropriate treatment.

Even Canada proposed certain changes to intra-group financial arrangements. Some of them include limiting the terms of intra-group loans to five years using the credit rating of the MNE group as a whole and removing subordination features and embedded options.

In India, the Central Board of Direct Taxes (CBDT), through a notification on 19 December 2023, introduced changes to safe harbour rules concerning intra-group financial transactions.[126] These rules will be effective from 1 April 2024.

Apart from specific legislative changes pertaining to financial arrangements, courts also extensively dealt with these transactions. One of such cases was decided by the UK Upper Tribunal in *JTI Acquisitions*.[127] Though the case did not specifically focus on TP aspects, it concerned issues pertaining to intra-group financing and the application of the 'unallowable purpose' rule. Another noteworthy case on the application of

124. Bundesministerium der Finanzen, *Verwaltungsgrundsätze Verrechnungspreise 2023* (6 June 2023), available at https://www.bundesfinanzministerium.de/Content/DE/Downloads/BMF_Schreiben/Internationales_Steuerrecht/Allgemeine_Informationen/2023-06-06-Verwaltungsgrundsaetze-Verrechnungspreise-2023.pdf?__blob=publicationFile&v=2 (accessed 12 March 2024).
125. BFH, ruling dated 18 May 2021, I R 4/17.
126. Notification No. 104/2023/F. No. 370142/26/2023-TPL.
127. UK: UK Upper Tribunal, 7 August 2023, *JTI Acquisitions Company (2011) Ltd. v. HMRC*.

anti-abuse rules to intra-group financial transactions is *Mylan Holding*, decided by the Australian Federal Court.[128]

3.6 Intangibles

Intangibles have been a complicated area to deal with both for taxpayers and tax authorities. In accordance with the BEPS Action Plans, the OECD TPG and the UN Transfer Pricing Manual (TPM) revamped the guidance for intangibles by adding concepts such as development, enhancement, maintenance, protection and exploitation (DEMPE) and hard-to-value intangibles (HTVIs). In recent years, many countries have incorporated these rules into their domestic legislation.

In 2023, Malaysia adopted the DEMPE concept, maintaining that income attributable to intangible property should be awarded to the party that performs functions and controls risks related to the DEMPE of such property.[129] It clarifies that legal owner of such property would not be entitled to the income arising from it if it fails to perform these functions. This is in accordance with the guidance provided in the OECD TPG. Similarly, the UAE's new Transfer Pricing Guide also relies on the DEMPE concept for the TP analysis of intangibles.[130] The Transfer Pricing Guide begins with the definition of intangible and provides a six-step framework for the TP analysis of intangibles. The guide also briefly discusses HTVIs without delving into much detail on the issue. Even the Canadian draft legislation acknowledges the issue regarding HTVIs; however, it ultimately suggests that the existing Canadian legislative framework, in combination with the OECD TPG, is sufficient for addressing concerns regarding such issues.[131] Finally, the new Brazilian rules have abolished the previous royalty cap, which is a contentious issue in many blocked income cases.[132] The new system allows for royalty deductions (including for technical, scientific, administrative, or similar payments) in the following three scenarios:[133]

(1) the same amount is already considered a deductible expense by a related party;
(2) the amount deducted is not treated as the beneficiary's taxable income in accordance with the legislation of its jurisdiction; or
(3) the amounts are intended for financial, directly or expressly, deductible expenses of related parties which include the scenarios referenced above.

Article 47 of Provisional Measure No. 1,152/2022 ameliorates this problem and, together with the 2021 law liberalizing royalty remittances, eliminates both the potential for blocked income and the risk of double taxation on payments that are

128. AU: Australian Federal Court, 21 June 2023, *Mylan Australia Holding Pty Ltd.*
129. Inland Revenue Board of Malaysia, *Income Tax (Transfer Pricing) Rules 2023 [P.U.(A) 165]* (29 May 2023).
130. *See* Federal Tax Authority, UAE, *supra* n. 104, at s. 7.3.
131. Department of Finance, Canada, *supra* n. 101, at p. 59.
132. First Security bank, P&G, Texaco, 3M.
133. *Supra* n. 98, at Art. 44.

neither deductible nor legally blocked. The provisional measure retains an amended anti-abuse provision stipulated in Article 45 but otherwise relies on the ALP to determine when an intercompany royalty payment is excessive.[134]

The Australian Taxation Office (ATO) released a Practical Compliance Guideline (PCG) on 17 January 2024 on intangible arrangements.[135] Its focus is on the structuring aspects of intangible arrangements that may then be relevant for applying the reconstruction provisions in the Australian TP rules and also the general anti-avoidance rules. The PGC is a risk assessment framework that enables taxpayers to assess the likelihood of the ATO applying resources to consider the potential application of the general anti-avoidance rules or the TP rules to cross-border related party intangible migration arrangements broadly comprising:

- migrations of intangible assets – reflecting any restructure or change associated with the taxpayer's intangible assets that allow another entity to access, hold, use, transfer, or benefit from them; and
- mischaracterization and non-recognition of Australian activities connected with intangible assets – primarily focusing on tax risks associated with a failure to appropriately recognize and tax Australian development, enhancement, maintenance, and protection activities carried out in relation to intangible assets held offshore.

The ATO makes it clear that the PCG does not focus on pricing aspects of intangible arrangements, although the TP methodology and profit outcomes can impact the risk rating under the PCG. The latter also does not cover the potential for embedded royalties and/or royalty withholding tax considerations. Another key change is the inclusion of the Australian traffic light risk assessment system for intangible structuring.

Apart from the various country developments, various important case laws also dealt with transactions pertaining to intangibles. One such important decision was rendered by the Danish Supreme Court in the case of *TotalEnergies EP Denmark* (formerly known as Maersk Oil and Gas AS – MOGAS).[136] The case involved MOGAS, a company owned by AP Moller-Maersk AS in Denmark engaged in shipping and oil and gas exploration. MOGAS specialized in regional surveys to confirm potential oil and natural gas reserves and possessed the required expertise and assets to conduct surveys and generate preliminary reports indicating their location. It also entered into negotiations with the respective governments to obtain a licence for further exploration activities. These activities constituted Phase 1 and Phase 2 of the business. These initial phases constituted an important aspect of the business that was conducted by MOGAS and crucial for its business.

134. R. Finley, *Brazilian Transfer Pricing Reforms Ease U.S. Tax Frictions*, 109 Tax Notes International 552 (30 January 2023).

135. ATO, *Intangibles Migration Arrangements: Practical Compliance Guideline (PCG 2024/1)* (17 January 2024), available at https://www.ato.gov.au/law/view/view.htm?docid=%22COG%2FPCG20241%2FNAT%2FATO%2F00001%22 (accessed 12 March 2024).

136. DK: Danish Supreme Court, 6 September 2023, *TotalEnergies EP Denmark A/S*.

In one such case, MOGAS conducted Phases 1 and 2 that led to the establishment of subsidiaries in Algeria (MOGAS DZ in 1990) and Qatar (MOGAS QA in 1992). These entered into agreements with state-owned oil companies, and their branches in these jurisdictions continued subsequent phases. The Algerian branch operated without employees, while the Qatari branch acted as an operator. MOGAS issued performance guarantees to state-owned oil companies, pledging support for the subsidiaries, timely performance, and full technical and financial assistance. Importantly, no performance guarantee fees were charged by MOGAS. It also provided various administrative and technical services (time-writing services) to the subsidiaries at cost. Additionally, it did not bill the subsidiaries for feasibility reports, which are critical elements for further exploration activities (*see* Figure 1.1).

Figure 1.1 Pictorial Depiction of the Facts of the Case

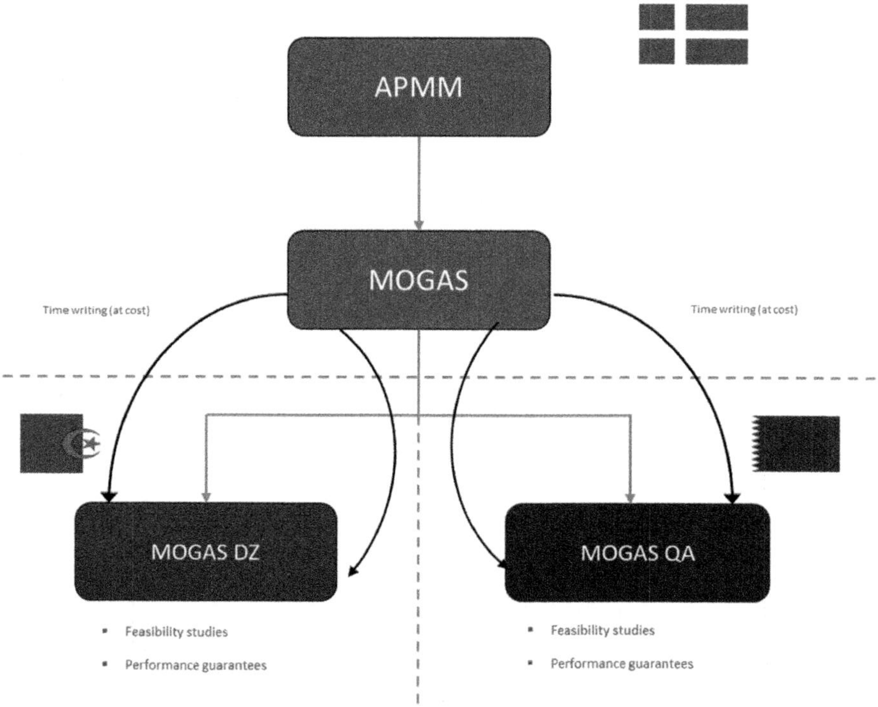

Despite incurring expenses for Phases 1 and 2, MOGAS did not receive compensation from the subsidiaries that received all of the profits from the highly profitable operation. The Danish tax authorities contested this structure for the assessment years 2006-2008 and carried out a discretionary assessment.

MOGAS argued that expenses related to preliminary surveys were not linked to existing group companies' work and should not be allocated to them. They claimed these costs were a natural part of their global business activities as the parent company in the oil sector. MOGAS emphasized that these surveys did not represent intangible assets provided to subsidiaries and considered themselves an investment company. Regarding performance guarantees, MOGAS asserted they held no economic value and aligned with the parent company's interests. They defended time-writing services at cost stating it followed industry norms and was considered a Comparable Uncontrolled Price (CUP). Tax authorities, however, highlighted MOGAS's chronic losses and suggested that these losses demonstrate income distortion within the group. They argued that preliminary surveys had economic value and emphasized MOGAS's ongoing role in generating income for local units through guarantees and expertise.

In 2022, the Danish Eastern High Court ruled in favour of MOGAS and adopted a very formalistic approach. The Eastern High Court determined that MOGAS DZ and MOGAS QA were the genuine proprietors of oil exploration licences after examining legal agreements and financial statements. It denied remuneration to MOGAS, considering there had been no intercompany transactions. The court acknowledged performance guarantees as an intercompany transaction but disagreed with the tax authority's valuation. Regarding time-writing services, it opined a profit element should be included, and the CUP used by the taxpayer lacked comparability.

However, the Danish Supreme Court reversed this decision and recognized the economic value in feasibility studies, time-writing services, and performance guarantees. It asserted that MOGAS's contributions were vital for subsidiaries to proceed and constituted an important 'know-how'. The court aligned with the Eastern High Court on time-writing services but endorsed the tax authorities' combined royalty rate of 1.7% for all transactions due to the absence of a comparability study by MOGAS.

The MOGAS case constitutes an important landmark in the oil and gas sector. Even though the feasibility studies constituted an important element for the functioning of the subsidiaries, the court failed to accurately delineate this transaction by simply agreeing to the arguments put forth by the tax authorities. MOGAS failed to fulfil the required burden of proof, and the court simply accepted the tax authority's proposal of applying a combined royalty of 1.7%. This case depicts the difficulty in assessing cases pertaining to intangibles.

3.7 Business Restructuring

Regarding business restructuring, not many specific legislative changes occurred in jurisdictions. However, Germany introduced some modifications to its existing rules on the change of functions. Building upon its previous decree on the Transfer of Business Functions published on 31 August 2022, the AP TP 2023 clarifies the definition of a 'transfer of function'. It discusses aspects relating to the secondment of employees, duplication of functions, transfer packages, termination clauses, valuation of functions, and a negative bargaining rate. The revised guidance retains its foundation in existing principles but omits several practical considerations. Notably, the clarification that certain transactions not perceived as a transfer of function by unrelated third parties should not follow the transfer of function principles has been removed. The '*de minimis*' rule of EUR 1 million serving as a threshold for a transfer of function and guidance on transactions meeting the criteria but not considered transfers under the ALP are no longer included. The helpful, practical guidance stating that timely contract terminations align with notice periods or that contractual expirations do not constitute a transfer of function has been omitted. Additionally, the updated guidance lacks specific examples of different restructuring types, such as the transfer of manufacturing or distribution functions, down-stripping from distributor to commissionaire/agent, etc., which were valuable for practical considerations. The MoF chose not to incorporate these examples into the updated guidance.[137]

Even the case laws dealing with business restructuring saw a decline in 2023. However, the Israeli court dealt with the issue of deemed transfer of functions, assets, and risks pursuant to a post-acquisition royalty arrangement and a research and development (R&D) contract in the *Medtronic Ventor* case.[138] The case concerned a US company acquiring a minority interest in an Israeli company that developed transcatheter heart valve technologies for treating aortic valve disease. Post-acquisition, the companies implemented royalty arrangements allowing the US company the issue of the Israeli company's IP and contract R&D services for which the Israeli company was compensated at cost-plus. The tax authorities claimed that this arrangement led to the transfer of the Israeli company's functions, assets, and risks to the US company that left it as an empty shell. The court sustained the arguments put forth by the tax authorities and held that post-acquisition, the Israeli company was stripped of its strategic and important activities and turned into a mere subcontractor. The court also examined the intercompany agreements and noticed that they were signed in 2011 retroactive to 2009. This issue of post-acquisition business restructuring has been contentious in Israel in recent years.[139]

3.8 Documentation/Country-by-Country Reporting

The sixth annual peer review of the BEPS Action 13 Minimum Standard of country-by-country reporting (CbCR) was published on 25 September 2023.[140] The CbCR requirements are subject to a peer review process to ensure timely and accurate implementation and to safeguard a balanced and fair situation.[141]

The sixth annual peer review covers 136 jurisdictions. For each jurisdiction, the review encompasses the domestic legal and administrative framework, the exchange of information framework, and the measures in place to ensure the confidentiality and

137. https://globaltaxnews.ey.com/news/2023-1095-german-ministry-of-finance-issues-updated-administrative-principles-regarding-transfer-pricing (accessed 12 March 2024).
138. IL: Israel Lod District Court, 1 June 2023, *Medtronic Ventor Technologies Ltd.*
139. *See* IL: Central District Court, 8 May 2022, *Israel v. Medingo Ltd.*; IL: Central District Court, 9 December 2019, *Broadcom Semiconductor Ltd v. Kfar Saba Assessing Officer*; IL: Israeli Central District Court, 6 June 2017, *Gteko Ltd. v. Kfar Saba Tax Assessor.*
140. OECD/G20 Base Erosion and Profit Shifting Project, *Country-by-Country Reporting: Compilation of 2023 Peer Review Reports* (OECD Publishing, Paris, 23 September 2023), available at https://doi.org/10.1787/21bd1938-en.
141. *Ibid.*, at p. 9.

appropriate use of the CbCR. The peer review process focuses on the following four elements of the minimum standard:

- domestic legal and administration framework;
- exchange of information framework;
- confidentiality; and
- appropriate use.

According to the report, over 110 jurisdictions have established a domestic legal framework for the CbCR. Even though this is a modest increase compared to the identified jurisdictions having a CbCR as of last year, this increase depicts their willingness to adopt these documentation requirements and their importance in the risk assessment framework. Apart from this, a number of jurisdictions have final legislation in place awaiting official publication. In this context, twenty-two jurisdictions have received a general recommendation to put in place or finalize their domestic legal or administrative framework, and thirty jurisdictions received one or more recommendations for improvements to specific areas of it. Additionally, eighty-nine jurisdictions have multilateral or bilateral competent authority agreements in place, whereas ninety-one have undergone an assessment by the Global Forum on Transparency and Exchange of Information for Tax Purposes concerning confidentiality and data safeguards in the context of implementing the automatic exchange of information standard and did not receive any action plan. Finally, seventy-three jurisdictions have provided detailed information, thereby enabling the IF to obtain sufficient assurance that measures are in place to ensure the appropriate use of the CbCR.

Many countries have also made changes to their TP documentation rules.[142] One such major change was introduced in the United Kingdom with the TP Records Regulations 2023.[143] These rules apply to MNE groups meeting the CbCR threshold. Moreover, on 12 September 2023, the Austrian MoF published updated guidance on the explanation and application of the DAC6 rules.[144] It provides additional clarifications on a number of key areas, including the meaning of tax advantage, TP structures, and the main benefit test. It also provides additional examples of persons who qualify as intermediaries. Apart from this, a few countries have also recommended increasing transparency with the public disclosure of their CbCRs. In March 2023, Australia proposed a draft legislation whereby certain entities (labelled as Significant Global Entities) are required to publicly publish their CbCR information.[145] According to the

142. Canada, France, Dominican Republic, Brazil, South Korea, UAE, Saudi Arabia, Malaysia to name a few.
143. Transfer Pricing Records Regulations 2023, No. 818, available at https://www.legislation.gov.uk/uksi/2023/818/contents/made (accessed 12 March 2024).
144. Update information letter on the application of the EU Reporting Obligation Act (EU-MPfG), Austrian Bundesministerium Finanzen, https://findok.bmf.gv.at/findok/volltext?execution=e100000s1&segmentId=34c7cbf8-9f66-48e3-9d8d-31c0e053c67c (accessed 12 March 2024).
145. US: Australian Government Treasury, *Treasury Laws Amendment (Measures 4 for Future Bills) Bill 2023: Financial 5 reporting by public companies* (16 March 2023), available at https://treasury.gov.au/consultation/c2023-373630 (accessed 12 March 2024).

draft legislation, failure to comply with the requirements would result in stringent penalties, including imprisonment.

3.9 Dispute Resolution

The OECD published a report on 14 November 2023 consolidating information about MAPs for IF member jurisdictions.[146] This manual serves as an exceptionally useful tool that offers a quick overview of a jurisdiction's current MAP situation, encompassing the MAP framework, recent developments, and a summary of MAP statistics. This contribution adds to the OECD's ongoing efforts post-BEPS Action 14.

The OECD released the 2022 MAP statistics on the same day. While the general figures saw minimal variations, a noteworthy improvement was observed – a reduction in the duration of MAPs dealing with TP from 32.3 to 28.9 months. This represents a significant step towards the 24-month duration target set by BEPS Action 14 in previous years. Conversely, the average duration for MAPs dealing with other issues increased from 20.7 to 22.17 months.

There was an 11% increase in access to TP MAP cases, rising from 1,015 to 1,166 new ones, highlighting taxpayers' interest in this format. The overall inventory of MAP cases increased by 49, and the percentage of cases closed with a major outcome – fully eliminating double taxation – increased by 6% thereby achieving 59% of closed cases.

Building on the MAP statistics, the OECD unveiled the 2022 MAP awards, identifying certain jurisdictions for their handling of MAPs based on considered proxies. The awards encompassed eight categories in this context:

(1) average monthly time to close TP MAP cases: the Netherlands (19.62), Switzerland (21.34), Denmark (22.03), Germany (25.37), and Spain (25.85);
(2) average monthly time to close other MAP cases: New Zealand (6.36), Ireland (7.5), Portugal (11.42), the United Kingdom (11.68), and Luxembourg (13.26);
(3) lowest pre-2016 cases inventory: Canada (1.04%), the Netherlands (1.14%), Switzerland (2.14%), Spain (3.26%), and Belgium (3.29%);
(4) closing ratio large inventory: Luxembourg (57%), Denmark (53%), Ireland (52%), the Netherlands (44%), and Switzerland (41%);
(5) closing ratio medium inventory: Norway (54%), Singapore (51%), Australia (51%), Hungary (42%), and Japan (38%);
(6) TP cases fully resolved by agreement: Denmark/Ireland (83), Italy/Spain (66), the Netherlands/Spain (47);
(7) other cases fully solved by agreement: Germany/Ireland (135), Ireland/United Kingdom (65), the Netherlands/United Kingdom (63); and

146. OECD, *2022 Mutual Agreement Procedure Statistics* (14 November 2023), available at https://www.oecd.org/tax/dispute/mutual-agreement-procedure-statistics.htm (accessed 12 March 2024).

(8) the most improved jurisdiction in relation to an increase in cases: the Netherlands (102).

Apart from the MAP statistics, various country developments also occurred in the area of APAs. In South Africa, the government introduced an APA program with the Tax Administration Law Amendment Bill 2023. This is set to begin in a pilot phase, offering potentially affected taxpayers an opportunity to gain insights into the APA framework. This initiative by the South African Government is to learn from other jurisdictions and expand its capacity before considering multilateral APA applications. Similarly, the UAE and Saudi Arabia also introduced an APA program while presenting the new TP rules. Changes were also brought about in APA regimes in Greece,[147] Malaysia, and the United Kingdom.[148]

3.10 Significant Domestic Case Law

The year 2023 saw several significant TP cases throughout the world. The WU Transfer Pricing Center conducted a survey of some of the important cases and noticed that the majority of them pertained to transactions of intra-group goods and services.[149] However, cases related to intra-group financing saw a decline compared to previous years. Nevertheless, cases relating to intangibles remain constant. For the issues observed, the majority of the cases dealt with the selection and application of the appropriate TP method as one of the important issues in most of the observed cases. Other important issues included burden of proof, comparability analysis, application of anti-abuse rules, non-recognition, losses, documentation, and attribution of profits to permanent establishments. Most of the observed cases were from the court of first instance, showcasing a surge in new TP cases being litigated worldwide. The end result was that the year 2023 exhibited a distinct trend from the preceding two years. Tax administrations secured victory in many of the analysed cases. Notably, the tax authorities achieved success in pivotal cases such as *3M*,[150] *Coca-Cola*,[151] *JTI Acquisitions Company*,[152] *ST Dupont*,[153] *MOGAS*,[154] *Eni Norge*,[155] and *Medtronic Ventor*,[156] among others. The post-BEPS guidance on TP has empowered tax authorities with tools to challenge transactions. Furthermore, issues such as burden of proof and inadequate documentation from taxpayers contributed to these victories. Additionally,

147. Decision A.1107/2023 of the Independent Authority for Public Revenues (AADE).
148. Transfer pricing: methodologies: Advance Pricing Agreements: introduction, *INTM422010, HMRC International Manual*, https://www.gov.uk/hmrc-internal-manuals/international-manual/intm422010 (accessed 12 March 2024).
149. *See* A. Padwalkar & M.B. Moura, *The Transfer Pricing World in 2023: A Review*, TPI 6 (December 2023).
150. *Supra* n. 111.
151. *Supra* n. 112.
152. US: UK Upper Tribunal, 7 August 2023, *JTI Acquisitions Company (2011) Ltd. v. HMRC.*
153. FR: French Conseil d'État, 5 July 2023, *ST Dupont.*
154. *Supra* n. 136.
155. NO: Norwegian District Court, 7 September 2023, *Eni Norge.*
156. IL: Israel Lod District Court, 1 June 2023, *Medtronic Ventor Technologies Ltd.*

establishing specialized teams in many tax administrations that are equipped with various instruments and databases has enhanced their ability to scrutinize and assess complex TP matters. However, it is essential to note that this trend may evolve as cases from the first instance are challenged, and decisions from higher judiciary bodies might differ, as was observed in the analysed cases from this and previous years.

The following are the important cases:

Argentina

- Case: Dart Sudamericana SA, Case No. 35.050 I (Argentina Tax Court)
  Keywords: Goods and services, comparability analysis, TP methods

Australia

- Case: Mylan Australia Holdings, Case No. [2023] FCA 672 (Australian Federal Court)
  Keywords: Financial transactions, GAAR, TP documentation

Belgium

- Case: RB NV, Case No. 2021/2991/A (Belgian First Instance Court)
  Keywords: Financial transactions

Bulgaria

- Case: Yazaki Bulgaria Ltd, Case No. 22/2022 (Administrative Court Bulgaria)
  Keywords: Goods and services, TP method, comparability analysis

Colombia

- Case: Bavaria SA, Case No. 25000-23-37-000-2017-00654-01 (25885) (Colombian Supreme Administrative Court)
  Keywords: Goods and services, burden of proof

Czech Republic

- Case: Argo Hytos sro, Case No. 2 Afs 66/2021 – 57 (Czech Supreme Administrative Court)
  Keywords: Goods and services, TP methods
- Case: ESAB CZ, Case No. 31 Af 21/2022 – 99 (Czech Regional Court)
  Keywords: TP methods
- Case: Stock Plzen-Bozkov sro, Case No. 10 Afs 93/2021 – 69 (Czech Supreme Court)
  Keywords: Goods and services, burden of proof
- Case: ERT Automotive Bohemia sro, Case No. 10 Afs 257/2022 (Czech Supreme Court)
  Keywords: Goods and services, TP methods, burden of proof, comparability analysis

- Case: Stora Enso Wood Products, Case No. 7 Afs 358/2021 – 34 (Czech Supreme Administrative Court)
  Keywords: Goods and services, accurate delineation, losses
- Case: Mayer & Cie, Case No. 10 Afs 162/2021 – 50 (Czech Supreme Administrative Court)
  Keywords: Goods and services

Denmark

- Case: IP ApS, Case No. SKM2023.135.LSR (Danish Tax Tribunal)
  Keywords: Intangibles, valuation (TP methods)
- Case: Soy A/S, Case No. SKM2023.316.ØLR (Danish Eastern High Court)
  Keywords: TP documentation, TP methods recharacterization/ discretionary assessment
- Case: Maersk Oil and Gas – TotalEnergies EP, Case Nos. BS-15265/2022-HJR and BS-16812/2022-HJR (Danish Supreme Court)
  Keywords: Intangibles, losses, goods and services

France

- Case: SA Exel Industries, Case No. 21PA06438 (French Administrative Court of Appeal)
  Keywords: Goods and services, TP methods, burden of proof, comparability analysis, accurate delineation
- Case: SAS Blue Solutions, Case No. 21PA06144 & 21PA06143 (French Administrative Court)
  Keywords: Financial transactions
- Case: SAS Weg France, Case No. 21LY03690 (French Administrative Court of Appeals)
  Keywords: Goods and services, TP documentation, TP methods
- Case: ST Dupont, Case No. 464928 (French Supreme Administrative Court)
  Keywords: Goods and services, losses, TP methods
- Case: SA Scala, Case No. 22LY03210 (French Administrative Court of Appeal)
  Keywords: Intangibles, TP methods

Germany

- Case: X-BR GmbH, Case No. 10 K 310/19 (German Tax Court)
  Keywords: Business restructuring
- Case: Z Pipeline, Case No. 3 K 1940/17 F (German Tax Court)
  Keywords: Attribution of profits to PE
- Case: MEAT PE, Case No. 7 K 1938/22 (German Tax Court)
  Keywords: Attribution of profits to PE

Greece

- Case: Loan Ltd, Case No. 1177/2023 (Greece Tax Board)
  Keywords: Financial transactions, TP methods, comparability analysis

India

- Case: Auronext Pharma Pvt Ltd., Case No. 486/Hyd/2022 (ITAT Hyderabad)
  Keywords: Goods and services, TP methods

Israel

- Case: Medtronic Ventor Technologies Ltd., Case No. 31671-09-18 (Israel District Court)
  Keywords: Business restructuring, intangibles, TP methods, recharacterization

Italy

- Case: Dolce and Gabbana SRL, Case No. 02599/2023 (Italian Supreme Court)
  Keywords: Goods and services, CCAs, burden of proof
- Case: SGL Carbon SPA, Case No. 11625/2023 (Italian Supreme Court)
  Keywords: Financial transactions, TP methods
- Case: Otis Servizi SRL, Sez. 5 Num. 23587 Anno 2023 (Italian Supreme Court)
  Keywords: Financial transactions, intangibles, TP methods, accurate delineation

Kazakhstan

- Case: KOR Oil Company, Case No. 6001-22-00-6aП/1563 (Kazakh Supreme Court)
  Keywords: Goods and services, TP methods

Liechtenstein

- Case: A Corporation, Case No. VGH 2022/099 (Liechtenstein Administrative Court)
  Keywords: Financial transactions, burden of proof

Malaysia

- Case: Sandakan Edible Oils, Case No. WA-14-2-02/2021 (Malaysian High Court)
  Keywords: Goods and services, TP methods
- Case: Watsons Personal Care Stores, Case No. WA-14-20-06/2020 (Malaysian High Court)
  Keywords: Financial transactions, recharacterization

Mauritius

- Case: Innodis Ltd, Case No. 2023 SCJ 73 (Mauritius Supreme Court)
  Keywords: Financial transactions, GAAR

Netherlands

- Case: Fertilizer BV, Case No. 22/01909 and 22/03307 (ECLI:NL:PHR:2023:226) (Netherlands Supreme Court)
  Keywords: Business restructuring, accurate delineation, burden of proof
- Case: X Shareholder Loan BV, Case No. 22/00587 (ECLI:NL:GHAMS:2023:1305) (Netherlands Court of Appeals)
  Keywords: Financial transactions, GAAR
- Case: Lux Credit BV, Case No. AWB-21_4016 (ECLI:NL:RBDHA:2023:12061) (Netherlands Tax Court)
  Keywords: Financial transactions, TP documentation, burden of proof

Norway

- Case: Pgnig Upstream Norway AS, Case No. LB-2022-52192 (Norway Court of Appeal)
  Keywords: Goods and services (commodities), TP methods
- Case: Eni Norge AS, Case No. TSRO-2022-185908 (Norway District Court)
  Keywords: CCA, Goods and services, TP methods

Panama

- Case: Tech Distributor SA, Case No. TAT-RF-006 Expediente: 115-19 (Panama Administrative Tax Tribunal)
  Keywords: Goods and services, TP methods, comparability adjustments
- Case: Banana SA, Case No. TAT-RF-048 (Panama Administrative Tribunal)
  Keywords: Goods and services, TP methods, losses

Poland

- Case: R SA, Case No. II FSK 2290/20 (Polish Supreme Administrative Court)
  Keywords: Goods and services, TP methods
- Case: ESA, Case No. I SA/Po 53/23 (Polish Provincial Administrative Court)
  Keywords: Intangibles, accurate delineation, GAAR, recharacterization
- Case: D sp zoo, Case No. II FSK 181/21 (Polish Supreme Court)
  Keywords: Financial transactions, recharacterization/non-recognition
- Case: KP, Case No. I SA/Po 475/23 (Polish Provincial Administrative Court)
  Keywords: Intangibles, non-recognition/recharacterization

Portugal

- Case: Gestao de Empresas de Retalho SGPS SA, Case No. 657/07.1 BELSB (Portuguese Administrative Court of Appeal)
  Keywords: Intangibles
- Case: Sociedade Unipessoal LDA, Case No. 036/21.8BALSB (Portuguese Supreme Administrative Court)
  Keywords: Financial transactions, GAAR
- Case: R Cash & C SA, Case No. 2579/16.6 BELRS (Portuguese Administrative Court of Appeals)
  Keywords: Intangibles, TP methods

Spain

- Case: SGGE WT, Case No. Rec. 00/07503/2020/00/00 (Spanish Central Administrative Court)
  Keywords: Attribution of profits to PE, goods and services, TP methods, burden of proof, comparability analysis
- Case: Ferroli Espana SLU, Case No. 3400/2023 (ECLI:EN:AN:2023:3400) (Spanish National Court – 1st instance)
  Keywords: Goods and services, TP methods, comparability analysis
- Case: Institute of International Research SL, Case No. SAN 3426/2023 (ECLI: EN:AN:2023:3426) (Spanish National Court – First Instance)
  Keywords: Intangibles, burden of proof
- Case: Tomas Bodero SA, Case No. STSJ CL 3218/2023 (Spanish High Court)
  Keywords: Goods and services, TP methods, comparability analysis
- Case: Compañía Española de Petróleos, S.A., Case No. STS 3507/2023 (ECLI: ES:TS:2023:3507) (Spanish Supreme Court)
  Keywords: Attribution of profits to PE

South Korea

- Case: Korean Clothing Corp, Case No. 조심 2022 중 2863 (Korean Tax Tribunal)
  Keywords: Financial transactions
- Case: Fuel Injection Corp, Case No. 2022 구합 50258 (Korean District Court)
  Keywords: Intangibles, TP methods

Switzerland

- Case: A AG, Case No. A-4976/2022 (Swiss Federal Administrative Court)
  Keywords: Goods and services, TP methods

Ukraine

- Case: LK Ukraine Group, Case No. 1340/3525/18 (Ukraine Supreme Court)
  Keywords: Goods and services, TP methods

UK

- Case: JTI Acquisitions Company, Case No. [2023] UKUT 00194 (TCC) (UK Upper Tribunal)
  Keywords: Financial transactions, GAAR

USA

- Case: 3M Company and Subsidiaries, Case No. 160 T.C. No. 3 (US Tax Court)
  Keywords: Intangibles, blocked income
- Case: Skechers USA Inc, Case Nos. 10-I-171 AND 10-I-172 (Wisconsin Appeals Commission)
  Keywords: Intangibles, GAAR, burden of proof
- Case: Coca-Cola, Case No. T.C. Memo. 2023-135 (US Tax Court)
  Keywords: Intangibles, blocked income

4 CONCLUSIONS AND INSIGHTS

The TP landscape of 2023, as discussed in the preceding sections, showcased a confluence of developments at both international and jurisdictional levels. Although diverse in nature, they underscored the ongoing evolution and refinement of TP frameworks worldwide.

At the international level, organizations such as the OECD and the UN played pivotal roles in shaping TP policies and standards. The progress made in the OECD's Pillar One project, particularly concerning Amount B, reflects a concerted effort to address the challenges faced by jurisdictions in addressing issues pertaining to routine distribution activities. While their outcomes remain subject to scrutiny and debate, they signal a proactive approach to adapting TP rules to contemporary economic realities. Additionally, adopting or committing to adopt Pillar Two by many jurisdictions is a welcome step. However, the emergence of digital services taxes and similar measures is concerning despite the almost global consensus on these developments. On the other hand, the UN Tax Committee's guidance on specific industries and transactions towards the application of the ALP to these transactions is appreciated and is beneficial for both tax authorities and MNEs. Its focus on various TP workstreams demonstrates a commitment to addressing emerging issues such as TP compliance assurance and the treatment of carbon offsets.

Within the EU, initiatives aimed at enhancing tax transparency and harmonization continued to be prominent. The proposed TP Directive and the BEFIT proposal represent significant steps towards standardizing TP rules across Member States. Additionally, judicial decisions in cases such as the Apple and Amazon disputes highlight the complex interplay between TP and state aid regulations. If the proposed TP Directive is indeed adopted in the future and the ALP is harmonized within the EU, the contentious issues in many of the state aid cases would be something that no longer exists. However, the core TP issues prevalent in these cases remain relevant. It remains to be seen how these proposals work out in the future.

On a jurisdictional level, countries around the world embarked on legislative reforms to modernize their TP regimes. Brazil's comprehensive adoption of TP rules aligned with the ALP exemplifies this trend, signalling a departure from 'fixed mark-up' practices towards international practices. This shift would also relieve many MNEs dealing with Brazil and facing blocked income issues. Similarly, other countries' efforts to update their TP rules reflect a broader global movement towards harmonization and alignment with OECD guidelines.

The case law of 2023 provided valuable insights into emerging trends and areas of focus in TP disputes. The shift towards intra-group goods and services transactions and increased scrutiny of TP methods underscored the evolving nature of TP audits. Since many of these cases were decided by the lower judiciary, there is a likelihood that there would be a change in the final outcome of some of these cases. As tax authorities adapt to the post-COVID-19 landscape, it is likely that TP enforcement efforts will prioritize issues such as business restructuring, intangibles, and intra-group financing.

Apart from the various developments at the national and international level, certain 'hot' trends and developments will be seen in the years to come. With the proliferation of remote work and high digitalization, attention will likely be drawn to matters concerning permanent establishments and the allocation of profits therein. Tax authorities and MNEs are grappling with questions surrounding whether remote employees constitute a permanent establishment and under what circumstances. Furthermore, the incorporation of environmental, social, and governance (ESG) considerations into business operations is gaining momentum. As MNEs increasingly embrace sustainable practices, TP policies must be adapted to accommodate these evolving dynamics. This includes assessing how the ALP applies to transactions that prioritize environmental sustainability, social responsibility, and corporate governance. Given the novelty of these issues, it remains uncertain how tax authorities and MNEs will navigate this changing landscape.

In conclusion, the developments in TP observed in 2023 underscore the dynamic nature of this field and the need for continuous adaptation to changing economic realities. Given the churn in the global tax landscape with the progress under Pillars One and Two, the importance of TP and the disputes concerning it will increase in the years to come.[157]

157. *Supra* n. 10.

CHAPTER 2

Transfer Pricing and Amount B

*Kirsty Rockall**

* The author would like to thank Anuj Khamar, Sonal Arora and Folakemi Ogunyemi for their contributions. The view of the author is solely her own.

1 OVERVIEW

There are three threads that have impacted the international tax landscape in recent years: the adoption of Base Erosion and Profit Shifting (BEPS) Project, the proliferation of unilateral measures, and the second BEPS movement. Before the Organisation for Economic Co-operation and Development (OECD) initiated its Action Plan on BEPS, many countries were concerned that companies were able to apply the arm's length principle (ALP) in a way that allowed them to move profits to no or low tax jurisdictions based largely on legal ownership, contractual rights, and funding. Under the ALP, multinational enterprises (MNEs) aim to set their intercompany transfer prices at the same levels as unrelated parties.

However, when the issue was debated during the first round of BEPS talks, the OECD concluded that the arm's length standard itself was not a problem. Rather, the actual issue was whether international income tax rules that were developed in a 'brick-and-mortar' economic environment were still sufficient for complex international arrangements.

Coordinated international action was therefore required, and a new approach to intangible property (IP) ownership and the allocation of associated profits among group companies was established. This approach considered intangibles in terms of their development, enhancement, maintenance, protection and exploitation (DEMPE) and dovetailed with revisions to the OECD Transfer Pricing Guidelines for Multinational Enterprises and Tax Administrations (OECD Guidelines) on risk allocation.

As work progressed on the other actions, the OECD delayed work on Action 1 – taxing the digital economy. By the time the OECD and the G20 were ready to attempt to effectively address these issues under the second BEPS movement, questions about taxing economic activity conducted electronically with no physical presence no longer seemed to only apply to purely digital companies. The consensus was that most businesses can be considered digital in some form, and any notion that the digital economy could be ring-fenced for international tax purposes was largely abandoned.

In the meantime, some countries believed they were failing to collect their share of tax from rapidly expanding digital economic activity, such as from profits generated by social media users within their borders. With no way to tax revenues from users contributing content or viewing ads, certain countries moved ahead with digital services taxes on digital transactions such as online advertising and sales of user data.

The tax landscape has shifted from the conventional way of charging tax on profit to taxation of decision-making, substance, value creation, and the recognition of the importance of implementation and data collection.

In January 2019, the OECD kick-started the second BEPS movement with the release of a policy note describing two pillars of work: Pillar One addressing the tax challenges of the digitalization of the economy and the allocation of taxing rights to market jurisdictions, and Pillar Two addressing the remaining concerns about potential

BEPS activity and tax rate competition among countries. The project is being conducted through the Inclusive Framework (IF), in which 145 jurisdictions are currently participating. In October 2021, a political agreement was reached on key parameters of both pillars, together with an implementation plan. Of the 145 participating jurisdictions, 139 members of the IF have joined this agreement.[1]

The key thing to note is the shift in focus of Pillar One. It originally began life as a form of a digital services tax focused purely on digital consumer-facing businesses. The 2020 Blueprint, for example, focused on revenue generated by automated digital services or consumer-facing businesses. However, following a statement on 8 October 2021,[2] it was made clear that Pillar One is applicable to all MNEs, not just those that are 'digital'. The statement introduced the Pillar One concepts of Amount A and Amount B.

Amount A provides a new taxing right to market jurisdictions by reallocating a portion of an 'in-scope' MNE group's residual profit based on a formulary approach. Only the world's largest and most profitable MNEs are likely to be encompassed within its scope.[3] Revenue derived from regulated financial services and extractive industry sectors are excluded. Market jurisdictions are those to which goods or services are supplied or where consumers or users are located.

Amount B simplifies the existing transfer pricing (TP) rules for all taxpayers.[4] It is intended to streamline the application of the arm's length standard for baseline marketing and distribution activities. The concept sounds simple, i.e., Amount B is a solution to problems of the old-fashioned tangible world where a physical presence exists, but the profits to be ascribed to it cannot be agreed upon;[5] however, the journey to finalizing the Pillar One – Amount B launch report (the Report) was littered with potholes.

On 8 December 2022, the OECD released a public consultation document on Amount B[6] that generated discussions more on what was not included in the document than what was. At the time, it was emphasized that it was not a consensus document,[7] which revealed the chasm in opinion on how to effectively address and streamline TP for marketing and distribution activities.

Once the public comments had been digested and the IF had conducted some additional work, a further public consultation (2023 Public Consultation) was released.[8] On 19 February 2024, the Report was published, and as a key deliverable of Pillar One, Amount B is expected to not only provide relief of compliance burdens for

1. Members of the OECD/G20 Inclusive Framework on BEPS joining the Statement on a Two-Pillar Solution to Address the Tax Challenges Arising from the Digitalisation of the Economy.
2. https://www.oecd.org/tax/beps/statement-on-a-two-pillar-solution-to-address-the-tax-challenges-arising-from-the-digitalisation-of-the-economy-october-2021.html.
3. OECD (2021), *The threshold for Amount A is Total Revenue of Greater than EUR 20 billion and Profitability Versus Total Revenues Measuring 10%.*
4. https://www.oecd.org/tax/beps/pillar-one-amount-b-in-a-nutshell.pdf.
5. Cooper, G.S., *Building on the Rubble of Pillar One, Bulletin for International Taxation* (2021).
6. Public Consultation Document Pillar One – Amount B, OECD, 8 December 2022.
7. Public Consultation Document – Pillar One Amount B, OECD, 2022.
8. Public Consultation Document Pillar One – Amount B, OECD, 2023.

taxpayers but also to enable tax administrations to allocate resources towards riskier and more complex transactions, thereby ensuring a more efficient and impactful approach to their work.[9]

The Report refers to the new guidance as the simplified and streamlined approach; since this is quite verbose, this chapter will continue to refer to the guidance as Amount B. It also explores the origins of Amount B, sets out the guidance included in the Report, and reflects on the road left to travel.

2 AMOUNT B

After the success of its simplified approach to remunerating and documenting low-value-adding services (LVAS), the OECD was keen to enhance tax certainty in other areas. It recognized that TP disputes for baseline marketing and distribution arrangements present administrative challenges for both tax administrations and taxpayers. Reports from some low-capacity jurisdictions, for instance, estimate that TP disputes relating to distribution activities represent between 30% and 70% of all of their TP disputes.[10] The OECD[11] considers that these often arise due to:

- defining whether or not activities can be considered baseline, i.e., 'limited risk' or routine in nature, as opposed to being more complex;
- selecting the TP method;
- the appropriateness of the benchmarking analysis; or
- the suitability of comparability adjustments.

The objective of Amount B is, therefore, to facilitate compliance, prevent TP disputes from arising, and help to more efficiently resolve those that do arise.

Concisely stated, Amount B focuses on standardizing the reward to be earned by baseline distributors by replacing the requirement to use a one-sided TP method with an agreed pricing framework. The one that is proposed is designed to address a long-recognized source of failure of the transactional net margin method (TNMM), especially in developing countries. A perceived problem with it is that it requires tax administrations to perform individualized, expensive, and often fruitless searches for uncontrolled comparables when conducting TP examinations.[12] The intention is that Amount B will reduce the amount of time spent focusing on the minutia of what could be considered 'simpler' transactions and enable tax administrations and taxpayers to focus on more complex cases. Tax administrations can choose to adopt and legislate on the guidance or abstain. If it is adopted, the OECD proposes that tax administrations choose to either make it an elective approach or mandatory.

9. Pillar One – Amount B Launch Report, OECD, 2024.
10. https://www.oecd.org/tax/beps/pillar-one-amount-b-in-a-nutshell.pdf.
11. Public Consultation Document Pillar One – Amount B, OECD, 2023.
12. Durst, M.C., *A Simplified Method for Taxing Multinationals for Developing Countries: Building on the 'Amount B' Proposal to Repair the Transactional Net Margin Method*, ICTD Working Paper 108 (2020).

Amount B consists of three broad steps: scope, applying the method, and determining the arm's length return. It will be incorporated into the OECD Guidelines as an annex to Chapter IV and come into effect from 1 January 2025 should tax administrations decide to adopt the approach (more on this later in the chapter).

2.1 Scope

Amount B only applies to related party transactions that can be 'reliably priced' using a one-sided TP method with the distributor, sales agent, or commissionaire being the tested party. Distribution in this context means the wholesale distribution of goods, therefore, digital goods and services are not included within it. Wholesale distribution[13] includes the sale of goods to any customer except the end consumers.

A one-sided method includes the comparable uncontrolled price (CUP) method, the resale price method (RPM), and the TNMM. These are applicable in cases when one of the parties makes all of the unique and valuable contributions involved in the controlled transaction while the other party does not make any unique and valuable contribution. In such a case, the tested party should be the less complex one,[14] and as such, Amount B focuses on the least complex entity that is party to a qualifying distribution transaction.

Distributors who might employ a one-sided approach to pricing their transactions but also engage in additional functions, utilize more assets or assume higher risks compared to a standard or 'baseline' distributor are identified under Amount B's scoping process and are considered out of scope. Only baseline distributors are considered in scope, and they are akin to low-risk distributors that perform core distribution functions. These functions change depending on the distributor's business model and vary in complexity depending on industry and geographic location. Core distribution functions may include 'buying goods for resale, identification of new customers and managing customers' relationships, certain after-sales services, implementing promotional advertising or marketing activities, warehousing goods, processing orders or performing logistics, invoicing and collection'.[15]

Therefore, the first step in understanding whether a distributor would be in scope for the Amount B approach is to accurately delineate the transactions in accordance with Chapter I of the OECD Guidelines. This means that the qualifying transaction must, as stated above, be able to be reliably priced using a one-sided TP method with the distributor, sales agent, or commissioner being the tested party. Determining that a two-sided TP method should not apply is particularly important[16] and directly relates to the application of Amount B, which stipulates the use of the TNMM with certain exceptions for the CUP method.

---

13. For the purposes of Amount B, a distributor that engages in wholesale and retail distribution is deemed to solely carry out wholesale distribution if its three-year weighted average net retail revenues do not exceed 20% of its three-year weighted average net revenues.
14. OECD (2022), *Transfer Pricing Guidelines for Multinational Enterprises and Tax Administrations*.
15. Pillar One – Amount B Launch Report, OECD, 2024.
16. Pillar One – Amount B Launch Report, OECD, 2024.

The Report points to Chapter II, Part III, section C.2.2 of the OECD Guidelines as containing useful examples that outline three key economically relevant characteristics of qualifying transactions that indicate when it may not be suitable to apply a one-sided TP method. The Report states that these should be applied to evaluate whether a qualifying transaction is appropriate for the simplified and streamlined approach. The examples are:

- when the contributions of each party to the qualifying transaction are 'unique and valuable', including contributions of unique and valuable intangibles;
- when the distributor and its counterparties carry out functions, use assets, and assume risks in the qualifying transaction with such a degree of integration that their contributions cannot reliably be evaluated in isolation from each other; and
- when the distributor and its counterparties share the assumption of one or more economically significant risks to the transaction or when the various economically significant risks in relation to the transaction are separately assumed by the parties, but those risks are so closely interrelated and/or correlated that the use of the risks of each party cannot be reliably isolated.

In essence, contributions to any DEMPE of any intangibles would render the tested party/transaction out of scope. Interestingly, the Report notes that holding a regulatory licence would only constitute an intangible in certain circumstances. If it is readily available and does not have the effect of restricting the number of competitors in the market, then this is unlikely to constitute an intangible asset and prevent Amount B from applying. This has ramifications for the life sciences industry in which marketing authorizations may or may not be considered intangible for the purpose of Amount B.

In addition, the tested party in the qualifying transaction must not incur annual operating expenses[17] (AOE) lower than 3% (over a three-year period or less as appropriate) or greater than 20% to 30% of its annual net revenues. This latter ceiling, as stated in the Report, is considered to act as a proxy to exclude qualifying transactions from the scope where the ratio of operating expenses to sales might indicate that additional functions are performed. The Report notes that care should be taken when assessing what costs are included in operating expenses, for instance, determining the appropriate treatment of revenues, rebates, and discounts. When the commissionaire or sales agent is not the entity making the sale, their counterparty's sales (i.e., whichever entity makes the sale to the third-party customer) will be utilized to compute the ratio of operating expenses to sales; however, the net operating expenses of the commissionaire or sales agent are always the sole item included in the numerator

17. Operating expenses refer to total costs excluding cost of goods sold, pass-through costs appropriately excluded under the accurate delineation of the transaction, and costs related to financing, investment activities, or income taxes calculated in accordance with applicable accounting standards. Moreover, operating expenses should not include any exceptional items that are unrelated to recurring business operations that should be quantified in accordance with applicable accounting standards.

of the ratios. The point in the range of annual net revenues will be specified by the tax administrations that adopt Amount B.

A tested party should also not be involved in the distribution of services, or the marketing, trading, or distribution of commodities or carry out non-distribution[18] activities (unless these non-distribution activities can be reliably priced separately from the distribution activities). If retail distribution activities are undertaken, then they will be incorporated into wholesale distribution activities if they fall below 20% of the tested party's three-year weighted average net revenues. If the additional functions can be priced separately, then the quantitative filter described above should be applied to the relevant allocation or apportionment of revenues and operating expenses to the distribution activity only.

For ease of assessing whether the tested party undertakes non-distribution functions, the Report suggests using the following objective measures:

- For manufacturing, the existence of manufacturing inventory (direct labour and/or work-in-process inventory) and/or the existence of manufacturing assets (e.g., property, plant, equipment);
- for research and development, the incurrence of research and development expenses, even if reimbursed;
- for procurement, the existence of procurement commission income;
- for financing, the existence of loan assets on the balance sheet; and
- for retail, the distributor's sales profile (for example, evidence of its sales channels and extent of sales made to retail customers) or holding or leasing retail storefront property.

If non-distribution activities are bundled with distribution activities for commercial purposes (for instance, services such as consumer financing are provided with the goods, but only one price is charged), then reliable separate pricing may be difficult to achieve and render the transaction out of scope. Tax administrations will need to assess the reliability of any allocation or apportionment of revenues, costs, assets, and liabilities between in-scope and out-of-scope activities.

2.1.1 Qualitative Approach

The second public consultation was published in 2023 that suggested the two alternative approaches of A and B. However, there were several jurisdictions that favoured a more qualitative approach to assessing whether transactions were in or out of scope. Ultimately, the more quantitative Approach A was chosen and is the one outlined in the Report. However, this has not been finalized as the Report states that the IF is working on an additional optional qualitative scoping criterion that jurisdictions may choose to apply as an additional step to identify distributors performing non-baseline activities for the purpose of the simplified and streamlined approach. This will appease

18. Examples of non-distribution activities include manufacturing, research and development, procurement, or financing that are non-incidental to a qualifying transaction.

jurisdictions, such as India, which have formally stated that it believes that an appropriately designed qualitative criterion is critical for ensuring that only baseline distributors are in scope of Amount B. India expresses an inability to support the Amount B work further if such a criterion is not incorporated as part of the scoping criteria in this report.[19]

2.2 Application of the Method

When assessing an appropriate method to apply to the qualifying transaction, it will not be necessary to review all of the methods. The Report assumes the TNMM will be the most appropriate method to use to test the pricing of a transaction using the net profit indicator of the return on sales.

The Report also recognizes that there may be rare instances in which the application of the internal CUP method could potentially be more appropriate; however, no other methods are considered appropriate.

2.3 Implementation and Determination of the Method

2.3.1 Pricing Matrix

The Report uses a pricing matrix to approximate arm's length prices and to avoid the need for a tailored benchmarking analysis. The pricing matrix was developed using a global dataset of companies and presents an approximation of arm's length operating margin results according to net operating asset to sales intensity (OAS), operating expense to sales intensity (OES), and industry groupings.

Industry groupings refer to the categorization of specific industries and industry sectors in which in-scope distributors operate into three predefined groupings based on the observed relationships between specific industries/products and the profitability attributed to baseline distribution of those products. The categories of goods falling into each of the three industry groups are:

(1) Group 1 – perishable foods, grocery, household consumables, construction materials and supplies, plumbing supplies, and metal.
(2) Group 2 – IT hardware and components, electrical components and consumables, animal feeds, agricultural supplies, alcohol and tobacco, pet foods, clothing, footwear and other apparel, plastics and chemicals, lubricants, dyes, pharmaceuticals, cosmetics, health and wellbeing products, home appliances, consumer electronics, furniture, home and office supplies, printed matter, paper and packaging, jewellery, textiles hides and furs, new and used domestic vehicles, vehicle parts and supplies, mixed products and products and components not listed in Group 1 or 3.

19. Pillar One – Amount B Launch Report, OECD, 2024.

(3) Group 3 - medical machinery, industrial machinery including industrial and agricultural vehicles, industrial tools, industrial components and miscellaneous supplies.

Industry Grouping / *Factor Intensity*	*Industry Grouping 1 (%)*	*Industry Grouping 2 (%)*	*Industry Grouping 3 (%)*
A] High OAS/any OES >45%/any level	3.50 +/- 0.5	5.00 +/- 0.5	5.50 +/- 0.5
B] Med/high OAS/ any OES 30% - 44.99%/any level	3.00 +/- 0.5	3.75 +/- 0.5	4.50 +/- 0.5
C] Med/low OAS/ any OES 15% - 29.99%/any level	2.50 +/- 0.5	3.00 +/- 0.5	4.50 +/- 0.5
D] Low OAS/ non-low OES <15%/10% or higher	1.75 +/- 0.5%	2.00 +/- 0.5%	3.00 +/- 0.5
E] Low OAS/ low OES <15% OAS/ <10% OES	1.50 +/- 0.5	1.75 +/- 0.5	2.25 +/- 0.5

A 3-step process will need to be applied to determine the arm's length return for a tested party:

(1) Step 1 Determine the relevant industry grouping for the tested party.
(2) Step 2 Determine the factor intensity classification (A to E). This should be calculated on a three-year weighted average.
(3) Step 3 Identify and apply the arm's length range that corresponds to the industry grouping and factor intensity of the tested party. If different industry groupings (>20% of sales are from products that fall outside of a single industry grouping) apply, then the weighted average return should be calculated by multiplying each return from the relevant cells of the matrix by the proportion of sales to be priced by reference to that cell and totalling these proportional returns to give a single weighted average return applicable to all sales by that distributor.

Taxpayers will need to apply and test the outcome of qualifying transactions to demonstrate consistency with the arm's length basis on an *ex post* basis. It is anticipated that the rates in the table above will be refreshed every five years. Two 'checks' will then be applied to assess the appropriateness of the return.

2.3.2 *Operating Expense Cross-Check*

After the return is identified, an operating expense cross-check is applied as a guardrail. If this produces a result outside of a predetermined cap-and-collar range, then the profitability of the tested party will be adjusted.

	Operating Expense Cap-and-collar range		
Factor Intensity	*Default Cap Rates (%)*	*Alternative Cap Rates for Qualifying Jurisdictions (%)*	*Collar Rate (%)*
High OAS (A)	70	80	10
Medium OAS (B + C)	60	70	
Low OAS (D + E)	40	45	

The operating expense cross-check applies to all in-scope transactions and requires a tax administration and relevant taxpayer to apply the following four-step process:

(1) Step 1 A tax administration and taxpayer will determine the return on sales for the tested party and compute an equivalent return on operating expense derived from that return.
(2) Step 2 The tax administration and taxpayer will determine the applicable operating expense cap-and-collar range, which is determined by reference to: (i) the factor intensity classification of the tested party, and (ii) whether the tested party is subject to the default cap rates or alternative cap rates for qualifying jurisdictions.[20]
(3) Step 3 The tax administration and taxpayer will compare the equivalent return on operating expense of the tested party against the operating expense cap-and-collar rate determined in Step 2.
(4) Step 4 When the equivalent return on operating expense of the tested party determined in Step 1 falls within the operating expense cap-and-collar range, no further adjustment is required to the return on sales per cent identified from the pricing matrix. However, when the equivalent return on operating expense of the tested party determined in Step 1 exceeds the operating expense cap, the return on sales of the tested party will be adjusted downwards until it results in an equivalent return on operating expense equal to the operating expense cap. Conversely, when the equivalent return on operating expense of the tested party falls below the operating expense collar, the return on sales of the tested party will be adjusted upwards until it results in an equivalent return on operating expense equal to the operating expense collar.

20. A list of qualifying jurisdictions will be published on the OECD website. This had not yet been published at the time of this writing.

2.3.3 *Data Availability Mechanism*

The data availability mechanism is intended to account for cases when there is no or insufficient data in the global dataset for a particular tested party jurisdiction, and it is defined as a qualifying jurisdiction by the OECD.

When a tested party is located in a qualifying jurisdiction, an adjustment will be made to the return initially determined by the pricing matrix and adjusted by the operating expense cross-check. A relevant taxpayer in an aforementioned qualifying jurisdiction will earn an adjusted return in accordance with the following formula:

$$\text{Adjusted return on sales} = \text{ROSTP} + (\text{NRAJ} \times \text{OASTP})$$

Where:

- ROSTP is the tested party's return on sales percentage that is calculated in accordance with the pricing matrix and after any cross-check adjustment.
- NRAJ is the qualifying jurisdiction's net risk adjustment percentage that is derived from the table below, for which the applicable category is determined by reference to the sovereign credit rating of the qualifying jurisdiction of the tested party applicable on the first day of the relevant fiscal year.
- OASTP is the tested party's net operating asset intensity percentage for the relevant fiscal year but will not exceed 85% for the purpose of computing the adjusted return on sales of the tested party.

Sovereign Credit Rating Category		*Net Risk Adjustment (%)*
Investment grade	BBB+	0.0
	BBB	0.0
	BBB-	0.3
Non-investment grade	BB+	0.7
	BB	1.2
	BB-	1.8
	B+	2.8
	B	3.8
	B-	4.9
	CCC+	5.9
	CCC	7.5
	CCC- (or lower)	8.6

It is anticipated that these rates will be reviewed annually by the OECD.

The adjustments proposed above could make a significant impact on the original matrix. It is unclear whether they would be policed, whether they would be mandated by certain tax administrations, or whether they would be considered optional if self-determined factors are met.

2.4 Documentation

Amount B will be contained within the OECD Guidelines and, as such, it is likely to be considered a safe harbour akin to the LVAS guidance. However, this is subject to local treatment by tax administrations. As a safe harbour, documenting the decisions in relation to identifying and characterizing qualifying transactions will be key including the context in which the transactions take place. The Report also suggests that there is other information that would be beneficial for the taxpayer to present to the relevant tax administrations. One is the calculations showing the determination of the relevant revenue, costs, and assets allocated or attributed to the in-scope transaction. Another is information and allocation schedules showing how the financial data used in assessing the applicability of the simplified and streamlined approach and applying the TP method ties to the annual financial statements.

The Report suggests that this evidence be incorporated into the local file accompanied by intercompany agreements that specifically discuss the delineation of roles and responsibilities between the tested party and its principal, as well as details of the calculations and allocation schedules. The Report implies that, as a safe harbour, a notification process would be advisable, but this has been left to the prerogative of local tax administrations.

The Report strongly suggests that a written contract is put in place; however, it also states that, regardless of whether there is one, tax administrations or taxpayers can assert or challenge the approach based on the accurate delineation of the transaction performed under the principles articulated in Chapter I of the OECD Guidelines. The Report also suggests that if the Amount B approach is applied, then it should be for a minimum of a three-year period unless the transactions fall out of scope.

Finally, the Report asserts that any advance pricing agreement (APA) should prevail prior to adopting Amount B, although, in the case of a unilateral APA, the counterparty's tax administration has the capacity to raise a TP adjustment under Amount B principles.

3 REFLECTIONS

The OECD received numerous responses to the 2023 public consultation. Some of those responses are reflected in the musings below. What is clear from reviewing the responses, discussions with taxpayers, and reading wider academic literature is that some of those concerns that were raised are still relevant following the Report's publication. The aim of the guidance is clear, but whether it will achieve its objective is still shrouded in uncertainty.

3.1 Spirit of the ALP

At the heart of the Amount B approach is the desire for simplification and streamlining,[21] but is this at the expense of the ALP? The OECD has long recognized that tax administrations often legislate local simplification measures adapting OECD guidance. More than 70% of those available, however, are directed at small- and medium-sized enterprises, small transactions, and LVAS, i.e. transactions that are deemed to carry a limited tax risk.[22] The Amount B proposals have no transaction cap, and any restrictions are placed on functionality rather than revenue size.

The Report expends a significant amount of effort to emphasize that the guidance to be included in the annex should not be regarded as a revision of the general ALPs articulated in the OECD Guidelines, nor should it be used to interpret the application of the rest of them regarding any transaction. Amount B instead approximates an arm's length outcome for a tested party by using the pricing matrix. However, does a single margin (albeit flexed by 0.5% either way) actually equate to the ALP? Its essence is that it is flexible so as to specifically account for the variety of circumstances and instances in which it is used by groups large and small operating in a myriad of industries and under a range of conditions.

If tax administrations choose to apply the Amount B approach, then the pricing matrix will be treated as providing an arm's length outcome. In jurisdictions that do not choose to apply the approach, the approach will not be treated as providing an arm's length outcome because it will be considered non-binding.[23] Taxpayers should, therefore, not rely on the Amount B approach to justify that a result should be treated as arm's length when filing a tax return in jurisdictions that have not adopted it.

However, there is a throwaway comment in the Report, which states that 'subject to their domestic legislations and administrative practices, members of the IF commit to respect the outcome determined under the simplified and streamlined approach to in scope transactions where such approach is applied by a low-capacity jurisdiction'.[24] This implies that a precedent should be established that if a low-capacity jurisdiction adopts the Amount B guidance, then the result will be deemed arm's length if the transacting jurisdiction is an IF tax administration regardless of whether it has adopted Amount B. This slightly contradicts the previous points regarding arm's length.

Amount B is to be designed with the needs of low-capacity jurisdictions in mind.[25] The term low-capacity jurisdictions that is used by the OECD is ambiguous. There are a variety of definitions that may apply, making assessments on the proposals in light of low-capacity jurisdictions difficult. They could simply be those where government resources for tax administration and collection are well below the group

21. The word simple, and derivations including simplification, is mentioned 146 times in the Report and derivations of streamline is mentioned 139 times.
22. OECD (2011), *Multi-Country Analysis of Existing Transfer Pricing Simplification Measures*.
23. Pillar One – Amount B Launch Report, OECD, 2024.
24. Pillar One – Amount B Launch Report, OECD, 2024.
25. Public Consultation Document – Pillar One Amount B, OECD, 2022.

average,[26] but this focuses on tax characteristics rather than the market or jurisdiction as a whole. A broader definition may use the following three elements to drive the designation 'low-capacity' in the context of a country or jurisdiction: administrative capacity (state capacity to govern and form effective public policy and deliver public services), human capacity (size and skill of the talent pool), and income capacity (gross domestic product (GDP)). This definition could be based on high-level data such as income thresholds or level of development as determined by institutions such as the World Bank, by very specific data such as the number of staff and skill levels of a tax administration's TP unit/team, or access, or lack thereof, to comparables. Regardless of the meaning, the focus on low-capacity jurisdictions is because implementing the ALP can often be more complex due to a lack of resources and a lack of comparables combined with less homogenous risk patterns within the low-capacity jurisdictions.[27]

Simplicity in applying Amount B is therefore considered to be beneficial for low-capacity jurisdictions, removing arguments over the delineation of transactions in addition to those that focus on the pricing considerations of marketing and distribution arrangements, focusing on areas such as the selection of the TP method, the appropriateness of the benchmarking analysis (especially the identification and selection of non-domestic comparables) or, when necessary, how to make appropriate comparability adjustments.[28] Simplicity, however, does have the potential to override the ALP and shift policy towards formulary apportionment. Embedding Amount B's guidance into the OECD Guidelines does not protect this from happening, and as such, some naysayers consider that Amount B has significantly exceeded its remit of providing tax certainty and reducing disputes.

Amount B is not meant to be a formulary apportionment, even if there are formulary aspects of it.[29] The guidance on it could be viewed as simplifying the implementation of the ALP rather than disregarding it. It breaks down practical barriers, such as enabling appropriate comparables to be identified, and ensures that a level of consistency can be achieved. The simplification targeted with Amount B might provide a significant upside in the application of the ALP in emerging and developing countries.[30]

The pricing matrix sits at the core of such a simplification, offering fixed net margin returns to distributors, thereby negating the need for benchmarking analyses should these distributors be determined to be in scope. Does using a fixed-margin approach make sense? The matrix removes the use of a range, or at least the range is hidden from view due to database restrictions[31] and only offers fixed margins with a

26. Eden, L., *Pillar One Amount B: Simplifying the Arm's length Principle for Baseline Distribution Activities*, Tax Notes International (2023) https://doi.org/10.2139/ssrn.4560131.
27. Steens, B. et al., *Pillar One Amount B: Issues for Emerging and Developing Economies*, Bloomberg Tax (2023).
28. Public Consultation Document Pillar One – Amount B, OECD, 2023.
29. Stewart, D. & Finley, R., *Pillar One Amount B: Disagreements and Divides*, Tax Notes International (2023).
30. Steens, B. et al., *Pillar One Amount B: Issues for Emerging and Developing Economies*, Bloomberg Tax (2023).
31. There is a distinct lack of detail included in the 2023 public consultation on the benchmarking analysis that drove the pricing matrix.

deviation. This contrasts with guidance in the OECD Guidelines, which indicates that because TP is not an exact science, all figures within a range may equally be reliable as opposed to a single one. Although the matrix attempts to address industry and operating intensity differences, it is still possible that a range would represent the fact that independent enterprises engaged in comparable transactions under comparable circumstances may not establish exactly the same price for a transaction.[32] Presenting a fixed margin removes this flexibility and, as such, is what prompts accusations of formulary apportionment. Some observers consider that Amount B should not be designed as a fixed rate of return regulatory policy but instead should follow the reference pricing approach.[33]

Comparisons can be drawn with the Australian Tax Office's (ATO) guidance on the TP outcomes associated with inbound distributors.[34] The framework is used by the ATO to assess the returns of inbound distributors distributing goods purchased from related foreign entities for resale and digital products or services for which the intellectual property of those products is owned by related foreign entities. It is a risk-based framework rather than a fixed-margin matrix. If the distribution arrangements fall within the low-risk category, then the taxpayer can be somewhat assured that the ATO will generally not instigate a review of the transactions. However, the latter could occur if the arrangements fall outside of that category. The inbound distributors are separated into four industry categories: general, life sciences, information and communication technology, and motor vehicles. Risk is considered low if taxpayers are above a certain earnings before interest and tax (EBIT) margin, medium risk consists of a range, and then high risk applies if taxpayers are below a certain EBIT margin. Taxpayers use these indicators as a guide, but it does not preclude them from establishing their own arm's length ranges and setting their own margins. The ATO is also clear that its approach has similarities with the TNMM but that it does not necessarily view this method as being the most appropriate to price such arrangements.

Advocates of a fixed-margin approach revert back to the objectives of Amount B and emphasize the fact that fixed margins could limit disputes by restricting the 'wiggle room' for both tax administrations and taxpayers in relation to a qualifying transaction. This is particularly relevant for low-capacity jurisdictions where enquiry teams may not be overly experienced in TP. Under litigation, a determination would, therefore, simply need to be made as to whether a taxpayer or tax administration had sufficiently demonstrated that the financial outcome derived from the pricing matrix was arm's length rather than argue a case on functionality. Supporters of the fixed margin approach consider that administrability issues are thus drastically diminished, making

32. OECD (2022), *Transfer Pricing Guidelines for Multinational Enterprises and Tax Administrations*.
33. Eden, L., *Pillar One Amount B: Simplifying the Arm's length Principle for Baseline Distribution Activities*, Tax Notes International (2023) https://doi.org/10.2139/ssrn.4560131.
34. Practical Compliance Guideline 2019/1, ATO.

the introduction of predetermined margins and methods more a necessity than an option, especially in developing countries.[35]

In conclusion, the Amount B guidance has been designed to simplify the implementation of the ALP, but this simplicity has the potential to override the principle and shift towards formulary apportionment. The pricing matrix, which offers fixed net margin returns to distributors, has been a contentious issue, with some arguing that it removes the flexibility necessary for TP. Despite these concerns, advocates of a fixed margin approach (which is what the Report determined was appropriate) emphasize that it could limit disputes and make the administration of TP more manageable, particularly in low-capacity jurisdictions. It is yet uncertain whether this will be the case or whether it is a safe harbour too far removed from the ALP to be commercially viable.

3.2 Battle of the Quantitative Versus Qualitative Scoping Approaches

An entity or functional characterization is one of the most critical and contentious areas of TP. Fundamentally, there is a direct correlation between a distributor's profit-earning potential and the level of risk borne by that entity. The core characteristics as identified by the OECD of purchasing goods and then marketing them still apply to a lower-risk distributor; it is just that other functions and risks will be transferred to a principal. The differences between the two scoping avenues are essentially the definition and treatment of 'baseline' and 'non-baseline' activities. The quantitative route potentially presents an oversimplified view, which is easier to implement but may not reflect reality. This characterization is often the primary basis for most distributor disputes, with tax administrations challenging the positions taken on low-risk distributors when, according to the tax administrations, they are less limited than how they are presented.

The focus on simplicity, while benefitting low-capacity jurisdictions, disregards the fact that these jurisdictions tend to bear operational risk that varies from industry to industry as well as within and between markets. For example, those arising from the sale and distribution of food can vary tremendously depending upon factors such as transport infrastructure, extreme weather, levels of crime, etc. Commentators tend to agree that this lack of homogeneity tends to be greater in low-capacity jurisdictions than in developed economies, mainly because these types of operational risks are often managed locally. Baseline distributors would consequently make any decisions regarding these risks with limited oversight from the principal. The Report's published scoping criteria may ignore these differences, subject to the country risk adjustment or, under the yet unknown qualitative scoping approach, may exclude the distributor due to the acquisition of expertise that is necessary in order to deliver those services to customers in the distributor's markets which would classify that entity as engaging in non-baseline activities. If this is the case, then many of the identified baseline

35. Navarro, A., *Simplification in Transfer Pricing: a Plea for the Enactment of Rebuttable Predetermined Margins and Methods Within Developing Countries*, Florida Tax Review (2019) https://doi.org/10.5744/ftr.2019.1588.

distributors in low-capacity jurisdictions may not be able to take advantage of Amount B, and therefore, the intended beneficiaries will not be able to benefit.

Is there a pivotal situation that can be defined? Would it not be of broader benefit to potentially allow some distributors that bear inherent risk through the net and include them in the scope as opposed to being overly strict with the baseline definition? If reflecting on what taxpayers do now when identifying a similar set to compare to a tested party that they consider bears a lower risk, the operating expenses to sales ratio is often applied as a screen along with a review of the website and financials for 'functional comparability'. It is highly likely that comparables in any final set may have a slightly different risk profile to each other and to the tested party.

Proponents of the qualitative scoping approach suggest that there is no statistical basis for using the operating expenses to sales ratio as a filter for excluding non-baseline activities, but as highlighted, this is standard practice for taxpayers when undertaking benchmarking analyses. Taxpayers do not use the screen as a reason to select a methodology, however, since this tends to be based on the functional analysis undertaken when the transaction is delineated.

Thus, although advocates of the quantitative approach are 'correct to observe that a controlled distributor's contributions can go beyond baseline distribution without being nonroutine',[36] is there a need for an additional qualitative assessment? A comparability (including functional) analysis must always be performed in order to appropriately characterize the transaction between the parties and choose the most appropriate TP method.[37] Such an analysis would be performed at the outset of starting any Amount B considerations in order to identify and appropriately delineate a qualifying transaction. At this stage, it is highly likely that any non-baseline activities would be identified and, if considered significant, they would be excluded from the analysis, or the transaction would be deemed unsuitable for Amount B. This analysis should be undertaken regardless of whether Amount B is being considered and, as such, should not add to the taxpayer's compliance burden.

This, of course, does not negate the fact that tax administrations may be critical of the conclusions of the quantitative analysis while, at the same time, dangling the qualitative carrot that still affords opportunities for disputes.

The 2023 public consultation indicated that the jurisdictions that supported the qualitative approach considered that an absence of an explicit requirement for qualitative considerations to identify non-baseline distributors creates a risk of BEPS.[38] The Report warned that although MNE groups are granted the discretion to organize their business operations as they see fit and that tax administrations do not have the right to dictate how groups design their structure or locate their business operations, the guidance in Chapter IX remains relevant regardless of Amount B. The Report also noted that attempts to artificially reorganize their arrangements to derive tax advantages from

36. Finley, R., *Scoping-Criteria Dispute Overshadows Amount B Progress*, Tax Notes International (2023).
37. OECD (2022), *Transfer Pricing Guidelines for Multinational Enterprises and Tax Administrations*.
38. Public Consultation Document Pillar One – Amount B, OECD, 2023.

Amount B would come under greater scrutiny.[39] Amount B is not perceived as a tool to prevent any nefarious tax planning. Indeed, the fact that it focuses on one-sided methods applied to entities that do not assume economically significant risks would indicate that the movement for any profit shifting is minimal. As stated by TP&C GmbH in its response to the 2023 public consultation: 'such [distribution] transactions do not offer an enticing lever for profit shifting'.[40] This is echoed in the OECD's own economic impact assessment where it states that 'at the global level, the revenue effect of Amount B is likely to be modest, as it does not provide market jurisdictions with a new taxing right, but is merely designed to simplify the administration of the current transfer pricing system'.[41]

In light of the differences between the two scoping approaches, the distributors eligible for Amount B and the potential challenges they pose, a balance needs to be struck between simplification and adherence to the ALP. The oversimplification of just using the current quantitative approach may lead to an unrealistic view of the risk borne by distributors, while the alternative focus on qualitative considerations may exclude many baseline distributors in low-capacity jurisdictions. Regardless, a comparability and functional analysis should always be undertaken to appropriately characterize the transaction and apply the most appropriate TP method, which is the TNMM in this case. Despite concerns over tax planning opportunities and the risk of base erosion, Amount B is designed to reduce the number of disputes, enhance tax certainty, and promote more efficient resource utilization. It is unlikely that this debate will be resolved until taxpayers and tax administrations field their first tax returns using the Amount B approach.

3.3 Products and Multifunction Entities

3.3.1 Digital

Many commentators were in favour of including digital goods and services within Amount B.[42] However, the scope of the Report is limited to wholesale distribution and does not include them.

The 2023 public consultation contemplated including digital goods within the simplified approach and defined their distribution as including the sale (including the perpetual royalty-free licensing) of e-books, movies, games, music, or computer software in digital format but not the rental of, royalty-bearing licence of, or subscription to such digital content.[43]

Although it is anticipated that further work will be undertaken to determine if a separate framework can be applied to the wholesale distribution of digital goods and to

39. Pillar One – Amount B Launch Report, OECD, 2024.
40. Kunz, T.-E. & Treidler, O., *A Risk Management Perspective on the OECD Amount B Proposal* (2023).
41. OECD (2020), *Tax Challenges Arising from Digitalisation: Economic Impact Assessment*.
42. For example, India's National Association of Software and Service Companies, BIAC, ACT, JFTC and WU per their submissions to the OECD.
43. Public Consultation Document Pillar One – Amount B, OECD, 2023.

consider whether services should be included, there was limited consideration of the method of delivery and the characterization of a digital wholesaler in the lead up to the publication of the final Amount B guidance. Delivery of a digital good can vary from one digital product to another, and a taxpayer may be a mix of a traditional wholesaler that also sells digital products or may be a purely digital one. These have vastly different risk profiles that the operating intensity screens may not fully capture. The different methods of delivery and wholesaler characterizations are discussed below.

There is a very narrow division between what could be categorized as a sale of a good versus what would be classed as a sale of a service. The definition in the public consultation was clear that a sale or licence of software would be included as a sale of a digital good but that a subscription would not. Where does that leave software as a service (SaaS)? It is labelled as a service but functionally could be perceived as digital distribution.

The SaaS is a subset of cloud computing when software is hosted on the cloud and accessible through the internet. Users can then access the software from anywhere as long as they have an internet connection. Updates and maintenance are managed by the software provider, and users pay a monthly or annual subscription fee that can be more affordable than purchasing a licence or one-time fee for traditional software. The latter is installed on premises, and updates and maintenance tend to be managed locally. Initially, direct user access may indicate a retail transaction rather than a wholesale transaction. It is unclear as to whether the term end consumers refers to individuals or corporate entities that also consume the goods. This is key as it will make a significant difference in whether a transaction would qualify as wholesale. If the definition refers to both individuals and corporate entities, then the direct SaaS distribution model, whereby the digital product vendor sells direct to customers, often through a website, would unlikely be caught by a simplified distribution approach. An indirect SaaS distribution model that involves group and third-party resellers, however, might depend upon whether the SaaS is perceived as a distribution or a service. This distinction may not present an issue, as Microsoft Corporation's commentary on the 2023 public consultation highlights by referencing an analysis undertaken by KPMG.[44] This analysis concluded that the 'returns for sales, marketing and distribution activities for goods and services are within a fairly narrow band and decrease as a share of system profits in highly profitable companies'.[45] Regarding the distribution of digital goods in conjunction with digital services (SaaS), there may, therefore, be little to distinguish between the returns. A digital service in its own right may be different as these are often value-added and non-routine in nature, thereby commanding a greater return than baseline distribution.

A digital wholesaler is an intermediary that purchases digital products from publishers (books, movies, etc.) and sells them to retailers. It often provides a 'managed service', which means that it might manage all aspects of the distribution

44. Transfer Pricing Analysis of Arm's Length Returns to Sales, Marketing and Distribution Activities, KPMG, 2020.
45. Comments on 17 July 2023 Public Consultation Pillar One – Amount B, Microsoft Corporation, 2023.

process, including pricing and marketing. This may also include additional value-added services such as analytics and reporting. Is this truly a 'service' or a sale as defined by the OECD? It is akin to the same physical process that a traditional wholesaler may ascribe to, but in a digital world, a digital wholesaler may have to modify their prices or volume in real time to adjust to market forces such as customer preferences or competitor movements. A digital wholesaler may also have to provide large amounts of data on consignment in advance, which can carry different risks than those of a physical wholesaler. Digital product supply chains differ markedly from their physical product counterparts.[46] Further work to understand these nuances will be important.

Often, digital wholesalers' returns are not priced using a TNMM approach and instead, an agency model may be used. The latter is much like revenue sharing or franchise models for which the baseline distributors are rewarded on a percentage of revenue basis. In this instance, the CUP method may be more appropriate rather than a return on sales.

Given the above, it is easy to understand why the distribution of digital products (even if exempting digital services) was removed from the Amount B guidance and pricing matrix. This author would encourage a separate branch of the Amount B framework to be devised to attempt to effectively address the distribution of digital goods *and* digital distribution.

3.3.2 Sales Agents

The 2023 public consultation prompted much discussion as to whether to include sales agents and commissionaires within the Amount B framework. Upon the Report's publication, they were retained in the guidance, and the operating expense cross-check is aimed at ensuring that they achieve an appropriate arm's length level of reward (*see* methods reflection below).

3.3.3 Multifunctional Entities

There are two aspects to the discussion on multifunctional entities. The first is the need for greater clarity to what extent 'non-core distribution' activities are acceptable for a tested party to still qualify for Amount B, and the second is whether including multiple industry groups overcomplicates the profit matrix.

For example, under the definition of core distribution, identifying new customers and managing customers' relationships, certain after-sales services, and implementing promotional advertising or marketing activities[47] were considered acceptable functions for a baseline distributor to be undertaking. However, conversely, the:

46. Chellappa, R.K. & Shivendu, S., *Pay Now or Pay Later? Managing Digital Product Supply Chains*, International Conference on Electronic Commerce (2003) https://doi.org/10.1145/948005.948036.
47. Public Consultation Document Pillar One – Amount B, OECD, 2023.

- design and control of marketing programmes;
- direction of and establishing priorities for creative undertakings relating to the marketing of the products distributed;
- control over strategic decisions regarding development programmes for marketing intangibles;
- management and control of associated [marketing] budgets; and
- defence and protection of marketing intangibles such as trademarks or trade names

were all considered unacceptable functions for a baseline distributor to be undertaking. The assumption is that they give rise to marketing intangibles that may require a greater than baseline return. If the products being sold are not considered to be consumable goods, then the activities listed above may not carry a significant additional return due to marketing intangibles tending to reflect a reduced value driver for business-to-business products. The distinction between the marketing activities may, therefore, not be warranted across all industries, and baseline distributors may be falling through the qualifying net.

Regarding the latter, Industry Grouping Two also includes any other distributor not specifically named in 1 or 3, so would it not be easier just to have a general distributor and one or two specific groupings as demonstrated by the ATO? This is particularly relevant if a distributor sells a variety of products and then potentially falls into more than one grouping. Conversely, some of the commentators mentioned that the groupings had little basis and were too broad. It is difficult to comment in detail on this point, however, because the OECD did not publish any evidence or rationale for the margins used or the grouping analysis.

3.4 Application

3.4.1 Methods

The Report and the public consultations focused on one-sided methods, precisely on the TNMM as the most appropriate method in the absence of a CUP to price a baseline distributor's return. It is interesting that the RPM only received a cursory glance despite its definition perfectly describing the qualifying transaction: 'a transfer pricing method based on the price at which a product that has been purchased from an associated enterprise is resold to an independent enterprise'.[48] It is understandable why the RPM was so readily rejected, given the evidence stacked against the appropriateness of comparing a tested party's gross margins with those of third-party comparables. Indeed, the weaknesses within the TNMM have already been highlighted, and these are only exacerbated in the RPM. An internal RPM should not be so readily dismissed, however. Like a CUP, these could provide valuable evidence as to appropriate pricing,

48. OECD (2022), *Transfer Pricing Guidelines for Multinational Enterprises and Tax Administrations*.

particularly in industries such as the wholesale of digital goods where third-party turnkey resellers may be used in equal measure to baseline distributors.

Could Amount B also be used in a residual profit split method to support the 'residual' aspect? Residual functions are often stripped of risk and IP and potentially could relate to baseline distribution activities. Would this be akin to treating the TNMM like the comparable profits method (CPM) and assessing the functions, assets, and risks at an entity level rather than at a transaction level? Can the CPM and the TNMM be used interchangeably in the context of Amount B? This has yet to be addressed by the OECD.

3.4.2 Start-Ups, Loss Makers, and Reduced System Profits

The Report mentions that if losses are in existence, the tax treatment of such losses is outside of the guidance and is subject to local tax administration considerations. The Report also notes that persistent[49] loss makers are screened out of the profit matrix benchmarking. Comparable companies that are incurring losses should be considered acceptable, albeit tax authorities may reject extreme results as comparables. While it may be a correct application of the ALP in some cases, the reasons for a loss may be genuine and may not always justify rejecting the loss-making company as a comparable. This status should be determined based on the facts and circumstances surrounding the company rather than its financial result. As such, this author considers that they should be included in the benchmarking. The profit matrix also disregards the prospect of a loss by focusing on a single margin. None of the post-matrix adjustments will push a profitable margin into a loss-making position.

An open question remains regarding MNEs in a start-up position or with reduced system profits as to whether they can 'afford' to guarantee a level of profit to their baseline distributors without the flexibility of being able to reduce it along a range if appropriate due to facts and circumstances. Situations may arise whereby the system profits are not sufficient for sustaining the number of distributors operated by a group and, thus, tax could end up dictating the commercial operating structure.

3.4.3 Data Availability Mechanism

One of the adjustments to the pricing matrix is the data availability mechanism. As touched on by the OECD Guidelines and other tax administrations, there are already known weaknesses with using the net profit indicator since it can be influenced by a number of factors that make comparing a tested party with another company very difficult if the latter is not affected by the same factors. For instance, the supposedly comparable company may have been managed and run very poorly, while the tested party may have been run very well. Would it be proper to draw any conclusions relevant to the transfer prices of the tested party from the fact that it made an x% operating margin, but the company that is said to meet the comparability criteria made

49. Losses for more than one year.

an operating margin of y%? It is easy to see from this simple example that incorrect conclusions can easily be drawn from using the TNMM (HMRC). Yet, it is one of the most popular methods, and besides using regional or local comparable sets, very few geographic adjustments are undertaken in practice. When they are, these are typically multifaceted (for example, using a combination of the living wage, the country's GDP, the country's sovereign risk, industry variations, and other economic factors) rather than a single broad-brush approach. To over-adjust may simply make a mockery of the initial benchmarking and consequently lead to more disputes.

3.4.4 Operating Expenses Cross-Check

This adjustment acts as a safeguard by keeping watch on the levels of functionality performed by the qualifying baseline distributor. The cross-check is similar to applying the Berry Ratio, which is the ratio of gross profit to operating expenses. Dr Charles Berry invented the method and stated that: 'for a distributor, who takes possession of a product in its final form and simply re-sells that product without change to retailers, gross profit is analogous to a firm's total revenues, and the distributor's operating expenses are analogous to a firm's total costs'.[50] In essence, the Berry Ratio is a variant of the cost-plus method that is not for manufacturers but for distributors.[51]

Commentators on the 2023 public consultation raised opposing views on using and adopting such a safeguard. Some disliked it outright as they viewed it as softening the stance to ensure that low-capacity jurisdictions recognized an appropriate level of reward. Others thought it should only be used to help identify those distributors with lower functionality, such as commissioners and sales agents. Ford Motor Co was an outlier in that its response heavily supported its inclusion, arguing that, in its absence, its distributors would be over-rewarded. Ford noted that its total system profits would not be large enough to sustain the levels of profits indicated in the profit matrix without the safeguard.

In practice, the Berry Ratio has been accepted by tax authorities as a corroborative method, and the OECD and UN support using it when the value of functions performed is proportional to the operating expenses and when sales driven by the distributor are not proportional to the expenses incurred. There is, therefore, some economic basis for using this type of cross-check as a safeguard to ensure that baseline distributors (aka sales agents and commissionaires) are not over-rewarded; however, there are limited arguments to support why it would be needed to increase rewards. The profit matrix should inherently be sufficient, particularly since it focuses on operational intensity, which, if high, would indicate that a Berry Ratio would not be applicable in any case.

50. Berry, C., *Berry Ratios: Their Use and Misuse, Journal of Global Transfer Pricing* (1999).
51. Eden, L. & Amba, T., *The Berry Ratio: More than a Profit Level Indicator?, Practical Guide to US Transfer Pricing* (2023).

3.5 Adoption

Amount B is intended to be incorporated into the OECD Transfer Pricing Guidelines rather than being implemented via the treaty network, but it is still unclear as to whether this will be considered a safe harbour or general guidance. The OECD Guidelines' definition of a safe harbour in a TP regime is a provision that applies to a defined category of taxpayers or transactions that relieves taxpayers from certain obligations otherwise imposed by a jurisdiction's eligible general TP rules. It substitutes simpler obligations for those under the general TP regime.[52] A safe harbour is supposed to provide certainty that the taxpayer's transfer prices will be accepted by the tax administration providing the safe harbour, but this depends on each local administration adopting the guidance.

Although the success of the LVAS was mentioned earlier in this chapter, many tax administrations do not specifically legislate on intra-group services within their local rules. Instead, the OECD Guidelines might simply be signposted as guidance. Commentators are therefore concerned whether including it as an elective provision in the guidelines is likely to have the same limited effect unless countries actually endorse it.[53] Other factors that will impact the level of adoption include the interest of a jurisdiction in maintaining the consensus over the application of TP rules exclusively based on the comparability analysis, the willingness to promote simplicity among taxpayers and tax administrations, the need to resolutely contend with profit shifting, its bargaining power vis-á-vis other relevant jurisdictions, and so on.[54]

Another way of looking at Amount B is to view it as a 'soft law' rather than a safe harbour. Soft law is a term that refers to rules or instruments that are not legally binding or have a weaker binding force than traditional law. Soft law could, therefore, also refer to guidelines such as the OECD Guidelines or the ATO's PCGs. Treating the framework as soft law, however, could potentially lead to the assumption that Amount B is to be applied automatically without checking whether tax administrations on either side of the transaction have actually adopted it. As Robyn Creyke states: 'A more significant danger is that agencies can attribute an inflated stature to their own policies. Agency policies are designed to structure discretion, provide certainty and consistency, and guide officials in decision-making. These are laudable objectives but if policies are couched in mandatory terms, this can obscure the fact that a more flexible application of rules is permissible.'[55]

The Report has taken a coward's way out by making it clear that it is leaving it up to the tax administrations to make the difficult decision while, at the same time, dangling the price matrix in front of them. Taxpayers will, therefore, need to spend

52. OECD (2022), *Transfer Pricing Guidelines for Multinational Enterprises and Tax Administrations*.
53. Steens, B. et al., *Pillar One Amount B: Issues for Emerging and Developing Economies*, Bloomberg Tax (2023).
54. Navarro, A., *Simplification in Transfer Pricing: a Plea for the Enactment of Rebuttable Predetermined Margins and Methods within Developing Countries*, Florida Tax Review (2019) https://doi.org/10.5744/ftr.2019.1588.
55. Creyke, R., *'Soft Law' and Administrative Law: A New Challenge*, AIAL Forum 15 (2010).

time and resources understanding if the jurisdictions in which they operate have implemented the guidance, weighing up whether it is a framework that they qualify for, and if it impacts and changes their current TP policies (does it mean their current policies are no longer arm's length if they are different?). There is, therefore, a danger for taxpayers that the framework may be 'dipped in' and 'dipped out' of when it suits a tax administration. Additionally, what happens when two tax administrations disagree on the qualification of a transaction? Is it the taxpayer's responsibility to prove that they are in or out?

In practice, it can be seen that tax administrations are acting too hastily and opening enquiries into low-risk distributors, arguing that the distribution margins currently being earned are too low based upon the profit matrix despite the existence of local comparable benchmarking analysis.

It would be advisable for the OECD to consider including some more detailed implementation instructions in the guidelines to manage the interpretation of the proposals by both taxpayers and tax administrations.

3.5.1 Interaction with Customs

Tax legislation tends to require prices in an MNE to be set for corporation tax and customs valuation purposes, respectively, as if group members are not related. One of the basic principles for determining the customs value is based on the World Trade Organisation (WTO) Valuation Agreement. It is based on the price actually paid or payable for the imported goods with certain adjustments. When the buyer and seller are related, the price can only be accepted if the relationship does not influence the price. This is similar to the direct tax principle of requiring the transfer price to be based on an arm's length price. However, the methodologies are not exactly the same, and a transfer price that has been accepted for direct tax purposes cannot be assumed to be acceptable for customs valuation purposes.

The amount of customs duty that is paid is often worked out as a percentage of the customs value of the goods, which is referred to as an 'ad valorem duty'. There are six methods stipulated in the WTO Valuation Agreement that can be used to work out the customs value of imported goods. Each method must be worked through before the most appropriate method is selected. Method 1 is considered the normal method of valuation and is used for over 90% of imports that are liable to an ad valorem customs duty. This does not initially appear to be an issue; however, certain tax administrations have registered dissatisfaction with using Method 1 if the TNMM has been used to support the transfer prices. UK guidance, for example, indicates that Method 1 cannot be used with a margin-based TP model because the real economic value for the imported goods cannot be assured at the time when they are sold for export to the United Kingdom. The interaction between customs valuation and the Amount B framework has yet to be addressed but has the potential to increase the level of disputes rather than reduce them.

3.6 Documentation

Pessimistically, it could be considered that Amount B simply removes the requirement for undertaking benchmarking searches but replaces that effort and cost with the requirement to put the work in to define and evidence the rationale for Amount B, which may ultimately be a more expensive exercise. Although the holy grail for a taxpayer is that Amount B will reduce disputes regardless of whether a written contract (or other documentation) is in place, tax administrations or taxpayers can assert or challenge the approach based on the accurate delineation of the transaction performed under the principles articulated in Chapter I of these guidelines.[56]

If the TP documentation is considered to be missing information relevant to assessing the simplified and streamlined approach, tax administrations may ask taxpayers to provide it. Doing so as part of annual requirements or upon request could result in fewer follow-up requests and audits as well as a more efficient use of tax administration resources. However, submitting the required information does not prevent tax administrations from examining the taxpayer's self-assessment of the scoping criteria and pricing methodology. For the first-time application of the simplified and streamlined approach, taxpayers are encouraged to include consent to apply the framework for at least three years unless transactions are no longer in scope or there is a significant change in the business. It is unlikely then, at least initially, that tax administrations will be freeing up their own resources as they will need to monitor and police the implementation of Amount B by both taxpayers and other tax administrations.

Considering the goal is to simplify and reduce the compliance burden to the uninitiated, the proposals as they currently stand resemble their own goal.

4 CONCLUSION

Considerable effort has been invested in developing the Amount B framework. It is likely to be well received by both taxpayers and tax administrations if it is implemented in a manner that does not compromise the ALP. The Report has created an overabundance of possibilities for tax administrations to choose from, however, ranging from whether to adopt or reject the guidance to introducing a more qualitative scoping criterion. The concern, therefore, is that, in the short term, more taxpayer and tax administration resources will be required to wade through the Amount B requirements, which may result in a spike in disputes.

Thus it is too early to comment upon whether the goal of introducing a simplified and streamlined approach has been achieved because there are still areas where additional clarity is needed (for example, defining what constitutes a low-capacity jurisdiction). Addressing these and other outstanding issues will be essential for ensuring that the proposed framework is implemented effectively and efficiently and that the desired outcomes are achieved.

56. OECD (2023), *OECD/G20 Inclusive Framework on BEPS Progress Report.*

CHAPTER 3

Transfer Pricing and BEFIT

Isabel Verlinden, Stefaan De Baets & Brendan Van Kets

1 INTRODUCTION

The European Commission's relationship with the arm's length principle (ALP) appears to be volatile, to state things mildly.

The idea of a formulary apportionment system is not something of the twenty-first century. Actually, the opposite is true quite on the contrary, as the first discussions were held on a formulary allocation of the tax base almost half a century ago. Indeed, an allocation-key-based system for multinational enterprises (MNEs) has long been on the agenda of the European Commission (EC). It published a proposal concerning the harmonization of systems of company taxation and of withholding taxes on dividends already in 1975.[1] Further, a committee of independent experts known as the Ruding Committee was commissioned in 1990 to evaluate the need and possibilities of harmonization of corporate tax. A further study on company taxation was performed in 1998[2] and led to the publication of a communication on a strategy for providing companies with a consolidated corporate tax base for their (European Union) EU-wide activities.[3,4] Finally, after an extensive number of technical working group discussions with Member States' representatives, the EC launched its first proposal for a Directive on a Common Consolidated Corporate Tax Base.[5] After achieving no consensus on the proposal (in particular on two important parts of it, i.e., the consolidated tax base and the formula), the EC withdrew it and relaunched the discussion in 2016 with two new proposals for a directive: a first one on a common corporate tax base (CCTB)[6] and a second on a common consolidated corporate tax base (CCCTB).[7]

---

1. Commission of the European Communities, *Proposal for a Council Directive Concerning the Harmonization of Systems of Company Taxation and of Withholding Taxes on Dividends*, COM (75) 392 final (23 July 1975). Bulletin of the European Communities, Supplement 10/75, COM(75) 392 (23 July 1975).
2. Commission of the European Communities, *Commission Staff Working Paper, Company Taxation in the Internal Market*, p. 3.
3. Commission of the European Communities, *Communication from the Commission to the Council, the European Parliament and the Economic and Social Committee*, Towards an Internal Market without tax obstacles, A strategy for providing companies with a consolidated corporate tax base for their EU-wide activities available at https://eur-lex.europa.eu/legal-content/EN/TXT/PDF/?uri=CELEX:52001DC0582 (accessed 8 January 2024).
4. An overview of the development on harmonization of corporate taxation, including the Report of the Ruding Committee and the 2001 study Company Taxation in the Single Market can be found in M. Lang et al., *Common Consolidated Corporate Tax Base*. Linde Verlag, contribution by M. Aujean, *The CCCTB Project and the Future of European Taxation* 13-35 (2008). For a short historic overview, *see also* P. Pistone et al., *Proposal for a Council Directive on BEFIT: an Initial Assessment*, IBFD 12-14 (2023) https://doi.org/10.2139/ssrn.4707439.
5. European Commission, *Proposal for a Council Directive on a Common Consolidated Corporate Tax Base (CCCTB)*, COM(2011) 121 final, Brussels, 16 March 2011.
6. European Commission, *Proposal for a Council Directive on a Common Corporate Tax Base*, COM(2016) 685 final, 25 October 2016, available at https://eur-lex.europa.eu/resource.html?uri=cellar:50e07d41-9b7f-11e6-868c-01aa75ed71a1.0002.02/DOC_1&format=PDF (accessed 8 January 2024).
7. European Commission, *Proposal for a Council Directive on a Common Consolidated Corporate Tax Base (CCCTB)*, COM(2016) 683 final, Strasbourg, 25 October 2016, available at https://eur-lex.europa.eu/resource.html?uri=cellar:ff337b5c-9b7d-11e6-868c-01aa75ed71a1.0002.02/DOC_1&format=PDF (accessed 8 January 2024).

The EC published a BEFIT package more recently on 12 September 2023 containing three proposals for a directive:

- Proposal for a Council Directive on Business in Europe: Framework for Income Taxation (BEFIT) to compute the tax base of company groups across the EU[8] (hereafter the 'proposed BEFIT Directive');
- Proposal for a Council Directive on transfer pricing (TP) to ensure a common approach to it within the EU;[9] and
- Proposal for a Council Directive on Head Office Tax system for SMEs to enable small businesses to interact with only one tax administration when operating cross-border in the EU.[10]

In this contribution, the authors focus on the TP aspects linked to the proposed BEFIT Directive. Its content is addressed in section 2. Section 3 will link the ALP with BEFIT. The proposed BEFIT Directive is commented upon in section 4. Section 5 briefly discusses the next steps, and finally, section 6 concludes.

2 THE PROPOSED BEFIT DIRECTIVE, WHAT IT IS ABOUT

2.1 The EC's Reasons to Launch BEFIT

In the proposed BEFIT Directive, the EC identifies several reasons why it would be beneficial to the European Market to introduce a common system to identify the taxable bases of MNEs. The first is that they must comply with (up to) twenty-seven different national tax systems, which makes it difficult and expensive for companies to do business across the EU. This leads to complexity and uncertainty, creates an uneven level playing field, and increases compliance costs.[11] The EC contemplates that compliance costs could be reduced by up to 65 %.[12]

The second reason is that the ALP's application results in higher costs and extended disputes. Its reliance on comparable transactions makes it less accurate for transactions involving intangibles that are often unique.[13]

8. European Commission, *Proposal for a Council Directive on Business in Europe: Framework in Income Taxation*, COM(2023) 532 final, Strasbourg, 12 September 2023, available at https://eur-lex.europa.eu/resource.html?uri=cellar:35311f2e-5210-11ee-9220-01aa75ed71a1.0001.02/DOC_1&format=PDF (accessed 8 January 2024).
9. European Commission, *Proposal for a Council Directive on Transfer Pricing*, COM(2023) 529 final, Strasbourg, 12 September 2023, available at https://taxation-customs.ec.europa.eu/system/files/2023-09/COM_2023_529_1_EN_ACT_part1_v7.pdf (accessed 8 January 2024).
10. Proposal for a Council Directive establishing a Head Office Tax system for micro, small and medium sized enterprises, and amending Directive 2011/16/EU, COM(2023) 528 final, Strasbourg, 12 September 2023, available at https://eur-lex.europa.eu/legal-content/EN/TXT/PDF/?uri=CELEX:52023PC0528 (accessed 8 January 2024).
11. European Commission, o.c. *supra* n. 8, p. 1.
12. European Commission, *Press Release*, 12 June 2023, available at https://ec.europa.eu/commission/presscorner/detail/en/ip_23_4405 (accessed 8 January 2024).
13. European Commission, o.c. *supra* n. 8, p. 1.

The EC reminds the reader that the international tax landscape has changed significantly as the (Organisation for Economic Co-operation and Development) OECD/Inclusive Framework (IF) uses consolidated financial statements under Pillar Two and a formulary apportionment to reallocate part of the taxable profits under Pillar One, Amount A.[14] A CCTB could also serve as a basis for the EU's own resources.[15]

The EC, therefore, concludes that:

> [t]he common framework will simplify the tax environment in the internal market as it will replace the current 27 different ways for determining the taxable base for groups of companies which have annual combined revenues exceeding EUR 750 million. Consequently, the common framework will create a level playing field, enhance legal certainty, reduce compliance costs, encourage businesses to operate cross-border and stimulate investments and growth in the Union.

These undoubtedly noble initiatives command a more comprehensive technical analysis and reflections as to the chances of success.

2.2 Scope of the Proposed BEFIT Directive

The proposed BEFIT Directive establishes a unified framework for corporate income taxation within the EU, specifically targeting groups of companies of a certain size. It outlines rules for forming what is referred to as a 'BEFIT group' calculating an aggregated tax base ('BEFIT tax base') and allocating this base to eligible members. Furthermore, it also aims to simplify TP risk assessments for transactions with associated enterprises outside of the group (EU and non-EU) and addresses the administration of the common legal framework.

The BEFIT framework encompasses a hybrid ambit characterized by a combination of mandatory and discretionary applications. BEFIT's scope mandates, including entities falling under the purview of the OECD/IF Pillar Two initiative, specifically those belonging to groups with minimum annual aggregate revenues of EUR 750 million. This is constrained to entities within the EU that satisfy a 75% ownership threshold forming the BEFIT group.[16]

In instances when the ultimate parent of a group operates outside the EU, applying BEFIT is contingent upon the BEFIT group's revenues within the EU constituting more than 5% of the total group revenues or amounting to at least EUR 50 million in combined revenue over two or more of the preceding four years. Specific methodologies are stipulated for revenue calculations in the context of intra-group reorganizations.[17]

To qualify as a member of a BEFIT group, the ultimate parent company must either directly or indirectly possess a minimum of 75% ownership rights in the

14. *See* s. 4.3.
15. European Commission, o.c. *supra* n. 8, p. 2.
16. European Commission, o.c. *supra* n. 8, pp. 12-13.
17. *Ibid.*

qualifying group company or in the head office of a qualifying permanent establishment. This condition must persist throughout the fiscal year.[18]

In addition to the mandatory ambit of BEFIT, the proposal includes a provision allowing MNE groups or domestic groups that compile consolidated financial statements yet fail to meet the EUR 750 million threshold to voluntarily opt into the BEFIT framework.[19]

2.3 Calculating the BEFIT Tax Base

Consistent with the Pillar Two Directive,[20] the initial phase in determining the tax base involves utilizing financial accounts belonging to a member of the BEFIT group as prepared in accordance with an accepted accounting standard of an EU Member State.[21]

Each constituent member of the BEFIT group is mandated to ascertain its tax base individually. Subsequent to this individual determination, the tax base necessitates adjustments involving both inclusive and exclusive modifications, albeit fewer in number compared to the stipulations under the Pillar Two Directive.[22]

The tax base includes items to be added back due to their prior deduction or non-recording in preparing financial accounting statements. Contrarily, certain items are to be excluded from the financial accounts. For a comprehensive view of the adjustments to the tax base, the authors refer to the table included in section 4.1.1.

Additional determinants influencing the tax base pertain to mandatory depreciation and temporal considerations. Specifically, tangible assets valued at less than EUR 5,000 require immediate depreciation in the acquisition year. Conversely, other fixed assets need to be depreciated over their economic life on a straight-line basis by the economic owner, except for immovable property that is ascribed a useful life of twenty-eight years and fixed intangible assets, including acquired goodwill for which the useful life is contingent upon the duration of legal protection or granted rights or, if indeterminable, is stipulated at five years.[23]

The proposed BEFIT Directive also incorporates provisions for calculating the depreciation base to be kept in a fixed asset register. Improvement costs are subject to depreciation in alignment with the applicable regulations to newly procured fixed assets. Financial assets are exempt from depreciation.[24]

A pertinent adjustment involves the valuation of stock and work-in-progress that is determined through the first-in-first-out method. Moreover, the financial accounting

18. *Ibid.*
19. *Ibid.*
20. Council Directive (EU) 2022/2523 of 14 December 2022 on ensuring a global minimum level of taxation for multinational enterprise groups and large-scale domestic groups in the Union (OJ L 328, 22.12.2022).
21. That is, national Generally Accepted Accounting Principles (GAAP) or International Financial Reporting Standards (IFRS).
22. European Commission, o.c. *supra* n. 8, p. 13.
23. European Commission, o.c. *supra* n. 8, p. 14.
24. *Ibid.*

net income or loss of a BEFIT group member needs to be adjusted to disallow any provision amount. Exceptions to this rule exist that are contingent upon the fulfilment of specified criteria. The proposed BEFIT directive contains explicit regulations for adjustments concerning bad debts, long-term projects, and hedging.[25]

Considering that BEFIT applies solely to group members being part of the fiscal year, it incorporates provisions relating to group members entering or exiting during the fiscal year. These provisions encompass considerations on both the timing and tax treatment of pre-existing long-term projects and pre-entry losses.[26]

2.4 Aggregation and Allocation of the BEFIT Tax Base

The process of aggregation and allocation within the context of the BEFIT framework involves consolidating the individually determined tax bases of BEFIT group members, denoted as *preliminary tax results*, at the level of the filing entity. The latter might be either the EU's ultimate parent company or a designated EU BEFIT group member. The outcome of this aggregation consequently permits the cross-border offsetting of losses against profits.[27]

The resulting aggregated tax base is referred to as the BEFIT tax base and may exhibit either a positive or negative value. In instances of the latter, the associated loss can be carried forward. As there are no explicit guidelines, it is reasonable to assume that losses could possibly be rolled forward indefinitely.[28][29]

For a positive BEFIT tax base, an allocation process is required among the individual BEFIT group members. In contrast to prior proposals, such as those in the CCCTB, the current BEFIT proposal introduces a transitional period of seven years. During this period, allocating the BEFIT tax base to BEFIT group members adheres to a baseline allocation percentage formula.[30]

This percentage is determined as follows:

$$(\text{taxable result of BEFIT group member} \;/\; \text{total taxable result of BEFIT group}) \times 100$$

The calculation considers the average of taxable results over the preceding three fiscal years. In the initial three years, BEFIT group companies' results realized during the pre-BEFIT period need not be recalculated according to BEFIT standards, with taxable results determined in accordance with national corporate tax rules being permissible for allocation purposes. This is treated as zero in cases when a preliminary tax result is negative.[31]

25. *Ibid.*
26. *Ibid.*
27. European Commission, o.c. *supra* n. 8, pp. 14-15.
28. *Ibid.*
29. P. Pistone et al., *Proposal for a Council Directive on BEFIT: an Initial Assessment*, IBFD 60 (12 October 2023) https://doi.org/10.2139/ssrn.4707439.
30. European Commission, o.c. *supra* n. 8, pp. 14-15.
31. Specific allocation rules may apply for EU Member States employing a distribution-based tax system, such as in Estonia.

During this transitional period, the EC is tasked with conducting a study on the potential composition and weight of selected formula factors to be applied in the post-transition period, with a report to be presented to the Council of the European Union by the end of 2031. Should the EC find it appropriate, a proposal to amend the allocation formula in the then-existing BEFIT Directive may be issued.[32]

Certain revenues, expenses, and deductible items associated with BEFIT group members are excluded from the BEFIT tax base. This exclusion encompasses group members predominantly engaged in the exploration or production of oil or gas as well as revenues, expenses, and other deductible items pertaining to (i) operating ships involved in international transport under an approved tonnage regime, (ii) flying aircraft in international transports, and (iii) operating boats engaged in inland waterways transport.[33]

After determining the allocated part, a BEFIT group member is eligible to deduct specific items from it, including expenses and losses incurred before entering the BEFIT group or deductible items as per domestic law, such as contributions to charitable bodies or pension provisions.

Furthermore, it is important to take into account that all intra-BEFIT group transactions are exempt from withholding taxes or other source taxation unless the beneficial owner is not a BEFIT group member.

2.5 Transactions Between BEFIT Group Members and Non-BEFIT Group Members: Traffic Light System

The proposed BEFIT Directive incorporates a TP risk monitoring framework that is commonly referred to as the traffic light system. It is designed to assess and manage TP risks associated with specific activities in BEFIT groups. This system is applied to facilitate TP risk compliance, particularly for low-risk distributors and manufacturers, for transactions with associated enterprises outside a BEFIT group.[34]

To facilitate ongoing risk monitoring, the EC will be tasked with establishing and disseminating public benchmarks based on the five-year average profit performance (EBIT margin) of comparable low-risk distributors and manufacturers. These public benchmarks will be periodically updated by the EC.[35]

The traffic light system employs a risk evaluation mechanism that categorizes activities into three distinct levels of low, medium, or high based on the EBIT margins in comparison to established benchmarks. The risk categories are determined by the profitability percentile of any member within the BEFIT group, with low-risk entities positioned above the 60th percentile, medium-risk entities falling within the 40th and 60th percentiles, and high-risk entities situated below the 40th percentile.[36]

32. European Commission, o.c. *supra* n. 8, pp. 14-15.
33. European Commission, o.c. *supra* n. 8, p. 15.
34. European Commission, o.c. *supra* n. 8, p. 16.
35. *Ibid.*
36. *Ibid.*

Fundamentally, the traffic light system aims to align risk assessment with compliance management. It classifies activities based on their inherent risk and utilizes benchmarks to ensure arm's length TP. Notably, this approach is strategically designed to alleviate administrative and compliance burdens for entities classified as low-risk within the BEFIT framework.[37] *See also* section 3.4 for further discussion on the traffic light system.

3 BEFIT AND THE ALP

3.1 BEFIT and the Pillar Two Directive

Will the formulary approach under the proposed BEFIT Directive make the ALP redundant? At least, that is what the EC has written on two occasions in the proposed BEFIT Directive.[38] It also refers to the Pillar Two Directive[39] on several occasions.[40] Strangely enough, reading the two directives together seems to make the redundancy statement quite a bold one. When delving deeper into the Pillar Two Directive, it appears as if, for the purposes of applying the Pillar Two Directive, the ALP is still existing and is prevalent.[41] According to Article 16, § 4 of the Pillar Two Directive, transactions between constituent entities in different jurisdictions should be recorded in the same amount and consistent with the ALP. If not, adjustments should be made to be consistent.[42] The text of said article reads:

> 4. Any transaction between constituent entities located in different jurisdictions that is not recorded in the same amount in the financial accounts of both constituent entities or that is not consistent with the arm's length principle shall be adjusted so as to be in the same amount and consistent with the arm's length principle.
>
> A loss from a sale or other transfer of an asset between two constituent entities located in the same jurisdiction that is not recorded consistently with the arm's length principle shall be adjusted based on the arm's length principle if that loss is included in the computation of the qualifying income or loss.

---

37. *Ibid.*
38. European Commission, o.c. *supra* n. 8, Explanatory Memorandum, p. 10: 'After the transition period, the need for pricing such intra-group transactions in consistency with the arm's length principle might even be made redundant for tax purposes.' Preamble, p. 4: 'That permanent mechanism could be based on a formulary apportionment and would render the need for intra-BEFIT group transactions to be consistent with the arm's length principle redundant.'
39. Council Directive (EU) 2022/2523 of 14 December 2022 on ensuring a global minimum level of taxation for multinational enterprise groups and large-scale domestic groups in the Union (OJ L 328, 22.12.2022), p. 1.
40. Reference to the Pillar Two Directive can be found in the Explanatory Memorandum p. 2, the Preamble (recitals (4), (6), (9) and (14) and text of the Proposed BEFIT Directive, Arts 17 (p. 15) and 77 (p. 44).
41. *See also* F. Scandone, L. Scordo & L. Marino, *Pillar One, Pillar Two and BEFIT: The End of an Unexpected Journey?*, 31(1) International Transfer Pricing Journal, IBFD (2024) https://doi.org/10.59403/2z2kyr1.
42. Council Directive (EU) 2022/2523 of 14 December 2022 on ensuring a global minimum level of taxation for multinational enterprise groups and large-scale domestic groups in the Union (OJ L 328, 22.12.2022), p. 25.

> For the purposes of this paragraph, 'arm's length principle' means the principle under which transactions between constituent entities are to be recorded by reference to the conditions that would have been obtained between independent enterprises in comparable transactions and under comparable circumstances.

This risks confusion and concerns. Indeed, for the purpose of the Pillar Two Directive, the MNE concerned should continue to apply the ALP while it should apply a formulaic approach to the proposed BEFIT Directive. It is unclear how this serves as a simplification. The EC might consider the ALP becoming redundant for the purpose of profit allocation between group members situated in different Member States; however, the MNE still has to apply the ALP to grapple with the Pillar Two Directive (and its transposition into the Member States' domestic law). It is equally difficult to see that the goals mentioned in the proposed BEFIT Directive (level playing field, enhance legal certainty, reduce compliance costs, encourage businesses to operate cross-border and stimulate investments and growth in the Union) could be met in the case of the parallel application of the ALP (Pillar Two Directive) and formulary apportionment (BEFIT).

3.2 TP under the Transitional Regime

In the initial phase of implementation of the proposed BEFIT Directive, the ALP will be a crucial factor. As the group members of a qualifying BEFIT group calculate their tax base on the basis of their financial accounting profits (losses) (and applying limited tax adjustments different from the Pillar Two Directive), TP is crucial for the group members concerned. These will then be pooled and allocated on the basis of a percentage in the three-year average of taxable results. *See* section 2.4 for the baseline allocation percentage formula. TP will hence have an impact on the weight of the group member in the overall base[43] during the transition period.

It is also useful to note that there is no guarantee that the transitional approach mentioned above will be replaced by a different allocation formula at a later stage, for example, based on factors such as payroll, assets, and/or sales. In such a case, the transitional approach may become the final approach[44] and will have TP incorporated into it.

This being said, in the proposed BEFIT Directive, the impact of TP and the ALP will be even more prominent. The former is used to determine the individual outcomes under BEFIT and will influence – through the formula used – also the outcomes of the other group members.[45] TP related to a certain transaction can thus influence the outcomes of a group member under BEFIT that has no bearing on the said transaction and subsequently impact the tax income of EU Member States that are not involved in the transaction.

43. P. Pistone et al., o.c. *supra* n. 29.
44. European Commission, o.c. *supra* n. 8, Art. 45(10), p. 29; P. Pistone et al., o.c. *supra* n. 29.
45. P. Pistone et al., o.c. *supra* n. 29.

3.3 Increase of More than 10% in Revenue or Costs

During the transition period, costs or revenue of the intra-group transactions of the members of an MNE under BEFIT that increase by at least 10% compared to the previous three fiscal years should be scrutinized and possibly adjusted.[46] The part exceeding the 10% increase would be considered not to be at arm's length. Stated otherwise, the 10% serves as a threshold test. This is considered a simplification of the TP risk assessment mechanism, leading to greater scrutiny.

With the proper mindset, it could perhaps be seen as a simplification of risk assessment. However, the point is whether this is a fair selection criterion.

The EC has opted to go further than risk assessment and considers that the part exceeding 10% should not only be examined as possibly not being at arm's length. It introduces a rebuttable presumption that excludes the part above 10% in the computation of the baseline allocation percentage. Through this rebuttable presumption, the EC places the burden of proof in all cases on the group member(s) concerned.

In some countries, the burden of proof rests with the taxpayer; in other countries, it is with the tax authorities, depending on domestic policy. It appears here that the EC intends to harmonize a procedural element. It is difficult, however, to marry this approach with the goals of simplification, enhanced tax certainty, and reduced compliance costs if the burden of proof switches from the tax authorities to the taxpayer.

In addition, as indicated by Pistone et al., does this mean that BEFIT group members have some discretion in determining TP as long as it falls with the ALP? Such a position would indeed seem strange as the 10% threshold should be calculated on an arm's length basis.[47] There seems to be circularity in the EC's reasoning.

It is also unclear why the threshold is set at 10% or how the EC has determined it. For certain cases, this rate could be aligned with the arm's length standard while, in others, it would not. The threshold is not only used as a risk assessment tool; but by making it a rebuttable presumption, it also becomes a taxation tool.

Finally, a valid question seems to be whether the introduction of a rebuttable presumption linked to an increase of a certain percentage of costs or revenue meets the standard of proportionality required by EU law.

3.4 Application of the ALP and BEFIT on Transactions with Group Members Outside the BEFIT Group (EU and Non-EU)

MNEs will generally have activities both in and outside the EU, with numerous transactions involving multiple entities situated in the EU and in third countries. These MNEs will be subject to several TP approaches:

- application of the ALP for the transactions or operations where all group members concerned are outside the BEFIT group (EU and non-EU);

46. European Commission, o.c. *supra* n. 8, Art. 45(3) and (4), pp. 27-28.
47. P. Pistone et al., o.c. *supra* n. 29, p. 71.

- application of the ALP for the transactions or operations between group members subject to BEFIT and group members (situated inside or outside the EU) not subject to BEFIT, including a traffic light system for low-risk distribution and manufacturing activities (*see* below);[48] and
- application of BEFIT for the intra-EU transactions or operations among group members falling within its scope.

Briefly stated, an MNE active in the EU may have to deal with applying the ALP and formulary apportionment under BEFIT at the same time. As TP between the group members not subject to BEFIT and BEFIT group members will affect the taxable bases of the BEFIT group members, it is key to have TP as accurate as possible because of its influence on the allocation under the formulaic approach.[49]

It is becoming even more cumbersome to delve deeper into a deemed simplification. The proposed BEFIT Directive contains a specific compliance framework for low-risk activities known as the simplified approach to TP. The title of Article 51 of the proposed BEFIT Directive calls this a compliance[50] framework. The text of the specific article indicates it is only a risk assessment framework. It is consequently unclear whether the enterprises concerned now have to *comply* with the simplified approach to TP, whether it serves as a rebuttable presumption or a safe harbour, or whether it is only a framework for establishing whether TP risk is present in a certain transaction. As it is unclear, it will be labelled as the compliance/risk assessment framework in this contribution.

The compliance/risk assessment framework uses the traffic light system approach of classifying transactions in a low (green), medium (orange/yellow), or high (red) risk zone.[51] This will be done on the basis of a public benchmark of which the details are not yet known but that will be determined by an implementing act. This appears as if the EC is operating under a proxy from the tax authorities. Perhaps this is an example of what is called the 'regulatory compulsion of command and control, giving Member States more control on the allocation of taxing rights'.[52] This is also recognized by Pistone et al. in the area of computing the BEFIT tax base.[53]

A particular area of concern is the extremely narrow margins that the traffic light system contains. This can be best illustrated by Figure 3.1 on how to interpret it:

48. European Commission, o.c. *supra* n. 8, Ch. IV Simplified Approach to Transfer Pricing Compliance, pp. 31-34.
49. P. Pistone et al., o.c. *supra* n. 29, p. 77.
50. According to the Cambridge Dictionary, compliance means the act of obeying a law or rule, especially one that controls a particular industry or type of work or the act of doing everything that someone tells or wants you to do; according to Merriam-Webster Dictionary, it is the act or process of complying to a desire, demand, proposal, or regimen or to coercion or conformity in fulfilling official requirements.
51. *See also* s. 2.5.
52. C. Peters, *A Governance Analysis of BEFIT: How the Member States' Wish to Obtain More Regulatory Authority is Driving a Revolution*, 5 EC Tax Review, Kluwer 199 (2023) https://doi.org/10.54648/ecta2023025.
53. P. Pistone et al., o.c. *supra* n. 29, p. 81.

Figure 3.1 BEFIT Range Compared to Full Range and Interquartile Range

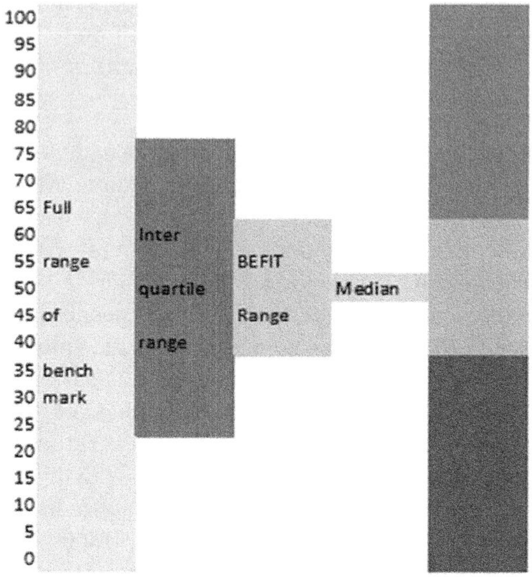

Source: No source available – author's comparison.

The authors assume that a generic benchmark will be performed that will serve as a basis for the compliance/risk assessment framework. Such a generic benchmark could well serve for risk assessment purposes but unlikely as a compliance tool as it should then align with the OECD TP Guidelines. The EC has likely been inspired by the work on Pillar A, Amount B and the matrix that has been developed for baseline marketing and distribution activities.[54] Additionally, in that context, it is anything but clear how the different figures in the Amount B matrix have been composed. This being said, it ordinarily contains a greater amount of selective criteria to determine the point that is likely best in the range, as it is currently not known how the benchmarking will be organized. Moreover, it would be helpful for the EC to develop these types of criteria to mitigate the risk of things becoming a one-size-fits-all exercise.

The traffic light system contains a major risk that transactions that perfectly meet the ALP will fall under the red or yellow/orange category and, hence, are liable to heightened scrutiny. A simple example will illustrate this. Assume the MNE has performed a best practice arm's length benchmarking analysis for its low-risk distribution and manufacturing. The outcome of the benchmarking indicates that the low-risk entity concerned is ranked below the 40th percentile but above the 25th percentile. This will lead to additional compliance costs and unnecessary use of resources from both taxpayers and tax authorities. The latter will identify (likely) false

54. OECD/Inclusive Framework on BEPS, *Public Consultation Document: Pillar One – Amount B*, 17 July-1 September 2023.

positives (i.e., the enterprises selected meet the standards of the traffic light system, but their transactions are at arm's length). The taxpayers concerned must respond to tax authorities' questions that could have easily been avoided and should demonstrate the arm's length conformity of their approach. It is also peculiar that the EC is contemplating a traffic light system to enhance compliance for transactions that basically carry a low TP risk and where the tax authorities have extensive experience.[55]

The approach also seems to potentially shift the TP outcomes to the higher ranges of the benchmark. If the group company proceeds in this way, the over-apportionment likely attracts scrutiny from tax authorities from countries on the other side.

4 COMMENTS ON THE PROPOSED BEFIT DIRECTIVE

4.1 Determining the BEFIT Tax Base

4.1.1 Adjustments under BEFIT and the Pillar Two Directive

'[T]he new rules are aligned as closely as possible with the Two-Pillar Approach.'[56] It is perfectly plausible that for simplification – one of the goals of the directive – the principles should be aligned as closely as possible. That would seem only natural. Deviations are always possible but should be kept to a minimum.

It is far from easy to conclude that the EC has succeeded in achieving this goal, as Table 3.1 illustrates.

Table 3.1 Comparison of the BEFIT Directive and the Adjustments in the GloBE Rules

BEFIT Adjustments	*Pillar Two Directive Adjustments*
Inclusions	
– Financial assets held for trading	– No equivalent
– Borrowing costs paid to parties outside the BEFIT group in excess of the interest limitation rule of the EU	– No equivalent
– Fair value adjustments and capital gains received by life insurance undertakings in the context of unit-linked/index-linked contracts;	– No equivalent
– Fines, penalties, and illegal payments such as bribes	– Policy disallowed expenses
– Corporate taxes that have already been paid or qualified domestic top-up taxes imposed in applying Pillar Two	– Net tax expenses

55. In a tax context, *see also* P. Pistone et al., o.c. *supra* n. 29, p. 80.
56. European Commission, o.c. *supra* n. 8, Explanatory Memorandum, p. 6.

BEFIT Adjustments	*Pillar Two Directive Adjustments*
Exclusions	
– Dividends and capital gains or losses on significant share or ownership interests other than interests held for trading purposes or by a life insurance undertaking	– Excluded dividends and equity gains or losses
– The profits or losses of permanent establishments	– No equivalent
– Shipping income subject to a national tonnage tax regime approved for state aid purposes	– International shipping income exclusion (Article 8 OECD Model Tax Convention-related issues, not related to tonnage tax)
– Rollover relief for gains on assets that are replaced	– No equivalent
– The costs of acquisition, construction, and improvement of depreciable assets (including directly related subsidies)	– No equivalent
– Unrealized gains or losses from currency exchange fluctuations on fixed assets	– Asymmetric foreign currency gains or losses
– No equivalent	– Net Tax expenses
– No equivalent	– Included revaluation method gain or losses
– No equivalent	– Gains or losses from the disposal of assets and liabilities
– No equivalent	– Prior period errors and changes in accounting principles
– Post allocations deductions	– No equivalent
– Pension provisions deductible under local CIT	– Accrued pension expenses

Source: No source available – author's comparison.

The concept, '[a]s closely as possible', is unspecified and unlikely to be felt satisfactory given the complexities imposed on both taxpayers and tax authorities to grapple with a complete overhaul of tax compliance already under Pillar Two.

The explanatory memorandum underscores the intention to align the new rules with the Two-Pillar Approach, ensuring coherence with the Pillar Two Directive through the uniform application of BEFIT rules to in-scope groups. However, a critical examination reveals material discrepancies between the two directives.

Primarily, adjustments made under both the Pillar Two Directive and the proposed BEFIT Directive lack alignment in their wording, introducing potential interpretational differences and corresponding legal uncertainties. It may only be hoped that these misalignments will be rectified in an amended version of the proposed BEFIT Directive.[57]

Furthermore, the divergence extends beyond mere textual variations, encompassing specific adjustments solely outlined in either the Pillar Two Directive or the proposed BEFIT Directive. This article does not aim to provide an exhaustive comparative analysis but rather focuses on some particular matters of attention.

A pivotal point of contention arises concerning remuneration derived from ownership interests in an entity, such as dividends and capital gains. Asymmetries emerge both between these income types and between Pillar Two and BEFIT rules. Article 8 of the proposed BEFIT Directive introduces an adjustment for ownership interests excluding 95% of dividend distributions and contingent upon the ownership interest meeting a minimum threshold of 10% and a holding period of at least one year.[58,59]

Notably, while the minimum participation threshold and holding period align with those specified in Article 16(1)(b) of the Pillar Two Directive for excluded dividends, the Pillar Two Directive provides a full (100%) exclusion if the conditions are satisfied. The tension created by this partial exclusion of dividends appears to extend to groups falling within the scope of application of the Parent-Subsidiary Directive.[60]

Substantial divergences are particularly evident concerning capital gains, introducing a bifurcated treatment with a 95% adjustment for gains (or losses) from a disposition and a 100% adjustment for fair value gains or losses. These adjustments again hinge on the same threshold and holding period conditions applied to dividends.[61]

A comparative analysis of the adjustments proposed by BEFIT and those outlined in the Pillar Two Directive shows that BEFIT introduces additional adjustments that are absent in the Pillar Two Directive. These supplementary adjustments appear to trace their roots directly from the original CCCTB framework or align closely with its aspirations for a comprehensive set of tax rules instead of a 'Limited Tax Adjustments Approach', indicating a methodological ambiguity in key aspects of base determination.[62]

The inherent risk in this ambiguity lies in requiring taxpayers within the scope of both the proposed BEFIT Directive and the Pillar Two Directive to compute three

57. P. Pistone et al., o.c. *supra* n. 29, p. 45.
58. P. Pistone et al., o.c. *supra* n. 29, p. 50.
59. According to the Pillar II Directive, 'excluded dividend' means a dividend or other distribution received or accrued in respect of an ownership interest, except a dividend or other distribution received or accrued in respect of either: an ownership interest that is held by the group in an entity that carries rights to less than 10% of the profits, capital, or reserves or voting rights of that entity at the date of the distribution or disposition (a 'portfolio shareholding'); and that is economically owned by the constituent entity that receives or accrues the dividend or other distribution for less than one year at the date of the distribution; or an ownership interest in an investment entity that is subject to an election pursuant to an election to apply a taxable distribution method; *Ibid.*
60. *Ibid.*
61. *Ibid.*
62. P. Pistone et al., o.c. *supra* n. 29, pp. 51-52.

distinct tax bases: One for the Pillar Two Directive, one for the proposed BEFIT Directive, and one for corporate income tax (CIT) due to an individual assessment under the proposal.[63]

In conclusion, the proposed BEFIT Directive, while aiming for alignment with the Two-Pillar Approach and coherence with the Pillar Two Directive, reveals substantial discrepancies and divergences upon closer examination. The lack of uniform wording in adjustments between the Pillar Two Directive and the proposed BEFIT Directive introduces potential interpretational challenges and legal uncertainties, as well as a risk of increasing the compliance burden with the obligation to compute three distinct tax bases. As the proposed BEFIT Directive undergoes further refinement, it will be essential to reconcile these discrepancies to ensure the effectiveness and coherence of an envisioned harmonized EU tax regime.[64]

To refresh memories, the aim of the Pillar Two Directive is different from the goal of BEFIT. The policy objective of the GloBE rules was to *deal with the remaining Base Erosion and Profit Shifting (BEPS) issues*. It is interesting to see how the political narrative has become the overarching theme. Indeed, stopping what is known as a 'race to the bottom' began to prevail at some point within Europe and beyond.[65] The Pillar Two Directive and the Global Anti-Base Erosion Model Rules (GloBE rules) essentially aim to introduce a minimum tax of 15%. The proposed BEFIT Directive, as explained, is a design for a common tax base followed by formulaic apportionment.[66]

Finally, the authors struggle to resist the temptation to flag that the 95% participation exclusion is probably not ideal when appreciating the policy objective of the EU to serve as a preferred location for investment. Indeed, attracting pan-European holding companies may be hampered by this provision. After all, investments in brick-and-mortar industries are important, but this is even more true if this encompasses decision centres (as part of holding companies) as a prerequisite for their captivity.

4.1.2 Losses

The proposed BEFIT Directive will allow groups to set off losses across borders. This is certainly welcomed, and the need for legalistic action is fueled by jurisprudence.[67] The measure accords well with the concept of a unified market.

63. *Ibid.*
64. J. Korving, *'BEFIT and HOT: FASTER and SAFE!' EU Law or Slogan for Slimming Pills?*, 63(12) Eur. Taxn., 515 (2023), Journal Articles & Opinion Pieces IBFD https://doi.org/10.59403/2jy6hxp.
65. Mrs Yellen, US Secretary of Treasury mentioned on 8 October 2021 further to the OECD Inclusive Framework Announcement: *As of this morning, virtually the entire global economy has decided to end the race to the bottom on corporate taxation, see* https://home.treasury.gov/news/press-releases/jy0394 (accessed 19 January 2024).
66. F. Scandone, L. Scordo & L. Marino, *Pillar One, Pillar Two and BEFIT: The End of an Unexpected Journey?*, 31(1) International Transfer Pricing Journal, IBFD (2024) https://doi.org/10.59403/2z2kyr1.
67. For an interesting overview of some milestone cases, *see* T.P. Rodrigues, *Cross-Border Loss Relief Jurisprudence*, 1 EC Tax Journal (2008), https://www.uria.com/en/publicaciones/2139-crossborder-loss-relief-jurisprudence.

There may, however, be some design issues. The cross-border relief is not applied to pre-BEFIT losses. These remain purely domestic[68] as they are deducted from the allocated part of a BEFIT group member. Such losses should then become deductible under the rules and limitations of the domestic CIT mechanisms.

In addition, issues may arise with regard to pre-BEFIT losses incurred by a BEFIT group member that is liquidated post-BEFIT. In this case, the loss should be transferred to the parent entity that has now become a BEFIT group member and is subject to BEFIT. This loss, however, cannot be taken into consideration as the parent entity is no longer subject to a local corporate tax system.

There is an apparent need for the design of the cross-border loss relief to be worked on in more detail. Should the BEFIT Directive be perceived as not serving as the ideal place to settle cross-border relief, then it might definitely be worthwhile to consider a specific dedicated directive.

4.1.3 Different Depreciation Rules

One of the aims of the proposed BEFIT Directive, as explained earlier, is to replace twenty-seven different tax systems with one coherent and consistent set of rules. It does so by creating a separate accounting system. BEFIT group members, for accounting purposes, are still required to follow the accounting principles of the different jurisdictions where they are situated. A parent company will also be required to file consolidated records under certain circumstances. For BEFIT purposes, the BEFIT group members must create new accounts honouring the mandatory depreciation rules. These will differ from the depreciation rules that the BEFIT group members have applied for accounting purposes, including consolidation. For the cynically enhanced, this might give an impression of simplification for tax purposes being realized by adding complexity in keeping accounting records. All in all, the different depreciation rules will more than likely add another layer of complexity and, hence, increase the compliance burden even more.

Enterprises choose certain options influenced by economic criteria that are judged differently by various players within the ambit of the legal framework in the design of their depreciation policy. Notwithstanding that EU Member States may have certain mandatory depreciation rules (even in their tax legislation), the rules under the proposed BEFIT Directive seem to step beyond certain boundaries. The question should be raised whether having a uniform depreciation mechanism for BEFIT purposes can be reconciled with the economic rationale of depreciation and the freedom of choice of the enterprises concerned. After all, the latter must explain their depreciation policy in their financial accounts.

68. European Commission, o.c. *supra* n. 8, Explanatory Memorandum, Art. 38 in conjunction with Art. 48(1)(a).

4.2 (Un)Certainty

4.2.1 Absence of Certainty Provisions

Tax certainty has always had a very prominent position on the agenda of various stakeholders, including taxpayers, tax administrations, and legislators. It is crucial to know what constitutes tax obligations as they not only impact the financial position of enterprises but are also examined by investors. Tax certainty is linked to avoiding double multiple taxation, but it is broader than that. It is also about having the correct approach being accepted by tax authorities. This is also the reason why certain groups are keen on adhering to real-time cooperative compliance programs such as the international compliance assurance program (ICAP).[69]

The EU has always been a forerunner regarding tax certainty, particularly with TP. The typical examples are, of course, the arbitration convention[70] and the dispute resolution directive.[71] However, also the European Trust and Cooperation Approach (ETACA),[72] the EU version of ICAP should be mentioned.

The proposed BEFIT Directive mentions enhancing legal certainty as one of its goals. It contains some aspects that can be linked to tax certainty, such as the traffic light system (*see* sections 2.5 and 3.4), alignment with the Pillar Two Directive, compatibility with the anti-tax avoidance directive (ATAD),[73] or a common administrative framework to allow tax administrations to agree on and achieve early certainty. On the other hand, the requirement (and subsequent separate audit) from all of the tax authorities involved for a local tax return next to the BEFIT tax return causes uncertainty. Although separate returns and audits seem logical in the current tax framework, it becomes less plausible when a cross-EU system is being implemented. Unfortunately and despite being one of the goals, the proposed BEFIT Directive does not contain a specific section on tax certainty for taxpayers.

For example, it is silent on whether advance certainty for the BEFIT group members can be achieved through (unilateral, bilateral, or multilateral) advance (pricing) arrangements. Early certainty, however, is mentioned as one of the proposed achievements. When harm is done and the application of BEFIT ends up in double or

69. International Compliance Assurance Program – ICAP. More information on ICAP can be found at https://www.oecd.org/tax/administration/international-compliance-assurance-programme.htm (accessed 10 January 2024).
70. Convention on the elimination of double taxation in connection with the adjustment of profits of associated enterprises (90/463/EEC), Official Journal of the European Commission, L 225/10, 20.08.1990.
71. European Commission Council Directive (EU) 2017/1852 of 10 October 2017 on tax dispute resolution mechanisms in the European Union, Official Journal of the European Union, L 265/1, 14.10.2017.
72. European Trust and Cooperation Approach – ETACA Pilot Project for MNEs. More information can be found at https://taxation-customs.ec.europa.eu/eu-cooperative-compliance-programme/european-trust-and-cooperation-approach-etaca-pilot-project-mnes_en (accessed 10 January 2024).
73. European Commission, Council Directive 2011/96/EU of 30 November 2011 on the common system of taxation applicable in the case of parent companies and subsidiaries of different Member States (recast), Official Journal of the European Union L 345/8, 29.12.2011.

multiple taxations, the question is whether access to a Mutual agreement procedure (MAP) or other dispute resolution instruments is guaranteed. For the time being, no reference to such a dispute resolution is considered in the proposed BEFIT Directive. It is also uncertain whether taxpayers under BEFIT will have access to the dispute resolution directive as reference is made in that directive to the application of double tax treaties or the arbitration convention.[74] The latter may not be applicable as BEFIT is not about TP or allocating profits but instead about allocating the (common) tax base. The question is whether BEFIT is a tax covered by double tax treaties (or an identical or substantially similar tax). It should definitely be considered an income tax. There is a pressing need for the proposed BEFIT Directive to be clear on what dispute resolution mechanisms are available.[75]

Within the EU, the ETACA pilot is dealing, in principle, with routine intra-group transactions such as low-risk activities (low-risk distribution, low-risk manufacturing, and low-risk research and development).[76] Hence, its scope may be too narrow. Should BEFIT be realized, it is highly recommended that a broader cooperative compliance approach would also be available, preferably one that is similar to ICAP with the possibility of covering both low- and high-risk transactions and operations. As the transactions and operations of BEFIT group members will likely stretch beyond the BEFIT group, the possibility of catching such transactions and operations under a larger tax certainty or comfort approach should certainly be envisaged.

4.2.2 One-Stop-Shop Approach

The primary objective of the proposed BEFIT Directive is to establish uniform procedural rules for the CIT across the EU, thereby promoting harmonization among Member States. This not only fosters collaboration among tax authorities from different countries but also introduces a key procedural innovation of the 'BEFIT team', which is a *central* body with representatives of the relevant EU tax administrations. Derived from the concept of joint audits, this European body possesses the authority to make conclusive decisions on tax matters within the BEFIT group.[77]

However, the effectiveness of this system without a centralized monitoring authority remains uncertain and raises questions about its ability to ensure consistent interpretation and application across various tax authorities (BEFIT teams). While harmonization may be a positive step, it is crucial to consider the other overarching goals, including simplification and reducing the compliance burden for MNEs.[78]

74. European Commission, Council Directive (EU) 2017/1852 of 10 October 2017 on tax dispute resolution mechanisms in the European Union, Official Journal of the European Union, L 265/1, 14.10.2017. For example, Art. 1 and recitals (1), (2), (3) and particularly recital (7) of the preamble: '[...] This Directive should apply to all taxpayers that are subject to taxes on income and capital covered by bilateral tax treaties and the Union Arbitration Convention.'
75. In that context, *see also* P. Pistone et al., o.c. *supra* n. 29, p. 90.
76. European Commission, *Guidelines European Trust and Cooperation Approach (ETACA)*, p. 5.
77. P. Pistone et al., o.c. *supra* n. 29, pp. 84-86.
78. *Ibid.*

The two-tier filing obligation system (filing with the lead tax administration (one-stop-shop) and local filing) proposed in the directive involving fact-finding at both the filing entity and individual group member levels is difficult to marry with the goal of simplification. Article 57(3)(d) suggests duplicative reporting requiring some information from the BEFIT information return to be reflected in each group member's individual tax return. This dual procedure introduces another level of complexity, posing a burden on group entities and tax authorities, thereby contradicting the intended one-stop-shop concept.[79] Again, for the cynically enhanced, Pistone et al. call it a 'one-more-stop approach'.[80]

4.2.3 *The BEFIT Allocation Formula*

The proposed BEFIT Directive describes a transitional formula only. The EC will launch a comprehensive study to determine the final formula 'by the end of the third fiscal year during the transition period'.[81] The transitional formula could well become the final formula if no agreement is reached on a different one (*see* section 2.4).

How the possible final formula will look is hence not known when the proposed BEFIT Directive is implemented during 2028 (if that date is kept, of course). Considering the three-year time lapse before the study is launched, the results might be realized sometime in 2031 or 2032. After that, there is then even no guarantee that the EU Member States will agree on a common formula (as has happened twice in the past). The fact of not knowing what formula will become final or even when it will be known when this will occur creates a factor of uncertainty for both MNEs and tax authorities.[82] In the meantime, EU Member States will, of course, have adhered to the principle of a formulary allocation of the tax base, and it may be difficult – if not impossible – to return to the pre-BEFIT stage.

While the political context and sensitivities are clear, it may be argued on pure tax technical grounds that it seems rather strange that the EC advocates a formulaic approach without a clear direction on the formula. It is more than an impression that the current atmosphere in international taxation favours brick-and-mortar activities. Some examples thereof are the return to a depreciation and payroll approach under the Pillar Two Directive (and GloBE rules) and the marketing and distribution safe harbour under Pillar One, Amount A. Without denying the importance of brick-and-mortar operations, the focus on only such activities could very well hamper the development of technology and research and development-driven groups in the EU. Striking a fair balance will hence be key. The old-school brick-and-mortar approach could likely trickle through in the formula because of the open-ended position of the EC on the potential formula. With having no clear direction on it or one that disfavours

79. In that context, *see also* P. Pistone et al., o.c. *supra* n. 29, p. 89.
80. P. Pistone et al., o.c. *supra* n. 29, p. 85.
81. European Commission, o.c. *supra* n. 8, p. 28.
82. J. Goulder, *BEFIT for Europe: Must We Do This Again?*, 112 Tax Notes International 304 (9 October 2023); J. Korving, *'BEFIT and HOT: FASTER and SAFE!' EU Law or Slogan for Slimming Pills?*, 63(12) Eur. Taxn. 515 (2023), Journal Articles & Opinion Pieces IBFD https://doi.org/10.59403/2jy6hxp.

technology-driven and research and development-oriented groups, it may impact the investment policy of such groups in the EU or the further development there. Is it not precisely this type of knowledge driven unicorns, although perhaps loss-making as a start-up, that the EU is currently lacking?

4.2.4 *And the BEFIT Proceeds Go to ...*

A valid question is whether the proposed BEFIT Directive leads to an equitable result, i.e., whether all EU Member States will derive benefits in a balanced way (in terms of tax base and taxes) from the formulaic apportionment. That also creates uncertainty. A high-level study performed by PwC colleagues G. Franssens and H. Polfliet[83] reveals that 'the implementation of BEFIT may result in the reallocation of corporate profits from smaller innovation- and service-oriented EU member states toward larger EU member states'.[84] This study was based on a formulaic allocation based on the traditional factors of payroll, assets (but not including intangibles), and sales. Another formula may, of course, lead to different results as the authors of the study recognize and indicate, '[I]t is possible that including intangible assets as a factor would benefit these smaller economies, but it is unlikely to fully offset the impact of the other three factors.'[85]

Taking the possible shift from smaller EU Member States to larger ones into consideration, it is not difficult to understand that the discussion on the final formula will be torturous.

4.3 BEFIT and the OECD/IF Two-Pillar Approach

With regard to Pillar Two, also referred to as GloBE, the Pillar Two Directive and the GloBE Model Rules are practically twins. The objective of Pillar Two (and the Pillar Two Directive) is different from that of the proposed BEFIT Directive. Pillar Two aims at installing a minimum tax of 15% to be introduced through domestic law provisions while the proposed BEFIT Directive is the determination and allocation on a formulaic basis of the taxable base (*see* section 4.1.1).

Regarding Pillar One, Amount A and Amount B should be distinguished. It could be argued that Amount A is ultimately also a formulaic apportionment of the tax base. After all, it reallocates a part of the profit before tax (25% exceeding 10% profit before tax) of the largest and most profitable MNEs (EUR 20 billion[86] revenue with 10% or more profit before tax) to market or user states. The goals of Amount A and the proposed BEFIT Directive are not the same. While Amount A only reallocates a part of the profits and acts as an overlay on the existing international tax framework, the proposed BEFIT Directive intends to replace, at least for the EU Member States, the

83. G. Franssens & H. Polfliet, *How the BEFIT Proposal May Disadvantage Smaller Countries*, 109 Tax Notes International 209 (9 January 2023). *See also* P. Pistone et al., o.c. *supra* n. 29, p. 77.
84. G. Franssens et al., o.c. *supra* n. 83, p. 212.
85. *Ibid.*
86. Possibly reduced to EUR 10 billion after a period of seven years and one year of review.

current international framework and – ultimately – the ALP. Additionally, Amount A reallocates only to market (or user) states, while the proposed BEFIT directive allocates the common tax base to all EU Member States involved. Finally, Amount A focuses on the redistribution of profits because of the economic footprint MNEs may have in a market state irrespective of a physical presence in the market or user state. The proposed BEFIT directive still maintains the physical presence approach.

Amount B intends to introduce a minimum return for what is referred to as baseline marketing and distribution activities as a simplification measure. This might particularly benefit emerging and developing economies. It is rooted in and represents an application of the ALP, at least according to the official OECD/IF communications. As indicated in footnote 38, the intention of the proposal is to make the ALP redundant whereas Amount B (and Amount A as well) keep the ALP as the gold standard.

5 BEFIT NEXT STEPS

The proposed BEFIT Directive will be submitted to both the European Parliament and the European Council. While the former holds a consultative role, allowing it to propose amendments to the directive, the latter is not obligated to incorporate these suggestions. Technical deliberations on the proposal, in view of potentially attaining a political consensus on the revised and amended BEFIT Directive, are to be conducted by the Council of the European Union and its associated working parties.

In light of the proposed BEFIT Directive's focus on direct taxation, unanimity within the European Council is imperative. Direct taxation is deemed a facet of Member States' sovereignty that affords each EU Member State the authority to exercise a veto and, thus, potentially obstructs the proposal's approval.

The requirement for unanimous agreement in the absence of sustained political impetus creates challenges.

The commission, however, expresses its optimism regarding the attainability of an agreement. Its positive vibe is grounded in the proposal's alignment with the accomplishments of the BEPS Project that culminated in the Two-Pillar solution agreed upon by some 140 countries and jurisdictions.

6 CONCLUDING THOUGHTS

BEFIT covers multiple aspects, of which TP is just one straw, albeit an important one, in a broader bundle.

Indeed, three proposals for a directive were published on the same date (BEFIT Directive, TP Directive, and Head Office Taxation Directive). A valid question is whether these constitute one 'package'.[87] Although they are labelled as separate directives, it could well be that they are technically (or politically) combined or linked

87. J. Korving, *'BEFIT and HOT: FASTER and SAFE!' EU Law or Slogan for Slimming Pills?*, 63(12) Eur. Taxn. 515 (2023), Journal Articles & Opinion Pieces IBFD https://doi.org/10.59403/2jy6hxp. In its Programme Belgian Presidency of the Council of the European Union – First half of 2024 – Protect, Strengthen, Prepare, the Belgian Government refers to the three directives as a

in one way or another. As the directives are related to direct taxation, unanimity is (still) required. Should they be considered one package, disagreement on any one of them would block unanimity on the others as well, which does not seem to be a desirable outcome. The EU Commission has already expended considerable effort into the drafting which commands the most viable way forward for each of them. Therefore, each of the proposed directives deserves to be considered and accepted (or not) on its own merits. The Netherlands and Finland have already indicated being supportive of the proposed BEFIT Directive but with serious reservations.[88] The Belgian Presidency of the Council only indicates that it welcomes the BEFIT package.[89]

The proposed goals of simplification, enhanced certainty, reduced compliance costs, and stimulation of investments and growth in the EU can only be embraced. A more comprehensive examination of the proposed BEFIT Directive effectuates mixed feelings as to whether it can realistically achieve those ambitious goals under the current text.

It can be perceived as another step in reforming the international tax landscape. The question is whether the proposed application from 2028 is not premature. Both companies and tax administrations have spent enormous amounts of time and effort to factor in and deal with the changes introduced through BEPS and the ATAD. The MNEs in the scope of the proposed BEFIT Directive are those who have to grapple with the Pillar Two directive (and, by extension, the GloBE rules worldwide). EU Member States very recently transposed the Pillar Two Directive into their domestic law. MNEs and tax authorities are now endeavouring to become well-informed about the Pillar Two directive requirements. Undoubtedly, this takes time from the most knowledgeable and experienced resources from all parties concerned.

Introducing a new system on top of the changes that have been introduced over the last decade might be the straw that breaks the camel's back. There may be more merit, at least for now, in developing simplified TP processes (such as under Amount B) and streamlining the approaches between countries through the principles rooted in the arm's length standard rather than initiating a likely difficult complete overhaul of the European tax system.

MNE and tax authorities have gained substantial practical experience in applying the ALP. It is extremely important to maintain and further leverage this rather than forfeit it because of some longstanding (political) desire to replace it with a system of formulary apportionment of which the outcomes are yet uncertain.

'package'. https://belgian-presidency.consilium.europa.eu/media/3kajw1io/programme_en.pdf, p. 19 (accessed 12 January 2024).

88. https://open.overheid.nl/documenten/e0787088-e0c7-428f-a932-0aa7f58cadf6/file; https://valtioneuvosto.fi/-/10623/hallitus-suhtautuu-varauksella-yritysten-tuloverotusta-euroopassa-koskevaan-befit-kehykseen?languageId=sv_SE. *See also* M. de Wilde, *BEFIT: A Company Tax System Layering Exercise for the Internal Market (Part 2)*, (Kluwer International Tax Blog, 28 January 2023), available at https://kluwertaxblog.com/2023/12/28/befit-a-company-tax-system-layering-exercise-for-the-internal-market-part-2/ (accessed 15 January 2024).

89. Belgian Presidency of the Council of the European Union, Programme, p. 19, available at https://belgian-presidency.consilium.europa.eu/media/3kajw1io/programme_en.pdf (accessed 15 January 2024).

The 2011 and 2016 proposals for a directive on the CCCTB now create a *déjà vu* effect for tax professionals. It may be wondered whether the attempt will be successful this time or rather fail again.[90] This contribution shows that it is imperative for the EC to undertake substantial work before the proposed BEFIT Directive is ready to pass the (unanimity) test.

Finally:

- the proposed implementation date of 2028 is overly ambitious, taking into account the implementation of the Pillar Two directive (and the GloBE Model Rules worldwide) on top of other recent (BEPS and ATAD) developments and will not allow sufficient time to understand and absorb the full impact and outcome of the rules; moreover, aligning the BEFIT rules *as closely as possible* with Pillar Two seems to lack ambition;
- further consideration should be given to allocating profits to or transactions with non-BEFIT group members (EU and non-EU); this is even more relevant when looking at the role that the EU (wants to) plays amid the current geopolitical challenges the world faces and, most importantly,
- simplification is welcomed, but the desired outcome by the EC cannot solely be achieved by the proposed BEFIT directive. It may offer some simplification, but it certainly needs further consideration in light of the overall international tax landscape and the ongoing reforms at various levels (OECD, UN, etc.). Examples are the introduction of a minimum tax into which *remaining BEPS issues* morphed, increased transparency requirements, real-time engagement between tax authorities and taxpayers and, finally, the likely elephant in the room: source versus residency taxation.

90. R. Goulder, *BEFIT for Europe: Must We Do This Again?*, 112 Tax Notes International 304 (9 October 2023).

CHAPTER 4

The EC's Transfer Pricing Directive Proposal*

Xaver Ditz

* For the first time in European history, transfer pricing could be regulated at European Union level in the wake of the European Commission's proposal for a directive. The attempt to achieve binding harmonization of the arm's length principle within the EU could be an important step towards reducing double taxation disputes in the Internal Market due to differences in national implementation and interpretation of the arm's length principle. However, the European Commission's proposal for a directive on transfer pricing also raises several issues that are not easy to resolve.

1 INTRODUCTION

For a standardized application of the transfer pricing (TP) principles, the majority of European Union (EU) Member States follow the Organisation for Economic Co-operation and Development (OECD) Transfer Pricing Guidelines (TPG) and have particularly enshrined the arm's length principle (ALP) in their national legislation. However, there are often differences in its interpretation, such as dealing with financial transactions, intangibles, and year-end adjustments, as well as avoiding double taxation.

At the EU level, TP has thus far not been regulated by legislation. Instead, the European Commission (EC) established the EU Joint Transfer Pricing Forum (JTPF) as an expert group with the objective of issuing practical recommendations on various TP aspects.[1] Although the intention was to harmonize TP practices within the EU, the JTPF recommendations were not legally binding. As the latter's work ceased in 2019, there is currently no standardized and coordinated EU guidance in the area of TP.

In order to alleviate this deficiency and to harmonize a broader range of corporate tax areas, the EC presented a joint package (Business in Europe: Framework for Income Taxation (BEFIT) package) of three proposals that were all published on 12 September 2023:

(1) The 'BEFIT' proposal[2] contains a new, standardized set of core rules for calculating the tax base of *all enterprises* operating in the EU *with a total annual turnover of at least EUR 750 million*. The regulations would be due to come into force on 1 July 2028.
(2) In addition, the 'Head Office Tax System' proposal (HOT)[3] is intended to simplify procedures for *small and medium-sized enterprises* operating across borders in the EU via permanent establishments. This would involve calculating the taxes payable solely based on the tax rules of the Member State in which the company has its head office and also submitting a tax return solely in its Member State. The approach would be comparable to the value-added tax (VAT) Mini-One-Stop-Shop Procedure. The regulations would apply from 1 January 2026.
(3) With the 'Council Directive on Transfer Pricing' proposal (TPD),[4] the EC's objective is to harmonize the interpretation of the OECD TPG within the EU's Internal Market, increase legal certainty, and reduce tax disputes between Member States for *all enterprises* operating in the EU. If approved, it would apply from 1 January 2026.

1. EU Joint Transfer Pricing Forum Report on compensating adjustments (JTPF/009/FINAL/2013/EN); EU Joint Transfer Pricing Forum Report on the use of economic valuation techniques in TP (JTPF/003/2017/FINAL/EN); EU Joint Transfer Pricing Forum Report on the use of comparables in the EU (JTPF/007/2016/FINAL/EN).
2. European Commission, COM(2023) 532 final.
3. European Commission, COM(2023) 528 final.
4. European Commission, COM(2023) 529 final.

The following analysis focuses on the TPD proposal.[5] Section 2 of this article presents the specific regulatory areas covered by the TPD proposal and provides an overview of its core aspects. Section 3 addresses the main challenges and critically examines the proposal by analysing the legal basis, the relationship with the OECD TPG, and the place of the proposal within the greater BEFIT package. Section 4 concludes with an outlook covering future developments.

2 STRUCTURE AND CONTENT OF THE EU TP DIRECTIVE PROPOSAL

2.1 General Remarks

The EC recognizes in its TPD proposal that complex and inequitable tax structures within the EU are leading to increased compliance costs, legal uncertainty, double taxation risks, and tax disputes for taxpayers within the EU. During the legislative process, the following options addressing these issues were discarded:[6]

- developing an ALP without including the OECD TPG. This would not achieve the objective as there would be no guidelines for uniform application; and
- including the ALP developed at the UN level.

Two options ultimately remained: either the incorporation of the OECD ALP and TPG into EU law (Option 1) or the incorporation of the OECD ALP and TPG, as well as ongoing coordination towards a common EU approach (Option 2). The second option was intended to include a specific anti-avoidance regime, although the form that this should take remained open.[7] As a result of the discussion with the TPD proposal, the EC developed twenty-two articles to address the issues mentioned above by implementing 'Option 1' and, therefore, by harmonizing the ALP under the inclusion of the OECD TPG.[8] The harmonization of TP rules is intended to strengthen the Internal Market and reduce the burden on tax administrations and businesses.[9]

Chapter 1 (General Provision) deals with definitional principles (Articles 1-3). Chapter 2 (TP Rules), as the core of the TPD proposal, provides guidance on the general application of the ALP (Article 4) and on specific issues such as the definition of associated enterprises (Articles 5 and 8), corresponding and year-end adjustments to avoid double taxation (Articles 6 and 7), TP methods (Articles 9 and 10), comparability analysis (Article 11), range restrictions (Article 12), and the documentation of transfer prices (Article 13). Chapter 3 (Organization) provides for further implementing acts of

5. *See also* R. Petruzzi & A. Myzithra, *The EC's Proposal for a Directive on Transfer Pricing: Paving the Road for a Common Application of the Arm's Length Principle*, 31(1) ITPJ (2024) https://doi.org/10.59403/6cd7v7. Among further findings, the authors provide a comprehensive article-by-article analysis under s. 4.
6. Cf., European Commission, SWD(2023) 308 final, p. 36.
7. Cf., European Commission, SWD(2023) 308 final, pp. 35 et seq.; European Commission, COM(2023) 529 final, p. 8.
8. Cf., European Commission, COM(2023) 529 final, pp. 9 et seq.
9. Cf., European Commission, COM(2023) 529 final, recitals 3 et seqq.

the Council of the EU to be introduced by the EC (Article 14). These implementing acts (e.g., planned for transferring intangibles and services as well as financial transactions) or implementing regulations should be in accordance with the OECD TPG 2022 while clarifying their application. As the EC states that additional guidance on applying the ALP will be published and that an expert group on TP will be established, the EU is taking steps beyond those of the OECD and allowing itself to concretize individual rules. Chapter 4 concludes with the final provision (Articles 15-22).

2.2 Associated Enterprises (Article 5 of the TPD Proposal)

The TPD proposal provides a much narrower interpretation of the OECD TPG regarding associated enterprises and related parties. Like Article 2(4) ATAD,[10] the holding of 25% of the voting rights or more than 25% of the profit shares qualifies as a connection to a related party and a 'significant influence' that is not explicitly defined.

The EC's proposal is significantly stricter than both Article 9 of the OECD Model Tax Convention on Income and on Capital (OECD MTC) and the rules in several Member States. Even larger EU countries such as France and Italy currently have less stringent rules in this respect.[11] In addition, other EU directives and directive proposals apply standards that are different from those of the TPD proposal (e.g., BEFIT and the Pillar-Two Directive).[12] Implementing the TPD may, therefore, result in a significant increase in the number of transactions that need to be captured in local TP documentation and increased coordination efforts for taxpayers.[13]

It should be noted that Article 5(7) of the TPD proposal qualifies permanent establishments within the meaning of Article 5 OECD MTC as associated enterprises.[14] This would codify the fiction of independence of permanent establishments for their profit allocation in EU law. This would be in line with Article 7(2) OECD MTC 2010, according to which only the ALP is to be observed between the permanent establishment in the residence state and the one in the other contracting state ('internal dealings'). However, not all double tax treaties (DTT) between EU Member States are

10. Council Directive (EU) 2016/1164 of 12 July 2016 laying down rules against tax avoidance practices that directly affect the functioning of the internal market, OJ L 193/1, 18.7.2016.
11. Cf., B. Heidecke & K. Smolka, *Richtlinienvorschlag der Europäischen Kommission zu Verrechnungspreisen vom 12.9.2023: Überblick und Abgleich mit deutschen Regelungen*, ISR 436 (437) (2023) https://doi.org/10.9785/isr-2023-121210.
12. Council Directive (EU) 2022/2523 of 14 December 2022 on ensuring a global minimum level of taxation for multinational enterprise groups and large-scale domestic groups in the Union, OJ L 328/1, 22.12.2022.
13. Cf., European Commission, COM(2023) 529 final, p. 2; R. Petruzzi & A. Myzithra, *The EC's Proposal for a Directive on Transfer Pricing: Paving the Road for a Common Application of the Arm's Length Principle*, 31(1) ITPJ (2024) https://doi.org/10.59403/6cd7v7, under s. 3.1 and s. 4.3.
14. Cf., European Commission, COM(2023) 529 final, p. 10; R. Petruzzi & A. Myzithra, *The EC's Proposal for a Directive on Transfer Pricing: Paving the Road for a Common Application of the Arm's Length Principle*, 31(1) ITPJ (2024) https://doi.org/10.59403/6cd7v7, under s. 3.4.

based on OECD MTC 2010 (e.g., DTT Germany/Austria). This is particularly relevant for the use of intangible assets.[15]

2.3 Corresponding Adjustments (Article 6 of the TPD Proposal)

TP adjustments in tax audits often result in economic double taxation. Mutual agreement procedures (MAPs) to reduce double taxation are often lengthy and not sought. Instead, corresponding adjustments are a practice to avoid double taxation in a less complex way. The TPD proposal on corresponding adjustments as part of a fast-track procedure is, therefore, an important step towards avoiding tax disputes and double taxation in a timely and efficient manner.[16]

If implemented, a primary upward adjustment at arm's length by one tax administration under Article 6 of the TPD should be followed by a corresponding downward adjustment by the other administration. This would mean that the other tax administration would have to reduce its tax base accordingly. The corresponding adjustment as an offsetting adjustment to a primary adjustment in a contracting state can be claimed at the taxpayer's request under certain conditions, which are as follows:

- the primary adjustment is at arm's length;
- if the primary adjustment was made in a third country, there must be a valid DTT with this country; and
- the primary adjustment must be final.

The legal basis for these procedures should be the familiar dispute resolution procedures in the EU, either a procedure under the Arbitration Convention[17] or the EU Dispute Resolution Directive[18] or a MAP under the respective DTT. Competent authorities should decide on the admissibility of the taxpayer's request within 30 days with a subsequent final decision on the adjustment being taken within 180 days of receipt of the request. If the correction is not granted, it must be ensured that the known procedural options for dispute resolution remain accessible.

The implementation of Article 6 of the TPD proposal would be an important step towards resolving tax treaty interpretation and application disputes more quickly and effectively than is possible under Article 9 OECD MTC.[19] However, questions regarding

15. Cf., B. Heidecke & K. Smolka, *Richtlinienvorschlag der Europäischen Kommission zu Verrechnungspreisen vom 12.9.2023: Überblick und Abgleich mit deutschen Regelungen*, ISR 436 (438) (2023) https://doi.org/10.9785/isr-2023-121210.
16. Cf., European Commission, COM(2023) 529 final, p. 10.
17. Convention of 20 August 1990 on the elimination of double taxation in connection with the adjustment of profits of associated enterprises (90/463/EEC).
18. Cf., Council Directive (EU) 2017/1852 of 10 October 2017 on tax dispute resolution mechanisms in the EU, OJ L 265/1, 14.10.2017.
19. Cf., OECD, *Transfer Pricing Guidelines*, paras 4.29 et seqq.; R. Petruzzi & A. Myzithra, *The EC's Proposal for a Directive on Transfer Pricing: Paving the Road for a Common Application of the Arm's Length Principle*, 31(1) ITPJ (2024) https://doi.org/10.59403/6cd7v7, under s. 4.4.

the effective implementation (including secondary adjustments)[20] and whether the primary adjustment is consistent with the ALP are likely to be controversial.[21]

2.4 Year-End Adjustments (Article 7 of the TPD Proposal)

The content of Article 7 of the TPD proposal is not new at the EU level.[22] Year-end adjustments should be recognized within the EU provided the following five criteria are met:

(1) the taxpayer has made reasonable efforts to achieve an arm's length outcome;
(2) the taxpayer makes the adjustment symmetrically in all EU Member States involved;
(3) the taxpayer applies the same approach consistently over time;
(4) the adjustment is made before filing the tax return; and
(5) the taxpayer can explain the deviation from its forecast.

In principle, the clarification and general acceptance of the year-end adjustments is a positive development and goes beyond Article 9 OECD MTC as well as the OECD TPG.[23] However, there is neither any guidance on how to deal with these adjustments from a customs and VAT perspective, which is often contentious, nor is there any clarification on what is meant by 'reasonable efforts'. The importance of operational TP management during the year is expected to increase.[24]

2.5 Arm's Length Range Determination (Article 12 of the TPD Proposal)

Determining a range of arm's length TP comparables under the TPD proposal goes well beyond the recommendations of the OECD TPG. While the OECD leaves how to determine an arm's length range to the taxpayer's discretion, Article 12(2) of the EU proposal deviates from this by specifying the use of the interquartile range, which is the range from the 25th to the 75th percentile of the results derived from the uncontrolled comparative values. In this respect, the TPD proposal states that this is the most

20. Cf., OECD, *Transfer Pricing Guidelines*, paras 4.68 et seqq.; R. Petruzzi & A. Myzithra, *The EC's Proposal for a Directive on Transfer Pricing: Paving the Road for a Common Application of the Arm's Length Principle*, 31(1) ITPJ (2024) https://doi.org/10.59403/6cd7v7, under s. 4.4.
21. Cf., B. Heidecke & K. Smolka, *Richtlinienvorschlag der Europäischen Kommission zu Verrechnungspreisen vom 12.9.2023: Überblick und Abgleich mit deutschen Regelungen*, ISR 436 (439) (2023) https://doi.org/10.9785/isr-2023-121210.
22. Cf., EU Joint Transfer Pricing Forum Report on compensating adjustments (JTPF/009/FINAL/2013/EN).
23. Cf., OECD, *Transfer Pricing Guidelines*, paras 4.38 et seq.; R. Petruzzi & A. Myzithra, *The EC's Proposal for a Directive on Transfer Pricing: Paving the Road for a Common Application of the Arm's Length Principle*, 31(1) ITPJ (2024) https://doi.org/10.59403/6cd7v7, under s. 4.5.
24. Cf., B. Heidecke & K. Smolka, *Richtlinienvorschlag der Europäischen Kommission zu Verrechnungspreisen vom 12.9.2023: Überblick und Abgleich mit deutschen Regelungen*, ISR 436 (438) (2023) https://doi.org/10.9785/isr-2023-121210.

appropriate method for determining a range of arm's length comparables in accordance with best international practice.[25]

In order to minimize disputes and ensure a consistent approach across the EU, Article 12(3) & (4) of the TPD proposal requires the following:[26]

(1) A taxpayer's TP results should not be adjusted if they fall within the interquartile range unless the tax administration or the taxpayer demonstrates that a particular different position within it is justified by the facts and circumstances of the individual case.
(2) If the results of a controlled transaction fall outside the arm's length range, the tax authorities must make an adjustment to the median of all results unless the taxpayer or the tax authorities can prove that another point in the range determines a more reliable arm's length price in the specific case.

This approach could lead to increased disputes and potential double taxation and is not in accordance with the OECD TPG.[27]

2.6 TP Documentation (Article 13 of the TPD Proposal)

Annex 2 of the TPD proposal provides for the creation of a common template for documentation under Article 13 of the TPD proposal. The EC intends to announce further details on TP documentation requirements at a later stage, whereby the OECD's three-tier approach (local file, master file, country-by-country reporting) is likely to be applied accordingly.[28]

A standardized documentation template would be a further step towards harmonization and may also reduce local specificities in TP documentation. The standardization of TP documentation would, therefore, be a significant simplification and a potential cost saving.[29] However, simplification measures such as thresholds could be considered to reduce the compliance burden.[30]

25. Cf., European Commission, COM(2023) 529 final, p. 16.
26. Cf., European Commission, COM(2023) 529 final, p. 16.
27. Cf., OECD, *Transfer Pricing Guidelines*, para. 3.55; R. Petruzzi & A. Myzithra, *The EC's Proposal for a Directive on Transfer Pricing: Paving the Road for a Common Application of the Arm's Length Principle*, 31(1) ITPJ (2024) https://doi.org/10.59403/6cd7v7, under s. 4.7.
28. Cf., European Commission, COM(2023) 529 final, p. 17.
29. Cf., B. Heidecke & K. Smolka, *Richtlinienvorschlag der Europäischen Kommission zu Verrechnungspreisen vom 12.9.2023: Überblick und Abgleich mit deutschen Regelungen*, ISR 436 (439) (2023) https://doi.org/10.9785/isr-2023-121210.
30. Cf., R. Petruzzi & A. Myzithra, *The EC's Proposal for a Directive on Transfer Pricing: Paving the Road for a Common Application of the Arm's Length Principle*, 31(1) ITPJ (2024) https://doi.org/10.59403/6cd7v7, under s. 4.8.

3 CRITICAL APPRAISAL OF THE EU TP DIRECTIVE PROPOSAL

3.1 Legal Basis

The EC relies on Article 115 TFEU as the legal basis for the TPD.[31] In the context of an explicit authorization basis for the area of indirect taxes in Article 113 TFEU, it is doubtful whether Article 115 TFEU provides the EU with a sufficient basis of competence in direct taxation. Therefore, the proposal requires unanimous approval by the EU Council.

The provisions of the TEU and the TFEU must constitute rules on the delimitation of competences between the Member States and the EU, and in accordance with the principle of conferral, the EU requires an explicit allocation in primary law for each legal act.[32] A distinction must also be made between the harmonization of substantive law on the one hand and procedural law on the other because, according to the principle of procedural autonomy, the EU has the power to regulate procedural law only in exceptional cases.

Despite these fundamental concerns, directives with effects in the area of direct taxation are increasingly being adopted on the basis of Article 115 TFEU[33] without this development being criticized by the Member States. The reason for this could be that it requires unanimity and, therefore, controversial proposals for directives can be averted during the legislative process. Whether this is sufficient is to be discussed.[34] However, the TPD proposal and the impact assessment contain a comprehensive analysis and explanation of how the TPD will reduce barriers that have a significant impact on the functioning of the Internal Market.[35]

3.2 Harmonization of the ALP for All EU Member States

The TPD proposal aims at harmonizing the ALP in the EU based on the OECD TPG. For the first time, it stipulates a supranational framework for applying and monitoring the ALP as well as regulating the procedures for making subsequent adjustments to transfer prices. The ALP has thus far mainly been tested under EU primary law.[36] The

31. Cf., European Commission, COM(2023) 529 final, p. 6.
32. Cf., R. Petruzzi & A. Myzithra, *The EC's Proposal for a Directive on Transfer Pricing: Paving the Road for a Common Application of the Arm's Length Principle*, 31(1) ITPJ (2024) https://doi.org/10.59403/6cd7v7, under s. 3.6; K. Ponomareva, *The Principles of Subsidiarity and Proportionality in European Tax Law*, 10(2) Financial Law Review, 64 (2018) https://doi.org/10.59403/6cd7v7.
33. Cf., Council Directive (EU) 2016/1164 of 12 July 2016 laying down rules against tax avoidance practices that directly affect the functioning of the internal market (ATAD), OJ L 193/1, 18.7.2016; Council Directive 2003/49/EC of 3 June 2003 on a common system of taxation applicable to interest and royalty payments made between associated companies of different Member States, OJ L 157/49, 26.6.2003.
34. Cf., C. Marburg & T. Ziegler, *Der EU-Richtlinienvorschlag zu Verrechnungspreisen – Ein Schritt zu einer Vereinheitlichung und mehr Rechtssicherheit?*, IWB (2023), 979 (981).
35. Cf., European Commission, COM(2023) 529 final, p. 7.
36. Cf., ECJ, Case C-324/00, *Lankhorst Hohorst GmbH*, 12.12.2002, ECLI:EU:C:2002:749. Concerning TP rules, cf., ECJ, Case C-311/08, *Société de Gestion Industrielle SA (SGI)*, 21.1.2010,

TPD proposal would make the ALP an integral part of EU secondary law. Once transposed into domestic law, it would have to be interpreted in accordance with the directive, and the primacy of EU law and the exclusive jurisdiction of the European Court of Justice (ECJ) would apply to ensure a uniform interpretation of EU law. In addition, the TPD proposal provides the legal basis for the adoption of tertiary legislation to further specify the ALP.

From the perspective of Member States with a dynamic reference to the OECD TPG in their domestic law, this approach may be well known. From the perspective of particularly German constitutional law, however, such a mechanism represents a significant innovation as it gives the OECD TPG a legally binding character for the interpretation of the ALP.[37] This leads to fragmentation of the interpretation of the ALP that the EC, however, intends to reduce by means of the TPD. The EU, as a supranational organization, has been authorized by its Member States to enact binding law within the scope of the competences transferred to it. By harmonizing the ALP, the EU has become a key player in legislating and monitoring the ALP by incorporating the ALP into the European multi-level system by adopting the directive as secondary legislation.

To be effective, the adopted TPD would require national implementation. Still, it is binding in terms of its objectives. Member States are, therefore, bound through the primacy of application and interpretation of domestic law in accordance with the directive. This means that, in this regard, national legislation and the application of DTTs incorporated into domestic law play only a supplementary role.[38] The Member States must implement the function of EU law, and the fiscal courts are obligated to refer questions on the compatibility of national legal acts with the directive to the ECJ.

3.3 First-Time Application of the TPD's ALP

In order to complete the TP framework set out in the TPD proposal, the OECD TPG 2022 are included in Annex 1. The objective is to provide a legally binding interpretation of the ALP contained in the OECD TPG. Assuming a binding national implementation on 1 January 2026 pursuant to Article 20(1) of the TPD proposal, Annex 1, including the

ECLI:EU:C:2010:26; ECJ, Case C-382/16, *Hornbach Baumarkt AG*, 31.5.2018, ECLI:EU:C:2018:366; ECJ, Case C-558/19, *Impresa Pizzarotti & C SPA Italia Sucursala Cluj*, 8.10.2020, ECLI:EU:C:2020:806; *see also* R. Petruzzi & A. Myzithra, *The EC's Proposal for a Directive on Transfer Pricing: Paving the Road for a Common Application of the Arm's Length Principle*, 31(1) ITPJ (2024) https://doi.org/10.59403/6cd7v7, under s. 3.5.

37. Cf., C. Marburg & T. Ziegler, *Der EU-Richtlinienvorschlag zu Verrechnungspreisen – Ein Schritt zu einer Vereinheitlichung und mehr Rechtssicherheit?*, IWB 979 (981), (2023). Concerning the legally binding character compared to the guidance nature of the OECD TPG, *see* R. Petruzzi & A. Myzithra, *The EC's Proposal for a Directive on Transfer Pricing: Paving the Road for a Common Application of the Arm's Length Principle*, 31(1) ITPJ (2024) https://doi.org/10.59403/6cd7v7, under s. 3.2.

38. Cf., ECJ, Case 6/64, *Flaminio Costa v. E.N.E.L.*, 15.7.1964, ECLI:EU:C:1964:66; ECJ, Case C-307/97, *Compagnie de Saint-Gobain, Zweigniederlassung Deutschland v. Finanzamt Aachen-Innenstadt*, 21.9.1999, ECLI:EU:C:1999:438, paras 57 et seq.; K. Holmes, *International Tax Policy and Double Tax Treaties: An Introduction to Principles and Application*, Ch. 4, 73 et seq. (2nd ed. IBFD 2014).

OECD TPG, could apply to all open cases for assessment periods from 1 January 2026 or earlier as the TPD proposal was published in September 2023.

However, the ECJ bases the principle of the protection of legitimate expectations on the principle of legal certainty.[39] Regarding substantive law, the legislature is therefore prohibited from enacting laws with effect for periods prior to their entry into force unless there is a legitimate purpose, such as combating tax fraud.[40] The ECJ also focuses on the protection of legitimate expectations that cease to exist if a *prudent and alert economic operator* could have foreseen the change in the legal situation, with the requirements for companies being lower than those for private individuals.[41] The ECJ distinguishes between the retroactive extension of legal consequences and the application of a new rule to circumstances that have not yet been finally determined.[42] Accordingly, in principle, the date of entry into force of the national legislation transposing the TPD would be the date of application of the substantive changes made by Annex 1.[43]

A distinction must be made as to whether the amendments by the TPD are to substantive law or procedural rules since the latter may be applicable to all litigation pending at the time of entry into force. Accordingly, the additional procedural rules would presumably be available to taxpayers, e.g., in the case of a corresponding adjustment under Article 6 of the TPD proposal for situations that occurred earlier.

3.4 Dynamic Reference to the OECD TPG

The OECD TPG are regularly updated as a result of the ongoing policy process. Article 3(18) of the TPD proposal provides in the definition of the term 'OECD Transfer Pricing Guidelines' that this includes the 2022 version contained in Annex 1 and a procedure for the dynamic incorporation of future amendments to the OECD TPG. Consequently, an amended directive at the EU level will not be required.[44]

The date of application in the event of a future amendment to the OECD TPG via Annex 1 is not explicitly stated. This dynamic element was deliberately included as the need to issue a new EU Directive in the event of future amendments to the OECD TPG was considered inefficient.[45] Assuming the intended direct effect in the absence of a clear provision on the date of application in the current draft, it could be assumed, in

39. Cf., ECJ, Case C-201/08 *Plantanol*, 10.9.2009, ECLI:EU:C:2009:539, para. 46.
40. Cf., ECJ, Joined Cases C-487/01, C-7/02, *Gemeente Leusden und Holin Groep*, 29.4.2004, ECLI:EU:C:2004:263, para. 77; ECJ, Case C-285/09 *R*, 7.12.2010, ECLI:EU:C:2010:742, para. 54; ECJ, Case C-251/16 *Cussens*, 22.11.2017, ECLI:EU:C:2017:881, para. 43.
41. Cf., ECJ, Joined Cases C-182/03, C-217/03 *Belgien, Forum 187*, 26.6.2003, ECLI:EU:C:2006:416, para. 147; ECJ, Case C-519/07 P *Koninklijke FrieslandCampina*, 17.9.2009, ECLI:EU:C:2009:556, para. 84; ECJ, Case C-201/08 *Plantanol*, 10.9.2009, ECLI:EU:C:2009:539, para. 53; ECJ, Case C-194/09 P *Alcoa Trasformazioni*, 21.7.2011, ECLI:EU:C:2011:497, para. 71.
42. Cf., ECJ, Joined Cases C-487/01, C-7/02 *Gemeente Leusden, Holin Groep*, 29.4.2004, ECLI: EU:C:2004:263, para. 62; ECJ, Case C-107/10 *Enel Maritsa Iztok 3*, 12.5.2011, ECLI: EU:C:2011:298, para. 39.
43. Cf., C. Marburg & T. Ziegler, *Der EU-Richtlinienvorschlag zu Verrechnungspreisen – Ein Schritt zu einer Vereinheitlichung und mehr Rechtssicherheit?*, IWB 979 (984) (2023).
44. Cf., European Commission, SWD(2023) 308 final, p. 54.
45. Cf., European Commission, SWD(2023) 308 final, p. 54.

accordance with the principles on the protection of legitimate expectations, that the earliest possible date for changes in substantive law could be based on the entry into force of the corresponding legal act. That raises the question as to which date is decisive.

It would be conceivable to base this on the final publication at the OECD level that would not have the character of a binding legal act. Weighing up the need to protect confidence in the continuity of the legal situation, an earlier date would be conceivable, e.g., the Council of the EU decision pursuant to Article 218(9) TFEU or the publication of a final OECD report prior to the integration into a consolidated version of the OECD TPG.[46]

In addition, the JTPF report should be used to interpret Article 7 of the TPD proposal.[47] Like the OECD TPG, as mentioned above, the JTPF reports and further recommendations[48] are not yet legally binding. It may be assumed that the contents of these reports and recommendations should also have greater legal force as interpretation aids for the TPD.[49]

3.5 Other TP Aspects Addressed in the BEFIT Package

The TPD proposal is part of the BEFIT package that consists of a total of three proposals including the BEFIT proposal and the HOT proposal. The latter two, in addition to the TPD proposal, are expected to have an (at least indirect) impact on TP.

However, while the HOT proposal would, at best, simplify the reporting process for groups that are adopting and implementing the BEFIT proposal, it would be much more far reaching. Within the EU, the TP topic would become much less relevant for groups with a turnover above EUR 750 million as the tax base would be harmonized and allocated between Member States. However, TP rules will remain relevant in relation to third countries. Here, the EC intends to simplify the definitions of contract manufacturers and low-risk distributors in Articles 50-53 of the BEFIT draft. If a company falls under these broad definitions, a safe harbour for target margins is envisaged. Like Amount B of OECD Pillar One, the target margins will be determined by searching an EU database to be published on the EC's website.

Even if the BEFIT proposal is not implemented, it is conceivable that the provisions in its Articles 50-53 on the definition of contract manufacturers and low-risk distributors, as well as safe harbour margins, will be implemented in an isolated draft or as part of the TPD proposal in the further procedure. This would be desirable as there is no definition of such functional profiles, which consequently repeatedly leads to conflicts. The proposal already provides at least an indication of how such profiles can be delineated. Safe harbour margins would also help to reduce conflicts. However,

---

46. Cf., C. Marburg & T. Ziegler, *Der EU-Richtlinienvorschlag zu Verrechnungspreisen – Ein Schritt zu einer Vereinheitlichung und mehr Rechtssicherheit?*, IWB 979 (985) (2023).
47. Cf., European Commission, SWD(2023) 308 final, recital 8.
48. Cf., European Commission, SWD(2023) 308 final, recitals 10, 12, 14.
49. Cf., C. Marburg & T. Ziegler, *Der EU-Richtlinienvorschlag zu Verrechnungspreisen – Ein Schritt zu einer Vereinheitlichung und mehr Rechtssicherheit?*, IWB 979 (985) (2023).

taxpayers should still be allowed to credibly demonstrate a different value in individual cases.[50]

4 CONCLUSION

TP could be regulated for the first time at the EU level with the EC's proposal for a directive. The TPD proposal is an important step towards a harmonized TP interpretation within the EU. The proposals on year-end adjustments and fast-track procedures for corresponding adjustments address two very practical issues by presenting viable solutions. If, in particular, an effective fast-track procedure for implementing corresponding adjustments is actually implemented, this will be a significant reduction in the risk of double taxation and legal disputes. Additionally, the EC's initiative in the BEFIT proposal to define contract manufacturers and low-risk distributors is welcome. The EC would, therefore, become an important factor in the international standardization of TP. Even if the application date still raises questions, it should be noted that the application of the OECD TPG would be significantly accelerated and standardized in all EU Member States.

Nevertheless, there is a lack of specific guidance on many topics. That being said, Article 14 of the TPD proposal provides an outlook on implementing acts. It is planned that these will be available within the next five years. It will be interesting to see how these implementing acts are structured, e.g., on financial or service transactions and intangibles. Safe harbour regulations should be adopted as much as possible. However, taxpayers should still always be afforded the opportunity to substantiate other values.

While the OECD currently still has the power of interpretation regarding TP, this could be changing due to the increasing role of the EC even if it will be guided by the OECD in many respects. A similar development can be observed at the UN level, which only recently announced that it intends to become a stronger participant in favouring the developing countries in the area of taxation.[51] For international corporations, this is likely to lead to more divergences between countries despite all efforts to harmonize the supranational organizations within their regulatory circle (the EC for the EU, the OECD for the Inclusive Framework, and the UN for developing countries). As a result, tax disputes can be expected to increase in the future if transactions take place between countries with different regulatory frameworks.[52]

However, adopting the directive at the EU level – and de facto its later transposition into domestic law – requires the unanimous agreement of all EU Member States, as the EU does not have any special authorization to harmonize direct taxes. This is,

50. Cf., B. Heidecke & K. Smolka, *Richtlinienvorschlag der Europäischen Kommission zu Verrechnungspreisen vom 12.9.2023: Überblick und Abgleich mit deutschen Regelungen*, ISR 436 (437) (2023) https://doi.org/10.9785/isr-2023-121210.
51. Cf., UN Secretary-Genera, *Promotion of Inclusive and Effective International Tax Cooperation at the United Nations* (2023).
52. Cf., B. Heidecke & K. Smolka, *Richtlinienvorschlag der Europäischen Kommission zu Verrechnungspreisen vom 12.9.2023: Überblick und Abgleich mit deutschen Regelungen*, ISR 436 (440) (2023) https://doi.org/10.9785/isr-2023-121210.

therefore, only possible if the Council of the EU unanimously adopts harmonization measures (Article 115 TFEU).

Finally, it is worth mentioning that, on 14 November 2023, the members of the Economic and Monetary Affairs Committee adopted their opinion on the TPD. They propose a major simplification of the directive that should be modelled as closely as possible on the latest OECD TPG (although space could be left for UN guidelines at a later stage). More importantly, MEPs propose that the EC, rather than the Council, should be empowered to propose further implementing measures in this area.

CHAPTER 5

Transfer Pricing and Profit Attribution to New-Age Permanent Establishments

*Mukesh Butani & Seema Kejriwal**

1 SUMMARY

This chapter discusses new-age permanent establishments (PEs) as two distinct concepts:

(1) new nexus rules or new PE recognition rules being developed under Pillar 1 and Pillar 2 of Action Plan 1 to the Organization for Economic Co-operation and Development (OECD) Base Erosion and Profit Shifting (BEPS) Inclusive Framework; and
(2) creating new-age PEs under traditional definitions of PE due to the digital transformation of the economy.

* The authors acknowledge the contribution of team members Rahul Agarwal, Shinjani Agnihotri and Pranoy Goswami.

2 INTRODUCTION

All countries retain the right to tax their residents' income. However, when a resident of Country A earns income from Country B, the question arises as to in which situations should Country B be entitled to tax this income as the primary right for this is granted to Country A. In order to agree upon the allocation of such taxing rights, countries enter into tax treaties, of which over 3,300 treaties are currently in force.[1]

Countries generally base their tax treaties on the OECD Model Convention or the United Nations (UN) Model Convention.[2] Under both the OECD and the UN Models, apart from either taxing or exempting specified sources of income (e.g., royalties and interest are typically taxed in source countries, and that of shipping and airlines is usually taxed only in residence countries), the existence of a 'PE' gives a source country the right to levy tax on the resident of another country. Even at the time these concepts were being developed, there was a divergence of views between capital-importing and capital-exporting countries as to what would constitute a 'PE'. The UN Model is considered a successor to the Mexico Draft of 1943; the meeting for this was mostly attended by capital-importing Latin American countries. The OECD Model is regarded as a successor to the London Draft of 1946.[3] The Mexico Draft suggests giving source countries the right to tax residents for anything beyond occasional or isolated involvement in their economy. However, in the London Draft based on which the 1963 OECD Model convention was drafted, the right of source countries to tax was restricted to the existence of PEs that were largely defined under the convention based on physical presence tests with some refinement over the years. However, one hundred years later, it is now possible for a multinational to have sustained and continuous engagement with an economy without having any presence there. This has also presented opportunities to place maximum income in countries with low tax regimes and continue business in high tax regimes. The OECD sought to attempt to effectively address these and other allied issues under the BEPS Inclusive Framework.

Separately, even if examining the traditional PE definitions alone, It is widely accepted that technology and the digital economy have redefined traditional business models and ushered in a new era of doing business. Consequently, the growth and global acceptance of the digital economy far outpaced the development of legislation to regulate it. In the context of tax regulation, as identified by the OECD,[4] there are three significant phenomena caused by digitalization that present significant challenges to the ecosystem of the extant international tax system – scale without mass, reliance on intangible assets, and the centrality of data. Innovations in information and communications technology are largely attributable to companies located in developed

1. The authors engaged in a search on the IBFD website to ascertain the number of treaties in force. Elliott Ash and Omri Marian, *The Making of International Tax Law: Empirical Evidence from Tax Treaties Text*, 24 Florida Tax Review (2023), Art. 3 identified a unique set of 4,052 bilateral treaties.
2. The US enters into tax treaties using its own template.
3. Ash and Marian (2023), *supra* n. 1.
4. Action 1 Tax Challenges Arising from Digitalisation, https://www.oecd.org/tax/beps/beps-actions/action1/ (accessed 9 January 2023).

countries. Given their digital nature, these businesses were able to effectively tap into source countries without actually having to create any type of physical presence, thereby rendering traditional concepts of PEs obsolete.

This led to concern among developing countries as corporate taxes continue to be a significant source of government revenues in developing countries.[5] To put things into perspective, the contribution of corporate taxes to the total revenue is 22.5% in Australia, 23.7% in Colombia, and 15.7% in New Zealand, as opposed to the OECD average of 10.2%.[6]

This chapter assesses the sufficiency of existing frameworks for tackling challenges of profit attribution to new-age PEs that are a phenomenon of the digital economy and investigates possible remedies for the fair distribution of profits from them.

3 IDENTIFICATION OF NEW-AGE PES CREATED BY ACTION PLAN 1 OF THE OECD BEPS INCLUSIVE FRAMEWORK

Pillar One: Allocation of Taxing Rights to Market Jurisdictions

The OECD stipulated in a report published in 2015 that a taxable nexus is formed in the event of a significant economic presence. The report stated:

> This option would create a taxable presence in a country when a non-resident enterprise has a significant economic presence in a country on the basis of factors that evidence a purposeful and sustained interaction with the economy of that country via technology and other automated tools. These factors would be combined with a factor based on the revenue derived from remote transactions into the country, in order to ensure that only cases of significant economic presence are covered.

The rationale provided was that a strong user network (and the attendant user data) is likely to result in enterprises either selling more or enterprises charging more for their core products/services or both. Under such circumstances, the revenues earned from customers in a country are a potential factor for establishing a nexus in the form of a Significant Economic Presence SEP in the country concerned. The report further noted that revenue would not be sufficient in isolation for establishing a nexus,

5. Corporate tax remains a key revenue source despite falling rates worldwide; available at https://web-archive.oecd.org/2019-01-15/504358-corporate-tax-remains-a-key-revenue-source-despite-falling-rates-worldwide.htm (accessed 9 January 2023). Pursuant to Action 11 of the OECD/G20 BEPS Project, the OECD has developed Corporate Tax Statistics as its flagship publication which is updated every year. The latest report contains information regarding corporate tax rates, revenues, ETRs, and tax incentives specifically related to research and development (R&D) and innovation and contains data up to 2020; it is available at https://www.oecd-ilibrary.org/taxation/corporate-tax-statistics-2023_f1f07219-en.
6. Revenue Statistics 2023 Tax Revenue Buoyancy in OECD Countries, https://www.oecd.org/tax/tax-policy/revenue-statistics-highlights-brochure.pdf (accessed 0 January 2023).

but it could be considered a basic factor that could potentially be used to do so when combined with other factors.[7]

The report identified a range of digital factors that could be used as part of a test for determining a significant economic presence, including a local domain name; a local digital platform; a local payment gateway; user-based factors, such as monthly active users, contracts concluded, data collected; etc.

Following this report, India introduced the SEP framework by adding it to the definition of 'business connection' (BC) in India.[8] It further expands its scope by providing that this income would include that derived from accessing an advertisement, sale of data, and goods or services using data collected from an Indian resident or person using an internet protocol in India.

Identification of New-Age PEs Created by BEPS Pillar Two

The model rules[9] for implementing Pillar Two require the ultimate parent company (UPE) of a multinational group to directly or indirectly have at least one foreign subsidiary or PE before the group is considered a multinational enterprise (MNE) group. The definition of a PE is:

- a PE as per a tax treaty;
- a PE as per domestic law of a source state when there is no tax treaty;
- a PE in a state that does not have a corporate tax income if the income has been taxable and if a PE would have been constituted under the OECD Model Convention giving the source state the right to tax under Article 7 of the OECD Model Convention (hypothetical PE); and
- a stateless PE – a state that has the right to tax the income but specifically exempts it from tax since it is earned outside that jurisdiction.[10]

A standalone legal entity that has a presence in multiple jurisdictions only through PEs (and thus technically does not constitute a 'group') is also covered under the Global Anti-Base Erosion Rules (GloBE Model Rules) for the application of a PE. However, exemptions are carved out, and stateless PEs of such a legal entity would not be considered.[11]

Correctly identifying a PE is thus important to ascertain the applicability of the GloBE Rules. Controversies abound in jurisdictions regarding the existence of a PE under the tax treaties, and businesses will now have to ascertain whether they also have hypothetical PEs and stateless PEs for the purposes of Pillar Two, which adds more complexity to this already vexed landscape.

7. The Task Force on Action Plan 1, OECD Base Erosion and Profit Shifting ('Action Plan') Report, 2015, para. 278.
8. Section 9 of the Indian Income Tax Act, 1961.
9. Article 1.2.1 of the GloBE Model Rules.
10. Refer to para. 112 of the GloBE Model Rules for an illustration at https://www.oecd.org/tax/beps/tax-challenges-arising-from-the-digitalisation-of-the-economy-global-anti-base-erosion-model-rules-pillar-two-commentary.pdf.
11. Article 1.2.3 of the GloBE Model Rules.

Income derived from PEs is considered when determining the effective tax rate (ETR) in a jurisdiction. The world is still grappling with disputes on income attributable to age-old concepts of a PE – the OECD recognizes the Authorised OECD Approach (AoA), which attributes profits based on the functions, assets, and risk (FAR) approach. However, developing countries such as India have expressed their reservation and want to instead consider the Functions, Assets, Risks and Market (FARM) concept. 'The same applies as in the previous paragraph regarding hypothetical PEs and stateless PE.

In these situations, the first sentence of Article 3.4.1 stipulates that the PE's financial accounting net income or loss must be reflected in its financial accounts (if they exist). This ensures that constituent entities that are PEs and subsidiaries are treated equally for the purposes of computing the ETR. However, following the principle in the GloBE Rules, such accounts must be prepared in accordance with an Acceptable Financial Accounting Standard or an Authorised Financial Accounting Standard subject to adjustments to prevent any material competitive distortions. 190. However, the PE will not have separate financial accounts in some cases. In that scenario, the second sentence of Article 3.4.1 provides that the financial accounting net income or loss is the amount that would have been reflected in its separate financial accounts if they existed. Therefore, accounts or reports will need to be prepared in these circumstances to compute the amount that would have been reflected in the financial accounts. Article 3.4.1 requires this determination to be based on the accounting standard used in the preparation of the UPE's consolidated financial statements.

The GloBE rules provide for the allocation of income or losses between the main entity and the PEs. The commentary on the GloBE rules provides that if financial accounts exist, they should be the starting point. However, the PE will not have separate financial accounts in some cases, for which accounts or reports will need to be prepared to compute the amount that would have been reflected in them.

Article 3.4.3 describes the attribution of income to a PE that arises under paragraph (d) of the PE definition in Article 10.1, i.e., the stateless PE. Article 3.4.3 attributes the income to the PE that the main entity jurisdiction exempts from tax that is attributable to activities occurring outside the jurisdiction. Similarly, Article 3.4.3 allocates any expenses to the PE that are not taken into account in the main entity's jurisdiction because they are attributable to activities occurring outside it.

4 IDENTIFICATION OF NEW-AGE PES CREATED BY DIGITAL BUSINESSES

In the absence of any universal definition of new-age PEs or those that are possible only due to the proliferation of information and communication technologies (ICT), the authors have identified concepts typically identified with ICT, tested them against the current PE definition, and attempted to hypothesize an arm's length profit attribution to such PEs even if the international tax framework could be amended to include the definitions of such new-age PEs:

- digital nomads;
- artificial intelligence (AI) and robotics;
- metaverse;
- online gaming; and
- e-commerce platforms and streaming services.

4.1 Digital Nomads

In 2022 in the European Union, almost six out of ten enterprises (57%) with ten or more employees or self-employed persons were offered access to remote work through all three types of identified enterprise resources: (i) access to an email system; (ii) access to documents; and (iii) access to the enterprise's business applications or software.[12] However, all remote workers do not qualify as digital nomads, defined by the Merriam-Webster Dictionary as 'someone who performs their occupation entirely over the Internet while traveling'.[13] It is appropriate, however, to state that digital nomadism is possible only because of the flexibility offered by remote working. As of 2023, 35 million people worldwide have reported being digital nomads, with an average age of 32 years.[14]

According to an article submitted by Brian Arnold to the UN Tax Subcommittee at its 27th session,[15] digital nomads are a unique subset of remote workers. They are individuals who have specialized skills and can work from almost anywhere with a laptop computer or tablet as long as there is a reliable Wi-Fi connection. They may spend years roaming the globe while spending only a few months in any particular country. Alternatively, they may follow a regular pattern of spending a few months in three or four countries every year. Still others may have a permanent home in one country but spend significant periods of time during the year working in other countries.

Digital nomads pose the following concerns from a tax standpoint when they travel between countries:

- due to their constant movement from one country to another, they are not treated as tax residents of any country; and
- they create PEs for the organization with which they are employed.

For this chapter, the authors have restricted the discussion to the latter statement.

12. https://ec.europa.eu/eurostat/en/web/products-eurostat-news/w/ddn-20230612-1.
13. https://www.merriam-webster.com/dictionary/digital%20nomad.
14. https://hir.harvard.edu/digital-nomadism-transnational-economic-relations-in-the-emerging-economies/.
15. https://financing.desa.un.org/sites/default/files/2023-10/CRP.40%20Digital%20Co-Coordinator%20Report%20and%20all%20annexes%20numbered%20Final-Copy.pdf.

Current Guidelines regarding a PE

OECD

While the Service PE concept found in tax treaties of many developing countries is a construct of the UN, the OECD Transfer Pricing Guidelines expressly provide in paragraph 144[16] for inserting a service PE article if the parties choose to do so on a bilateral basis. However, paragraph 143 clearly states that, even in this situation, taxation should not extend beyond services rendered outside the territory of a state and should be limited to profits from services rather than the payments for services itself. Paragraph 169 further goes on to state that, in any event, if the services are preparatory and auxiliary in nature, the same would not constitute a PE.

UN

In his article submitted to the UN tax Subcommittee, Brian Arnold further recommends that one way to reduce or eliminate this risk for MNEs would be to change the definition of a PE to provide an additional exemption for the activities of remote working employees. However, it is not clear why an MNE should not be considered to have a PE or fixed base as a result of these kinds of activities by remote working employees, and there was little support expressed at the 26th session of the Committee of Experts for such an additional exemption. It might be preferable for countries that wish to reduce the risk of an inadvertent PE or fixed base resulting from the activities of remote working employees to provide an advance ruling procedure or to change their domestic law so that multinationals can obtain the necessary certainty. However, PE determinations in these situations are highly dependent on the facts and may not be suitable for advance rulings. Moreover, it is unclear why countries should be expected to eliminate the risk that remote working employees might create a PE or fixed base where they should be able to minimize the risk themselves.

Another possibility for reducing the risk of an inadvertent PE created by remote-working employees would be to clarify the UN Commentary on Article 5 (and also perhaps on Article 14) that remote-working employees would not create a PE or fixed base for their employer except in clearly specified circumstances. Such additional guidance would be helpful for both employers and tax officials and does not present any obvious disadvantages.

---

16. Paragraph 144 of Commentary to Art. 5 of the UN Model Tax Convention:

> a PE may exist due to the provision of services, if one of the following conditions is met:
>
> - The services are provided through an individual who remains in the recipient state for a period or periods totalling more than 183 days in any 12-month period, and more than 50% of the gross revenue from the company's activity in that period or periods comes from the services provided in that other state through that individual.
> - Or the services are provided during a period or periods totalling more than 183 days in any 12-month period, and those services are provided for a single project or related projects through one or more individuals who are present in the recipient state and provide their services there.

Although the concept of a fixed base in Article 14 is similar in part to the concept of a PE in Article 5, the two concepts are apparently not exactly the same, and there is uncertainty about how the two concepts differ. For example, there are no exceptions to the concept of a fixed base equivalent to the exceptions in Article 5(4) for preparatory or auxiliary activities. Consideration could be given to adding an exception for preparatory or auxiliary activities to the concept of a fixed base or, at least, clarifying whether or not equivalent exceptions can be incorporated into Article 14 through changes to the Commentary on Article 14. However, since the term 'fixed base' is not defined in the UN Model Convention, such a change would probably require the addition of a complete definition of a fixed base and Commentary, which would be a formidable challenge.

Thus, under both the OECD and UN Model conventions, a PE constituted by a digital nomad could be equated to a service PE. To the extent that the activities of the digital nomad are preparatory and auxiliary to the enterprise, the presence of the digital nomad would not constitute a PE.

4.2 AI and Robotics

According to a recent IMF study,[17] almost 40% of global employment is exposed to AI. Historically, automation and information technology have tended to affect routine tasks, but one of the things that distinguishes AI is its ability to impact highly-skilled jobs. As a result, advanced economies face greater risks from it – but also more opportunities to leverage its benefits – compared with emerging markets and developing economies. In advanced economies, approximately 60% of jobs may be impacted by AI. Almost half of the exposed jobs may benefit from AI integration by enhancing productivity. For the other half, AI applications may execute key tasks currently performed by humans, which could decrease labour demand, thereby leading to lower wages and reduced hiring. In the most extreme cases, some of these jobs may disappear. In emerging markets and low-income countries, by contrast, AI exposure is expected to be 40% and 26%, respectively.

Using robots in manufacturing has been prevalent since the late 1930s; the first industrial robot that met the ISO definition of the word was created in 1937 by Griffith 'Bill' P. Taylor. George Devol submitted the first industrial robot patent in 1954. His robot could transport things from one place to another within a radius of 12 feet or less. He founded Unimation in 1956, and it created UNIMATE which is the first robot utilized by the prominent manufacturer General Motors in 1962.[18]

A new development referred to as the third wave of AI in this sphere is the concept of 'autonomous AI' (AAI). According to a Forbes article:[19]

17. https://www.imf.org/en/Publications/Staff-Discussion-Notes/Issues/2024/01/14/Gen-AI-Artificial-Intelligence-and-the-Future-of-Work-542379?cid=bl-com-SDNEA2024001.
18. https://www.universal-robots.com/in/blog/impact-of-robotics/.
19. https://www.forbes.com/sites/bernardmarr/2022/03/21/a-short-history-of-the-metaverse/?sh=11f8ac885968.

Autonomous artificial intelligence is defined as routines designed to allow robots, cars, planes and other devices to execute extended sequences of manoeuvres without guidance from humans. The field is still very new, and researchers are continually refining their algorithms and their approaches to the problem, but it's common to break the job into these layers.

Sensing – Building a model of the constantly shifting world requires a collection of sensors that are usually cameras and often controlled lighting from lasers or other sources. The sensors usually also include position information from GPS or some other independent mechanism.

Fusion – The details from the various sensors must be organized into a single, coherent view of what's happening around the vehicle. Some images may be occluded. Some may be failing. They may not always be consistent. The sensor fusion algorithms must sort through the details and construct a reliable model that can be used in later stages for planning.

Perception – After the model is constructed, the system must begin to identify important areas like any roads or paths or moving objects.

Planning – Finding the best path forward requires studying the model and also importing information from other sources like mapping software, weather forecasts, traffic sensors and more.

Control – After a path is chosen, any device must ensure that the motors and steering work to move along the path without being diverted by bumps or small obstacles.

In general, information flows from the top layer of the sensors down to the control layer as decisions are made. There are feedback loops, though, that bring information from the lower layers back up to the top to improve sensing, planning and perception.

The systems also bring in data from external sources. One big advantage of autonomous systems appears when the devices communicate with each other, exchanging information in a process sometimes called 'fleet learning'. Being able to fuse the sensor readings allows the devices to make smarter decisions using historical data from other devices that may have been in the same position earlier. Detecting moving objects like pedestrians can be difficult with only a few seconds of video because people may be standing still, but it gets easier when it's possible to compare the sensor data with similar images taken earlier in the day.[20]

Following is an example to illustrate PE issues created by using AAI:

An MNE headquartered in Country X sets up a fully automated factory functioning with robots in Country Y under a separate legal entity. The servers on which the robots operate are in Country Z. Robots deployed in Country X are occasionally sent to Country A and Country B. The IP for all of this is centralized in Country C including the containment method for the AAI.

In this situation, will both Country X and Country Y then have a PE in Country Z, where the servers are located? Assuming the robots are of a particular level of intelligence and enable Country X to generate revenues from Country A and Country B, how will the latter two obtain the right to tax such revenues at source?

It is important to understand technology nuances around how these AAIs function and their ability to continually interact with each other before categorizing

20. https://venturebeat.com/ai/what-is-autonomous-ai/.

these into machines, software, or servers. These are issues that would need deliberation and guidance by policymakers as digital technologies continue to evolve. Extending a legal personality and thereby being able to tax such AAIs or robots is also widely debated among tax academicians.[21]

Metaverse

The term 'metaverse' was first used in Neal Stephenson's 1992 novel, Snow Crash. It was a virtual place where characters could go to escape a dreary totalitarian reality.[22]

In the metaverse, while participants may feel that they are situated in a different plane of existence due to the immersive capabilities of the metaverse, their physical selves remain firmly rooted in the same spot. More importantly, the user remains in the same tax jurisdiction according to the law. Regardless of how real the experience may be, domestic and international tax law does not currently grant any special status to a meta realm as a distinct jurisdiction.[23]

The taxable event in the case of the metaverse is when its participants receive profits from activities such as operating a virtual store or purchasing or selling digital property with real economic value. Furthermore, this income fits within the statutory definition of 'income' worldwide, which is somewhat similar to 'from whatever source derived.[24]

The tax issues posed by the metaverse are further exaggerated when all dealings in it use cryptocurrencies. According to a report by Standard & Poor,[25] market participants still debate whether cryptos behave like currencies, commodities, or financial securities or are something else, such as synthetic financial instruments backed by new technology and an algorithmic trading protocol. According to this study, cryptocurrencies do not exhibit any correlation to traditional financial assets, fiat currencies, or even gold.

Given that the values of cryptocurrencies cannot be easily identified with underlying traditional financial assets, the taxability of transactions in the metaverse using them will lead to a more nuanced analysis in terms of ascribing values to these transactions. No accounting standard currently exists to explain how to account for cryptocurrency. According to the Association of Certified Chartered Accountants (ACCA), digital currencies appear to meet the criteria for intangible assets in the most

---

21. *See*, for example, Vikram Chand, Svetislav Kostić and Ariene Reis, *Taxing Artificial Intelligence and Robots: Critical Assessment of Potential Policy Solutions and Recommendation for Alternative Approaches – Sovereign Measure: Education Taxes/Global Measure: Global Education Tax or Planetary Tax*, 12 World Tax Journal 4 DOI: https://doi.org/10.59403/2sjxe4d, available at https://research.ibfd.org/#/doc?url=/collections/wtj/html/wtj_2020_04_int_5.html).
22. https://www.forbes.com/sites/bernardmarr/2022/03/21/a-short-history-of-the-metaverse/?sh=11f8ac885968.
23. Vincent Ooi and Daryl Loy, *Virtual Worlds, Real Money: Tax Issues in the Metaverse* (23 January 2023). The Business Times, 23 January 2023, Singapore Management University School of Law Research Paper, available at SSRN: https://ssrn.com/abstract=4395545.
24. The OECD had released reporting framework for cryptocurrency in 2022. The report is available at https://www.oecd.org/tax/exchange-of-tax-information/crypto-asset-reporting-framework-and-amendments-to-the-common-reporting-standard.htm.
25. https://www.spglobal.com/en/research-insights/special-reports/understanding-crypto-valuation.

favourable view.[26] IAS 38 provides for recognition of intangible assets at cost or revaluation. Thus, transactions in the metaverse, if and when they eventually make their way into business accounts, may not reflect the true market value of transactions.

Even assuming that solutions regarding allocating taxing rights could be agreed upon between countries, actually ascribing values to the attributable profits would need significant enhancement in the reporting framework against which the same can be verified by tax administrations. Both tax and accounting policies thus need to evolve to effectively address such new-age business models attributable to the metaverse and the use of cryptocurrencies for this.

Online Gaming

The online gaming market is estimated to reach approximately USD 876 billion by 2026, evolving at a compound annual growth rate (CAGR) of 3.6% over the assessment period. The European online gaming market is expected to increase by 9.20% by 2025, fuelled primarily by software and hardware innovations and the rising popularity of gambling.[27] As such, the gaming industry shows no signs of decelerating. In this regard, it becomes imperative to understand the double conduit of taxable events from the user and platform perspectives, respectively. One key factor that must be noted is that, especially in online role-playing games, there is a market for virtual goods that only exists within the boundaries of the respective game. The German Federal Fiscal Court (BFH) has now addressed the question[28] of whether trading virtual goods effectuates sales tax. The BFH deems there to be no sales tax liability in the virtual world, but only when virtual money is exchanged for real money. This leaves the question of a taxable event in a bit of quicksand, a conundrum.

An examination of the user's perspective would highlight entry/registration charges that the user must pay while signing up for these single or multi-platform games. Winnings from the game form an additional element kernel to the event that would qualify as a taxable activity. In India, the Finance Act 2023 inserted two new provisions,[29] i.e., section 115BBJ (tax on winnings from online games) and section 194BA (withholding tax on net winnings) in the IT Act. They provide for a specific tax regime and the withholding tax obligation on any income derived from winnings in any online game from a user-centric perspective. In Italy, an on-game activity that leads to an event constituting a win for users of the game would qualify as a taxable transaction under 'allied income'.

An examination invigoration from the platform's perspective shows a varied picture. Transactions in gaming are essentially a contractual right. To accentuate the benefit arising out of such a contract, the commissions received from gaming entities

26. https://www.accaglobal.com/gb/en/student/exam-support-resources/professional-exams-study-resources/strategic-business-reporting/technical-articles/cryptocurrencies.html.
27. Primus Partners, *Online Gaming in India: Taxation Quandary*, available at https://primuspartners.in/docs/documents/ltOAZaeMVPLOkrH54fDe.pdf (accessed on 12 January 2024).
28. *See also*, Oppenhoff, available at https://www.oppenhoff.eu/en/news/detail/gaming-e-sport-die-virtuelle-welt-bleibt-vorerst-umsatzsteuerfrei/ (accessed on 12 January 2024).
29. Nishith Desai Associates, *News Details*, available at https://www.nishithdesai.com/NewsDetails/10609 (accessed on 13 January 2024).

through user accounts ('User Account' shall include every registered account of the user with the online gaming intermediary and when any taxable deposit, non-taxable deposit or the winnings made by the user is credited, and the withdrawal by the user is debited) form an element of the taxable event. The other taxable event under consideration is an obligation to withhold tax from the person responsible for paying any income by way of winnings from any online game during a financial year (FY) at the rates in force.

To determine how these transactions would be taxable, one of the ideas mooted by tax experts[30] is to consider taxing activities related to online gaming as profits and gains from business and profession (PGBP). Legislations such as the Interactive Gaming Act[31] lay the cornerstone for the same. The impetus for determining the PE would be found in the server based in the host precipice, and hence, the attribution challenge is less as compared to a blockchain transaction where the element of determinability and certainty is nearly negligible.

5 CURRENT FRAMEWORK FOR PROFIT ATTRIBUTION

OECD

Under Article 7 of the OECD Model Tax Convention, the profits to be attributed to a PE are those that it would have derived if it was a separate and independent enterprise performing the activities that cause it to be a PE.

UN

The UN Model Tax Convention also states that profits attributable to a PE are those that it might be expected to make if it was a distinct and separate enterprise engaged in the same or similar activities under the same or similar conditions and dealing wholly independently with the enterprise of which it is a PE. Importantly, however, the UN Model also provides a formulary apportionment by stating that it has been customary in a contracting state to determine the profits to be attributed to a PE based on an apportionment of the total profits of the enterprise to its various parts. However, nothing in paragraph 2 (dealing with the arm's length standard) shall preclude that contracting state from determining the profits to be taxed by such an apportionment as may be customary. The method of apportionment that is adopted, however, shall be such that the result shall be in accordance with the principles contained in this article.

30. *See also* Olena Demchenko, *Electronic Commerce in the Gaming Industry. Legal Challenges and European Perspective on Contracts Through Electronic Means in Video Games and Decentralized Applications*, available at https://ceere.eu/pjiel/wp-content/uploads/2019/12/pjiel-2019-1-2-olena-demchenko.pdf (accessed on 13 January 2024).
31. *See also* Kahlil S. Philander, *A Normal Analysis of Online Gaming Policy*, available at https://digitalscholarship.unlv.edu/cgi/viewcontent.cgi?article=1280&context=grrj (accessed on 13 January 2024).

Multilateral Developments

Multilateral Development under the Aegis of the OECD

To effectively address the allocation of profits from a PE that constitutes a new-age business due to engaging with a country's population, one solution narrowed down by the International Framework (IF) members was to redistribute a portion of profits of multinational corporations (MNCs)[32] to the countries where they sell their products and offer their services that cater to their consumer base. In the absence of this regulation, these corporations can generate substantial financial gains in a particular market while evading a significant portion of their tax obligations. This proposal has yet to attain finality. In any event, given its extremely narrow coverage of in-scope companies, this would not assuage the concerns of developing countries regarding the loss of taxation due to new-age business models, especially when these create new-age PEs. In addition, although simplicity and ease of administration are identified as objectives, there was a reasonable apprehension that these concepts may not attain unhindered implementation in countries with limited administrative capacity.

Multilateral Development under the Aegis of the UN

The UN provides an alternative perspective complementing the efforts of the OECD. While sharing foundational principles with the OECD Model, the UN Model often emphasizes the interests of developing nations and seeks to ensure a fair distribution of taxing rights. The principles outlined in the UN Model are of particular relevance in the context of the digital economy.[33] The UN has introduced Article 12B[34] pursuant to the determination that taxing rights for income generated by automated digital services (ADS) should be distributed among treaty partners. Broadly, Article 12B allows the source jurisdiction to tax income earned from the provision of ADS by a non-resident (NR). The source jurisdiction would levy the tax on gross revenue at a rate that is bilaterally negotiated between the source and residence jurisdictions. However, it is crucial to trace developments, especially in the context of PEs and the attribution thereof.

---

32. This initially only targeted MNCs with a turnover of EUR 20 billion.
33. Unlike the OECD's focus on the place of business or significant economic presence, the UN Model places priority on other relevant considerations such as user participation, data localization, or the impact on the developing country's economy. This model acknowledges the evolving nature of commerce and aims to strike a balance that accommodates the interests of both developed and developing nations.
34. During the 20th session of the UN Tax Committee, a drafting group was formed to develop an additional provision in the UN MC to allocate additional taxing rights in order to supplement developing countries' resources. It presented a proposal for a new Art. 12B ('Income from Automated Digital Services') in the UN MC that was distributed for comment to all members of the UN Tax Committee. *See also* UN Committee of Experts on International Cooperation in Tax Matters, Twentieth session, Update on work on taxation issues related to the digitalization of the economy, E/C.18/2020/CRP.41, available at https://financing.desa.un.org/sites/default/files/2023-03/CRP41_Digitalization%2010102020A.pdf.

In a 2019 UN report,[35] it was observed in relation to the first two proposals under consideration by the IF (user participation and marketing intangibles) that an assumption has been made that the principle of 'value creation' (usually focusing on the supply side) is the guiding factor for profit allocation in taxation. The report notes that modern business models in the digital era warrant rethinking where and how value creation occurs. From the perspective of developing countries, 'value creation' may mean various things to different people. Sales involve two parties, i.e., the buyer and seller, who interact to create value and profits. Demand and supply factors affect market price and sales volume. The supply-side factors involve production and marketing, while the demand-side factors include consumer paying capacity, impact prices, and profitability. This is subsequently influenced by the availability of public goods, law and order, market facilitation, infrastructure, and redistribution of resources (income support and subsidies) to the extent that it can directly or indirectly affect consumers' paying capacity in an economy. The state and public resources play a vital role in generating profits and value for enterprises in a jurisdiction by stabilizing, promoting, preserving, and enhancing consumer paying capacity. Profits are only made when consumers purchase a supplier's economic goods. The same was also advocated by the Indian Tax Administration (ITA), i.e., the Central Board of Direct Taxes (CBDT), in a public consultation document[36] released on 18 April 2019. The article recommended a formulary balanced approach that allocates profits between the jurisdiction based on both demand and supply side factors with necessary safeguards to prevent excessive attribution on the one hand and to protect the interests of Indian revenue on the other. With India being a capital import country, the report recommended a formulary approach that included demand-side factors such as the number of employees, wages paid to them, assets deployed and located in India, and the user base there. The report recommends profit attribution for an NR in India with a BC there broadly based on two approaches: (a) An NR with a BC that derives sales revenue from India; and (b) an NR with a BC in India due to the user base beyond a prescribed threshold.[37]

Another novel concept of 'location saving' was proposed in the 2019 UN report for further discussion wherein factors such as the relatively inexpensive labour and real estate housing in developing nations are considered in the analysis of 'value creation'.

---

35. Tax Issues related to the Digitalization of the Economy: Report, Committee of Experts on International Cooperation in Tax Matters Eighteenth session, E/C.18/2019/CRP.12 https://www.un.org/esa/ffd/wp-content/uploads/2019/04/18STM_CRP12-Work-on-taxation-issues-digitalization.pdf.
36. https://incometaxindia.gov.in/hindi/Lists/Latest%20News/Attachments/261/Report_of_the_Committee_on_Profit_Attribution_to_PE_in_India_18_4_19.pdf.
37. The formulaic approach recommended by ITA under both of the scenarios is reproduced hereunder:

    (a) An NR with a BC that derives sales revenue from India:
    Step 1: Determine profit derived from India, i.e., the higher of the following amounts: (a) The revenue derived from India x global operational profit margin (b) 2% of the revenue derived from India.
    Step 2: Apportionment of the profits derived from India based on three equally weighted factors of sales, employees (manpower and wages), and assets.

This was pursuant to the view that these demand-side factors provide value to multinationals that are not always taken into consideration when performing transfer pricing analyses. This was caveated by stipulating that, with no agreed-upon definition of 'value creation', a difference in interpretation will be inevitable, leading to a potentially confusing investment climate and the possibility of double or even triple non-taxation. The UN report noted that this is one danger of the present focus on 'value creation' as a cornerstone. In light of this, changes to the PE definition were proposed for further consideration to capture remote activities performed by MNEs for interacting with market jurisdictions, especially without the presence of human intervention.

In this regard, the UN has noted that the acceptance of formulaic approaches is a significant and encouraging development. The international community may initially be more amenable to formulaic allocation approaches in a limited area due to their novelty, as these methods necessitate significant information sharing. Since all countries aim to calculate the same amounts for allocation, smaller countries may benefit from others' efforts.

Profits attributable to operations in India = Profits derived from India x [SI/3 × ST + (NI/6 × NT) + (WI/6 × WT) + (AI/3 × AT)

Where,
SI = Sales revenue derived by Indian operations from sales in India;
ST = Total sales revenue derived by Indian operations from sales in India and outside India;
NI = Number of employees employed with respect to Indian operations and located in India;
NT = Total number of employees employed with respect to Indian operations and located in India and outside India;
WI = Wages paid to employees employed with respect to Indian operations and located in India;
WT= Total wages paid to employees employed with respect to Indian operations and located in India and outside India;
AI = Assets deployed for Indian operations and located in India;
AT = Total assets deployed for Indian operations and located in India and outside India.
Step 3: If the BC is due to the activities of a resident associated enterprise (AE) and it any payments (as below) on accounts of sales or services from any resident person and the activities of that AE have been fully remunerated by the NR enterprise by an arm's length price: (a) Payments less than or equal to INR 1 million (approx. USD 14,000) – no further profits will be attributable to the operation in India; (b) payments more than INR 1 million – profit attributable to the Indian operation will be derived by apportionment and deducted from the same profits that have already been subjected to tax by the AE.

(b) An NR with a BC in India constituting a user base beyond a prescribed threshold:

The approach is as above; however, Step 2 will be replaced by a four-factor approach consisting of sales, employees (manpower and wages), assets, and users (with weights assigned to each)

(a) Formula for low and medium intensity – Profits derived from India × [0.3 × SI/ST + (0.15 × NI/NT) + (0.15 × WI/WT) + (0.3 × AI/3 × AT)] + 0.1]
(b) Formula for high intensity – Profits derived from India × [0.3 × SI/ST + (0.125 × NI/NT) + (0.125 × WI/WT) + (0.25 AI/3 × AT)] + 0.2]

The report therefore concluded that the option of 'fractional apportionment' based on apportionment of profits derived from India would be acceptable under tax treaties and the Indian ITL.

Interestingly, utilizing withholding taxes was to be investigated as a means to facilitate implementing new profit allocation regulations and enhancing effective compliance. Some factors for further consideration would include whether such taxation could be imposed on a net basis. This approach was aimed at enhancing tax certainty by mitigating conflicts between tax authorities and taxpayers.

Country-Specific Norms for Profit Attribution

In this section, the authors discuss some approaches adopted by countries for profit attribution to digital activities.

Nigeria

Nigeria has been proactive in its approach to taxing the digital economy. In 2020, it introduced SEP provisions[38] that became the new 'nexus rule' for deciding whether an enterprise providing digital services or a foreign enterprise providing technical services is liable to income tax on enterprises in Nigeria. A ministerial order[39] provides that a non-resident company (NRC) shall be considered to have a SEP in Nigeria if it satisfies any of the following conditions:

(a) derives gross turnover or income of more than *N25 million* or its equivalent in other currencies in that year from any or combination of the following:
   (i) *streaming or downloading* services of digital content, including but not limited to movies, videos, music, applications, games and e-books to any person in Nigeria,
   (ii) transmission of *data collected about Nigerian users*, which has been generated from such users' activities on a digital interface, including website or mobile applications,
   (iii) provision of goods or services other than those under sub-paragraph(5) of this paragraph, directly or indirectly through a *digital platform to Nigeria*, or:

38. The Nigerian revenue authorities amended s. 13(2) of CITA on 13 January 2020 by inserting new paras (c and e) that introduced the concept of the SEP under Nigerian law. Section 13(2)(c) of CITA now provides that the profits of a company other than a Nigerian company from any trade or business shall be deemed to be derived from Nigeria:

    c) if it transmits, emits or receives signals, sounds, messages, images or data of any kind by cable, radio, electromagnetic systems or any other electronic or wireless apparatus to Nigeria in respect of any activity, including electronic commerce, application store, high frequency trading, electronic data storage, online adverts, participative network platform, online payments and so on, to the extent that the company has significant economic presence in Nigeria and profit can be attributable to such activity; c) ...
    e) if the trade or business comprises the furnishing of technical, management, consultancy or professional services outside of Nigeria to a person resident in Nigeria to the extent that the company has significant economic presence in Nigeria ... .

39. While the concept of the SEP was introduced by the Companies Income Tax (Significant Economic Presence) Order, 2020 (SEP Order), it, failed to expand on what constitutes the SEP. Thus, bearing in mind the need for clarification of the concept and its localization, the Minister of Finance, Budget, and National Planning issued the Companies Income Tax (Significant Economic Presence) Order, 2020 on the 29 May 2020 (also referred to as 'Ahmed Order').

(iv) provision of *intermediation services* through a digital platform, website or other online applications that link suppliers and customers in Nigeria;

(b) uses a *Nigerian domain name (.ng)* or registers a website address in 'Nigeria; or

(c) has a purposeful and sustained *interaction with persons in Nigeria* by customizing its digital page or platform to target persons in Nigeria, including reflecting the prices of its products or services in Nigerian currency or providing options for billing or payment in Nigerian currency. {emphasis added}.

Consequently, an amendment was also brought into section 30 of the act to assess NRCs with a digital SEP in Nigeria. A fair and reasonable percentage of their turnover attributable to the SEP would be taxed in the instance when there is no assessable profit, that profit is less than what is to be expected from that type of business, or it cannot be ascertained. While this amendment should (to an extent) address the pending issue of profit attribution for digital businesses in Nigeria, it is unclear what percentage of turnover should be deemed as taxable profits for such companies.

What constitutes a fair and reasonable percentage is neither defined nor explicitly stated in the law - not in the 2021 act or any other tax law. Nigeria's Minister of Finance, however, has confirmed that the fair and reasonable percentage is 6%.[40]

The above methodology adopted by the Nigerian authorities is similar to DSTs adopted by other jurisdictions, such as France and the United Kingdom, that impose a 3% and 2% DST, respectively. The 6% ad hoc rate imposed by Nigerian authorities has been criticized for its general application to all businesses without considering their unique features and economies. There does not seem to be any scientific basis for undertaking such allocations. Further, the 6% rate seems to be on the higher side, especially in a scenario where economies like Kenya, a comparable developing economy in the same region, have a DST rate of 1.5%.

India

India has also introduced SEP provisions in its domestic law, an equalization levy (a digital services tax) that operates beyond the realm of the Income Tax Act and thus does not violate existing tax treaties. India's SEP provisions effectuate a BC in India;

40. This principle of fair and reasonable percentage is not novel in the Nigerian taxation regime. The origin of this doctrine is traced to the Nigeria's budget press briefing in 1996 which stated the government's position to tax NRCs on their turnover at 6% rate. Since then, the Nigerian tax authority has been using the 6% tax rate for turnover assessment. This principle assumes that 20% of revenue of a taxable entity is profit while the remaining 80% is operating costs. The 20% deemed profit is taxed by the standard corporate tax rate of 30% to obtain the 6% ETR. Rather than waiting for the company to assess and ascertain profit that will be taxed at 30%, the tax authority will simply apply a 6% tax rate on the turnover.
    https://www.afronomicslaw.org/category/analysis/nigerias-finance-act-2021-and-digital-tax-framework-another-attempt-boil-ocean.

however, the tax office has yet to release any guidance on profits attributable to such SEPs. The extant law[41] provides for-profit attribution in the following manner:

- at such a percentage of turnover accruing or arising as the revenue officer considers reasonable;
- the ratio of total profits to total receipts computed under the provisions of India's Income Tax Act; or
- any manner that the officer deems suitable.

What emerges from the above is that the current framework under both the OECD and the UN propagates an arm's length return to a PE. This inevitably instigates a value chain analysis of the PE.

From a value chain standpoint, its analysis in these situations would be extremely critical and would need refined, extensive, and in-depth documentation, including the nuances of the activities of nomads and, in other situations of technology, interplay with the location of servers, frequency of live contact with them, and the characterization of the transactions. Given the complexity involved and the significance of every subtlety in the value chain, it intuitively appears that finding reasonably accurate comparables would be difficult, which is a prerequisite to arriving at an arm's length price.

Various authors have critically analysed in numerous articles the deficiencies of the current profit attribution norms using the arm's length standard based on a value chain analysis and considering the risk and control framework under the development, enhancement, maintenance, protection, and exploitation (DEMPE) analysis. However, none of the alternative suggestions provided seem to be viable propositions either.[42]

A formulary apportionment based on user engagement might be a simpler solution to relieve uncertainties for taxpayers at the time of audits and to keep tax administrations from devoting enormous amounts of time and energy that may be disproportionate to the outcome on many occasions. This would also assuage the concerns of developing countries about no weight being given to the demand side in profit attribution.

Additional Profit Attribution Due to 'Force of Attraction' Principle

The force of attraction principle permits taxing profits that are not attributable under normal rules to the PE but relate to sales of the same or similar goods or merchandise in the source state and other business activities of the same or similar carried on by the enterprise in the source state. This principle is recognized in the UN Model Convention[43] but is expressly prohibited in the OECD Model Convention.[44] Interestingly, though, India has several treaties with OECD member countries where the limited force

41. Rule 10 of the Income Tax Rules 1962 read with s. 9 of the Income Tax Act, 1961.
42. *See* a critique of various scholarly writings on the topic in the article: I. Verlinden, *Article 7: Business Profits – Global Tax Treaty Commentaries*, Global Topics IBFD (accessed 23 January 2024).
43. Paragraph 15.10 of UN Model Double Taxation Convention between Developed and Developing Countries.
44. Paragraph 12 of OECD Model Commentary on Art. 7.

of attraction principle is present – for example, treaties with Belgium, Canada, France, Germany, Italy, Japan, Singapore, the United Kingdom, and the United States.

In the context of profit attribution to new-age PEs, applying such a limited force of attraction principle could constitute significant challenges. To give a simplistic example, if the presence of a robot creates a PE for Company A in Country X, would Company A's income from other robots not constituting a PE and performing different functions be encompassed within the attraction principle?

6 CONCLUSION

The term 'PE' was first used in the tax treaty between Austria/Hungary and Prussia (1899): 'The following are considered Betriebsstätten: Branch offices, factories, storage facilities, offices, purchase and sale facilities and other business establishments used for the performance of standing enterprises by the entrepreneur himself, business partners, authorized agents or other permanent agents.' A PE was used in a model in the first League of Nations Draft (1927).[45]

Betriebsstätten was thus linked to the concept of 'business premises' that has been completely upended in this digital era of conducting business.

Unfortunately, international tax policy has failed to maintain similar progress as this rapid evolution in the ways and means of conducting business. This complexity is further exacerbated by the fact that over 70% of global trade is intra-group, thereby affording opportunities for profit shifting and tax base erosion from high-tax countries.

A constant catch-up game by tax policy markets is proving disastrous for businesses as they are becoming encumbered with both unilateral levies and tax controversies. It is, therefore, important that the definition of a PE be supplemented with that of a 'deemed PE' with no nexus to physical presence but instead to revenues, presence, or engagement with the population of a country. As technology becomes all permeating in businesses, another debate in this sphere would be concerning what constitutes 'preparatory and auxiliary' vs 'core' business activities for a company. The Commentary on Article 5 of the OECD Model states that the reason for the exclusion of preparatory or auxiliary activities is that such activities 'are so remote from the actual realization of profits that it is difficult to allocate any profit to the fixed place of business in question'. While anti-fragmentation rules have since been built in, further guidance needs to be developed in the context of digital presence.

Consensus at a multilateral level on what are adequate profits attributable to deemed PEs caused by digital businesses seems elusive, but given that countries have come a long way at the negotiating table, the present Pillar One seems to be a

45. The Origins of Concepts and Expressions Used in the OECD Model and their Adoption by States by John F. Avery Jones (United Kingdom), Luc De Broe (Belgium), Maarten J. Ellis and Kees van Raad (Netherlands), Jean-Pierre Le Gall (France), Sanford H. Goldberg (United States), Jürgen Killius (Germany), Guglielmo Maisto (Italy), Toshio Miyatake (Japan), Henri Torrione (Switzerland), Richard J. Vann (Australia), David A. Ward (Canada) and Bertil Wiman (Sweden). Published in IBFD Tax Treaty Monitor – June 2006.

better-than-nothing option for attaining certainty around profit attribution to new-age PEs.

The attribution of profits to such new-age deemed PEs needs to consider the four canons of taxation stipulated by Adam Smith – equality, certainty, economy, and convenience. The current international tax framework seems to have none of these for digital businesses!

CHAPTER 6

Transfer Pricing and ESG

Paolo Ludovici & Luca Tortorella

1 AN INTRODUCTION TO ENVIRONMENTAL, SOCIAL, AND GOVERNANCE

The philosophy behind environmental, social, and governance (ESG) aspects has been a driver of relevant events in human history, such as improving labour conditions, increasing awareness regarding social projects, and adopting sustainable practices to reduce the impacts on the environment. The ESG has always been here, has gradually risen, and is influenced by several causes.

Currently, discussions regarding ESG primarily refer to a set of guidelines that investors and stakeholders take into account to evaluate the impact that companies and their activities have on the world. It originated as a concept of socially responsible investing (SRI) and corporate social responsibility (CSR), which gained significant relevance over the years during the twentieth century and was demonstrated in many different ways, as described below:

- SRI. With the SRI, a group of investors began incorporating ethical and social factors into their investment choices. In the 1960s and 1970s, they began avoiding companies engaged in activities considered socially irresponsible.
- CSR. In the last part of the century, businesses began embracing CSR practices that help companies to be socially accountable to themselves, their stakeholders, and the public beyond financial performance. The CSR is a self-regulating business model.
- Global Reporting Initiative (GRI). The GRI was established in 1997 and developed a set of guidelines for sustainability reporting. It exists to help organizations be transparent and take responsibility for their impact on society. Indeed, companies started using such guidelines to disclose their ESG performance. Several other initiatives were then introduced. One is the International Integrated Reporting Initiative (IIRI) that was founded in 2010. Its goal is to encourage businesses to provide a more comprehensive view of their value creation over time. This exceeds standard financial reporting by including information on ESG factors that could affect an organization's ability to create value in the short, medium, and long term. According to the IIRI, 2,500 companies across seventy countries have currently embraced it.[1]
- The UN report titled 'Principles for Responsible Investment'. It was initially addressed to investors and business leaders to begin familiarizing and discussing the message behind the ESG principles. It was released as a response to the then-UN Secretary's call for action. The report was part of an effort under the UN Global Compact supported by financial institutions like the International Finance Corporation (IFC) and the Swiss Government.

The development of ESG principles, especially for the letter 'E', then continued over the years:

- In 2015, the Paris Agreement to hold 'the increase in the global average temperature to well below 2°C above pre-industrial levels' and pursue efforts 'to limit the temperature increase to 1.5°C above pre-industrial levels' was

1. The GRI published GRI 207 in 2019 that entered in force in 2021. It addresses the topic of taxation acknowledged by the UN to play a vital role in achieving the sustainable development goals. According to the GRI 207, companies that adopt such principles must provide an overview of their tax strategy, including 'the use of tax havens, the types of tax incentive it uses, or [their] approach to transfer pricing' as well as their approach to mitigate risks engaging tax authorities (e.g., the participation in cooperative compliance programs or APAs in force).

signed. There are 196 parties that agreed to it. The treaty is legally binding and requests all nations to combat climate change together and adapt to its effects.
- In the same year, the United Nations created the United Nations Sustainable Development Goals. The 2030 Agenda for Sustainable Development that was adopted by all United Nations Member States provides a shared blueprint for peace and prosperity for people and the planet both now and into the future. The goals are to face poverty, inequality, climate change, and environmental degradation and reach peace and justice. To achieve such goals, businesses are influenced to align their operations with sustainable practices. Taxation is linked to achieving several of these goals (e.g., goal 1 regarding no poverty for which fair taxation may contribute to reducing income inequality and poverty; goal 4 concerning quality education for which education initiatives depend on the amount of taxes collected; goal 8 for decent work and economic growth; or goal 13 for climate action).
- The EU introduced the European Green Deal in 2019 by adopting a package of proposals to make the EU's climate, energy, and land use, as well as transport and taxation policies, suitable for reducing net greenhouse gas emissions by at least 55% by 2030 compared to 1990 levels and no net emissions of greenhouse gases by 2050.[2] Under the umbrella of the European Green Deal, the European Commission has crafted a sustainability policy agenda. One of its components is the EU Taxonomy that came into effect in 2020. Both of them are vital for attempting to effectively address climate change, promoting sustainability and facilitating a shift towards a more robust economy.
- Finally, it was agreed in the recent COP28 that a 'transitioning away' from fossil fuels and reducing global emissions by 43% would occur by 2030.

The increasing awareness of climate change and its potential effects on businesses and communities has resulted in an emphasis on environmental considerations. Investors have begun acknowledging the risks connected to climate change, including regulatory modifications, physical risks, and changing consumer preferences. In relation to this, it should be recalled that the CEO of BlackRock, the world's largest asset manager, affirmed in 2020 that 'climate change has become a defining factor in companies' "long-term prospects"'. The CEO sent a letter to its clients outlining some steps they are taking in order to prioritize sustainability in their investment strategies. These actions include incorporating sustainability into their portfolio construction and risk management processes; divesting from investments with sustainability risks like thermal coal producers; introducing new investment products that screen for fossil fuels; and reinforcing their dedication to sustainability and transparency in their investment stewardship activities.[3]

2. The UN has similar goals. 'Race to Zero' is indeed the UN-backed global campaign that calls on non-state players – including companies, cities, regions, financial, and educational institutions – to take rigorous and immediate action to halve global emissions by 2030 and achieve a healthier and more equitable carbon-neutral world on time.
3. (...) 'ESG investing has become a leading form of sustainable finance and has shifted from early stages of development toward mainstream finance in a number of OECD jurisdictions, and

The insistent urge for increased transparency and accountability has compelled companies to prioritize practices. The ESG is widely recognized in the current business landscape and impacts the value chains of company communities and their reporting.

2 ESG AND TAXATION

ESG considerations and taxation often operate within distinct paradigms and sometimes result in divergent approaches. Consider, for instance, a multinational enterprise (MNE) opting to invest in a jurisdiction with favourable tax regimes. While this choice might draw criticism from a tax standpoint and be seen as an endeavour to minimize tax liabilities in its home country, it could simultaneously attract commendation through the ESG perspective for its implementation of progressive welfare schemes, promotion of diversity and inclusivity, attainment of zero carbon emissions objectives, and active involvement with local communities. These endeavours positively impact the social and environmental landscape of the regions in which the MNE operates and are often hailed as exemplary corporate stewardship.

Although ESG and taxes may follow different rationales, they are interconnected, and the importance of the latter on the former is very clear: tax revenues are a significant means for funding the achievement of sustainable development goals and contributing to a country's public households. Taxation has a direct impact on the wealth of communities, and tax becomes one of the foundations of trust with citizens. In the long run, this may even become a tool to make states and revenue agencies accountable for how they use resources when investing money collected by corporations that implemented ESG tools. Accurate reporting and disclosure of the tax strategy to the stakeholders are essential for aligning businesses with social communities. In fact, the disclosure of a tax policy:

- not only has financial impacts since it allows comparing the environmental and social performance of companies with their peers;
- but it can also lead to a competitive advantage when customers recognize the adoption of specific policies and efforts undertaken, thus rewarding the virtuous company over its direct competitors.

In summary, the interplay between ESG and taxation is becoming increasingly intertwined as businesses navigate evolving regulatory landscapes, investors demand

---

generally refers to the process of considering environmental, social and governance (ESG) factors when making investment decisions. ESG ratings, which are applied to companies representing around 80% of market capitalisation in 2020, have evolved in recent years to incorporate long-term financial risks and opportunities in investment decision making processes. At the same time, the environmental "E" pillar score of ESG rating is being increasingly used as a tool to align investments with a low-carbon transition, and a range of financial market products and measurement approaches have developed to help investors align portfolios with specific climate-objectives and strategies in line with the Paris Agreement.' OECD (2021), *ESG Investing and Climate Transition: Market Practices, Issues and Policy Considerations*, OECD Publishing, Paris, https://doi.org/10.1787/7b321b7a-en.

transparency and, in general, the need is emerging to align tax practices with broader sustainability goals.

3 ESG AND TRANSFER PRICING: A QUALITATIVE AND QUANTITATIVE BLENDING

The majority of global trade consists of international transfers of goods, services, capital, and intangibles within a multinational group that is operating in more jurisdictions.[4]

Intercompany trades require applying the correct transfer pricing (TP) rules: a proper TP policy enables MNEs to accurately determine the prices for goods, services, intangibles, or financial transactions that occur between affiliated parties. This ensures that these transactions are conducted as if they were taking place between independent entities and ultimately guarantees a fair allocation of taxation rights between jurisdictions.[5]

It is crucial for states to focus on TP aspects, to defend their taxation rights, and to ensure that MNEs pay the proper amount of taxes based on the functions performed, risks assumed, and assets employed in their jurisdiction. Effective TP prevents double taxation but also tax evasion and ensures fair distribution of profits among the involved jurisdictions. Applying the arm's length principle (ALP) also allows wealth redistribution in countries where a multinational group conducts business, which is especially significant when operations are carried out in less developed areas.[6]

The question at this point is what the interconnections are, if any, between TP and the ESG. They initially indeed appear to be two perfect strangers: the Organisation for Economic Co-operation and Development (OECD) Transfer Pricing Guidelines (TPG) and the OECD Model Tax Convention never mention the term 'ESG'. The only reference to environmental and social concepts in the OECD TPG is included within the paragraph regarding identifying economically significant risks. At the same time, databases commonly used for TP studies do not report ESG-driven information.

However, ESG is now a fact, and MNEs are assessing how ESG awareness can be reflected in their TP policies in terms of impact on both value chains and their social responsibilities towards citizens of the countries in which they operate.

4. According to the OECD, in 2002, related party trade accounted for 60% of all international trade. According to the *World Investment Report (2013): Global Value Chains, Investment and Trade for Development* report by the UN, the percentage increased, and approx. 80% of global trade took place within the value chains of large global organizations.
5. As known, TP is not an exact science (or, as stated in the UN Practical Manual on Transfer Pricing, TP is 'an art, not a science'). Compliance with the ALP cannot always be reflected by one single figure, such as a price or a margin, therefore, there might be occasions when the application of the most appropriate TP method produces a series of values, i.e., the arm's length range.
6. The ALP was indeed established to tentatively objectify transfer prices and to allocate taxation rights properly between jurisdictions. It is based on economic principles, and it is supposed to ensure an equally advantageous situation between associated and unrelated enterprises. The ALP requires that related entities set their prices in a manner consistent with what unrelated parties would agree upon under comparable circumstances. *See also* S. Greil, C. Schwarz & S. Stein, *What's ESG Got to Do with Transfer Pricing?*, Kluwer International Tax Blog (2023).

Multinational corporations embracing ESG principles aim to align their operations with standards to engage responsibly with society. However, it is crucial to note that – especially – for the social ('S') and governance ('G') aspects, the focus is not on immediate financial returns but rather on qualitative and reputational gains, much like an ethical code. Unlike traditional business plans that prioritize short-term economic advantages, ESG initiatives take a long-term perspective, emphasizing sustainable practices and accountability. This difference highlights a contradiction between the short-term focus of taxation and the long-term orientation of ESG strategies. Moreover, the ESG is shifting the focus of TP from profit allocation across the value chain to the allocation of (extra) costs among the group companies. Indeed, not all ESG initiatives currently lead to an increase in revenues and profits, but, as better explained in the following sections, additional costs deriving from implementing ESG policies might be expected. Under certain conditions, this is dispersed over the group companies following the accurate delineation of the transaction and the proper analysis for contractual risk reallocation.

While the results of ESG-aligned practices on TP are predominantly qualitative in nature – since the outcome of ESG-compliant activities cannot generally be easily measurable in terms of financial impacts – companies that do not proactively consider ESG consequences in their operations may suffer reputational damages directly impacting their market standing. This is particularly true now as MNEs are in the process of adopting new ESG policies and still operate in unequal circumstances. Those who proactively initiate a review of their policies in principle can gain an initial advantage as pioneers in this evolving environment. However, this advantage does not necessarily translate into selling ESG-compliant goods or services applying an ESG premium price. It might instead happen that non-compliant ESG goods or services require applying additional discounts for companies to remain competitive.

The influence of the above aspects on TP policies is then predictable: TP is the tax discipline that has the most intrinsic connections with business and is the tool that establishes intercompany prices based on actual value creation within the multinational group.

However, MNEs lack specific guidelines to reflect ESG strategy on TP policies; therefore, they will have to rely on existing tools to address this new consideration. To assess and acknowledge the influence of ESG factors on TP policies, it is crucial to:

- set up a proper tax control system by updating the documentation accordingly and consider taking measures like disclosures and advance pricing agreements (APAs) to effectively handle any potential disputes;
- evaluate how business initiatives can promote sustainability and responsible business practices;
- review the value chain and weigh the impacts of green technologies on the value of products and services; and, in general
- ensure that TP practices are aligned with substance and value creation and that specific ESG costs – and risks – are sustained by those who are able to control them.

Certain aspects are to be considered when integrating the ESG into TP operations. For example, when performing external benchmarks, it appears difficult, if not impossible, to have evidence of the structure of costs of third-party companies and their observation of ESG best practices (e.g., in terms of respecting their workforce and plants' safety regulations or the environment and their impacts on social communities). Moreover, in the case of business restructurings required by clients' and stakeholders' increased awareness of ESG aspects, what amount of exit charge could potentially be due if a company moves from one country to another due to an inability to fully comply with ESG policies in the original country thereby exiting from underperforming operations with limited profit potential?

MNEs must be able to navigate the evolving tax landscape. The inclusion of ESG factors in their TP frameworks requires a holistic approach. This exceeds the parameters of tax compliance and incorporates sustainability and responsible business practices towards socially and environmentally conscious corporate strategies and the involvement of the executive-level managers within a company whose titles begin with the letter C, such as CEO, CFO, COO, and CIO (C-suite).

The following sections will initially examine the unique challenges that MNEs need to consider when aligning TP policies with ESG strategies across each ESG pillar in the order of G, S, and E. Subsequently, recognizing the intricate interconnections among specific aspects that transcend individual pillars, paragraph 7 will present a unified overview of common elements.

4 TP AND G OF GOVERNANCE

4.1 An Introduction to Reporting Requirements and Trends

Reporting holds importance for MNEs. It is currently increasingly expected that companies are transparent about their ESG practices to investors, customers, employees, and regulatory bodies. Companies can effectively communicate their performance in sustainability areas to stakeholders through reporting. Compliance purposes aside, it is also a factor in shaping the companies' reputation and serves as a tool for continuous improvement. Regularly assessing and reporting on ESG performance enables companies to establish goals, track progress over time, and demonstrate a commitment to ongoing sustainability initiatives.[7]

The importance of tax reporting in the United States was emphasized back in 2006 with the introduction of Financial Accounting Standard (FAS) No. 109 by the

7. In the realm of 'tax reporting', the trajectory indicates that ESG reporting is transitioning from being a discretionary practice to a more obligatory one. Consequently, the business ramifications of ESG initiatives may create tax complexities necessitating ongoing dialogue between taxpayers, communities, and regulatory bodies. To navigate these challenges effectively, companies must establish robust tax risk management protocols. Concurrently, governments and tax authorities are enhancing collaborative compliance initiatives to facilitate voluntary disclosures that are more streamlined and effective pertaining to advanced tax matters. The role of tax directors is then changing, and they now frequently sit in strategic steering committees.

Financial Accounting Standards Board (FASB), subsequently followed by FASB Interpretation (FIN) No. 48 titled 'accounting for uncertainty in income taxes'. The latter addresses how uncertain tax positions taken by companies should be treated and establishes a framework for recognizing and measuring tax implications resulting from such uncertainties. It also deals with how companies handle situations in which they are uncertain about their tax positions. It establishes guidelines for assessing and quantifying the tax consequences of these uncertainties and guidance on measuring the potential tax benefit or liability associated with these uncertain tax positions. This involves estimating the likelihood of those being sustained based on the technical merits of the position and considering the amount that would be recognized or settled. Companies must provide evidence to support their positions that serves as the commencement for recognizing and evaluating them. Furthermore, companies must acknowledge the impact of uncertain tax positions in their financial statements,[8] both in terms of their nature and amounts as well as their potential effects. They are then requested to reassess their uncertain tax positions on a regular basis as new information becomes available and adjust these when warranted. When the FIN 48 states that 'the term tax position also encompasses ... an allocation or a shift of income between jurisdiction', there is a clear reference to TP.[9]

Always in terms of proper reporting and accurate management of tax risks, the OECD issued a document[10] in 2013 prepared by the Forum on Tax Administration (FTA)[11] based on a detailed examination of the practical experiences of countries that have established a relationship of trust and cooperation with large business taxpayers. It also identified certain features such as the part played by the tax control framework used by a large business in providing an objective basis for trust, the internal governance of an enhanced relationship (definition then changed into 'cooperative compliance') within revenue bodies, the importance of making a sound business case for the approach, and how to measure the results of cooperative compliance programs. Then, as part of the OECD/G20 international tax agenda, the OECD published a report[12] in 2016 in which it provided specific guidance for tax cooperation and for the importance of a tax control framework, including elements for establishing a concrete system of tax risk control. Requirements are articulated in six essential points: (a) tax strategy, (b) roles and responsibilities, (c) procedures, (d) monitoring, (e) adaptability to the internal and external context, and (f) reporting to management bodies.

At the European level, the commission initiated the 'Fiscalis programme' in 2010, which is an EU cooperation project that enables participating countries, their tax administrations, and their officials to work together in the fight against tax fraud, tax

8. An uncertain tax position is one taken or expected to be taken in a tax return that is not certain to be sustained upon examination by tax authorities.
9. According to M.L. Friedlich, *FIN 48 Answer Book*, Chicago (2009), 'This means that all transfer pricing positions must undergo the FIN 48 recognition and measurement process.'
10. OECD, *Co-operative Compliance: A Framework – From Enhanced Relationship to Co-operative Compliance*, OECD, Paris (2013) https://doi.org/10.1787/9789264200852-en.
11. The FTA was created in 2002 with the objective of promoting dialogue between tax administrations and identifying good tax administration practices.
12. OECD, *Co-operative Tax Compliance: Building Better Tax Control Frameworks*, Paris (2016), https://doi.org/10.1787/9789264253384-en.

evasion, and aggressive tax planning.[13] In this regard, the DAC directive (Council Directive 2011/16/EU, which repealed Directive 77/799/EEC and has undergone a series of amendments in recent years to align with the Union's new initiatives in the realm of tax transparency) seems to have proceeded in this direction. Initially, it was aimed at granting Member States the power to efficiently cooperate at international level as stated:

> There is a tremendous development of the mobility of taxpayers, of the number of cross-border transactions and of the internationalization of financial instruments, which makes it difficult for Member States to assess taxes due properly. ... A single Member State cannot manage its internal taxation system, especially as regards direct taxation, without receiving information from other Member States.[14]

The revisions that occurred over the various years to the 2011 Council Directive primarily incorporated reporting requirements along with the obligation to communicate such information to other Member States. The focus then was on financial accounts, advance cross-border rulings, TP advance pricing arrangements, country-by-country reporting (CbCR) (e.g., DAC4),[15] and reportable cross-border arrangements (i.e., DAC6). These amendments expanded the scope of automatic information exchange. Member States' tax authorities now possess a more extensive array of cooperative tools for identifying and addressing instances of tax fraud, tax evasion, and tax avoidance.[16]

---

13. For the period 2021-2027, such a programme has a budget of EUR 269 million available.
14. Whereas (1) and (2) of the Council Directive 2011/16/EU.
15. In this context, reference should be made also to Council Directive 2021/2101 dated 24 November 2021 where it is stated that 'Public country-by-country reporting is an efficient and appropriate tool for increasing transparency in relation to the activities of multinational undertakings and for enabling the public to assess the impact of those activities on the real economy. It also improves shareholders' ability to evaluate properly the risks taken by undertakings, leads to investment strategies being based on accurate information and enhances the ability of decision-makers to assess the efficiency and the impact of national legislation' and also 'By introducing public country-by-country reporting with this Directive, the Union becomes a global leader in the promotion of financial and corporate transparency. More transparency in financial disclosure will be advantageous for all, since civil society will become more involved, employees will be better informed and investors less risk-averse. In addition, undertakings will benefit from better relations with stakeholders, which will lead to greater stability, along with easier access to finance due to a clearer risk profile and an enhanced reputation.' The directive makes it mandatory from 2025 for groups with a consolidated turnover exceeding EUR 750 million to draw up, publish, and make a report on their income tax information accessible on their corporate website. With such a directive, information that, according to the OECD (Action 13 of the BEPS Project), should have been shared across the tax administrations only is now publicly available to everyone in Europe.
16. In 2021, the OECD Secretary reported to G20 Finance Ministers and Central Bank Governors, among various arguments, an update on the 'tax transparency developments' (*OECD Secretary-General Tax Report to G20 Finance Ministers and Central Bank Governors*, OECD, Italy, 2021, https://www.oecd.org/tax/oecd-secretary-general-tax-report-g20-finance-ministers-february-2021.pdf). Regarding the automatic exchange of information, a peer review published by the Global Forum in December 2020 showed that '88% of jurisdictions committed to commence exchanges by 2017 or 2018 have satisfactory legal frameworks in place'. In his report, the OECD Secretary confirmed that the network of exchange relationships is increasing over the years, reaching 115 jurisdictions in 2023. The mentioned report also analysed the impacts of tax and the environment specifically related to carbon pricing (effective carbon rates and taxing energy

Multinational groups are now transforming these requirements into an opportunity to make their tax strategy and their impact on society public, e.g., by publishing their total tax contribution (TTC).[17]

With the implementation of Council Directive 2021/2101 on public CbCR, it can be expected that the number of companies providing more details about their total tax figures will increase.

According to the European Business Tax Forum,[18] the European Free Trade Association (EFTA), and the United Kingdom, sixty-seven of the largest one hundred MNEs operating in Europe participated in the study in 2022 (the number of participating companies was sixty-one in 2021) disclosing their TTCs.[19] Those companies with robust ESG reporting and, in general, companies that are able to manage tax risks may

use) as well as the implementation of the BEPS measures and tax certainty (tools analysed regarded the developments on BEPS Action 5 – countering harmful tax regimes; BEPS Action 6 – prevention of tax treaty abuse and countering treaty shopping; BEPS Action 13 – improving transparency through CbCR; and BEPS Action 14 – mutual agreement procedures) but also updates on the ICAPs, on APAs, standard benchmarks used by the tax administrations for particular sectors, and activities and joint audits. As stated by the OECD Secretary, 'in an increasingly uncertain world, providing tax certainty is becoming even more important to facilitate global growth and cross-border investment'.

17. Several voluntary tax transparency measures have been developed over the years. Among these, the most relevant are:

    - GRI 207 (report prepared according to the GRI must detail management's approach to tax, tax governance and control framework, stakeholder engagement and management of concerns in relation to tax, and country level tax information – *see supra* n. 1).
    - World Economic Forum (WEF) white paper titled 'Measuring Stakeholder Capitalism Towards Common Metrics and Consistent Reporting of Sustainable Value Creation' dated 2020 (reports prepared according to the WEF must detail total taxes paid by the group globally and any tax relief received by governments, total taxes collected on behalf of others, and total taxes paid in the most relevant countries for the group).
    - B Team Responsible Tax Principles launched in 2018 according to which information to be shared covers MNEs' tax strategy, their approach to tax risk management (including relationship with authorities), the approach they take to implement their strategy, the taxes they pay, and the tax incentives accepted all in a meaningful and understandable way.
    - The Dow Jones Sustainability Indices (DJSI) that has taken into account a company's approach to tax since 2014. A DJSI report includes tax strategy and tax governance, the tax information for each jurisdiction in which the MNE's single entities are tax resident, and the reported tax rate and cash tax rate for the past two financial years.

18. A body of European businesses dedicated to raising the standards of the public tax debate formed in 2017 and composed by some of the most relevant MNEs based in Europe.
19. According to the results of the fifth edition of the study (2022 report available at https://ebtforum.org/wp-content/uploads/2023/12/TTC-Study-2022.pdf), the global TTC of the largest companies headquartered in the twenty-seven Member States of the European Union, the EFTA, and the United Kingdom amounted to EUR 505.6 billion, comprising EUR 235.7 billion in taxes borne (actual costs for the MNEs), and EUR 269.9 billion in collected taxes (payments made as a result of recourse mechanisms, substitution, etc.). The total amount of taxes borne by the companies that participated in the study for three years in a row has increased by 48.8% over the three-year period from EUR 109.5 billion in 2020 to EUR 162.9 billion in 2022.

have better access to capital as they are considered to be more sustainable and better positioned for long-term success.[20]

According to a McKinsey report:

> more private markets managers are incorporating considerations for ESG factors into their corporate policies, operating procedures, and investment decisions. In 2022, 1,069 more investors committed to the United Nations Principles for Responsible Investment (PRI), and a further 88 asset owners became PRI signatories, bringing the total to 681. The proportion of total private capital fundraising that came from managers with an investment policy that includes ESG issues rose to 66 percent in 2022, a new high.[21]

It emerges from a PwC survey that 37% of respondents have refused an investment opportunity because of ESG concerns, and one-third of respondents stated that ESG was a primary driver of value creation in more than half of their organization's recent deals. For the majority of respondents, risk mitigation ranks among the first three ESG benefits.[22]

Companies are currently not required to undertake ESG reporting as few, if any, compulsory regulations are in effect.[23] As better described in the following sections of this chapter, the most recent reporting obligation imposed in the EU refers to the Corporate Sustainability Reporting Directive (CSRD) (Directive 2022/2464) as part of the European Green Deal. According to this directive that entered into force in January 2023, all large companies and all listed companies (except listed micro-enterprises) will

20. It should be mentioned, however, that certain investors now opine that aggregating ESG data for reporting purposes increases costs that funds are reluctant to sustain. Speaking at the Infrastructure Investor Global Summit that occurred in March 2023 in Berlin, Ben Alves Walters, senior investment director at Cambridge Associates stated, 'with respect to the quality of data, there is definitely an elephant in the room, which is: the more quality it is, the more costly it is to extract' (https://www.newprivatemarkets.com/the-cost-of-esg-data-is-an-elephant-in-the-room/#: ~ :text = Speaking%20at%20last%20month's%20Infrastructure,costly%20it%20is%20to%20extract.%E2%80%9D accessed on 2 January 2024). The same article quotes a report published by the French management consultancy company Opimas which affirms 'many portfolio companies are reluctant to embrace ESG initiatives, because they see them as a costly compliance exercise with little direct or immediate financial benefit'. Adam Gillett, head of sustainable investment at Willis Towers Watson PLC, shares the same opinion, believing that 'the costs involved in meeting the standards of the European Union's Sustainable Finance Disclosure Regulation are significant' and also 'where permitted and appropriate, managers may be including some of the expenses in fund costs directly. Other costs will have to be borne by the managers, which in effect is likely to place an indirect cost on end investors. So however the costs are dealt with, end investors will likely feel the impact in some form'. (https://www.pionline.com/esg/european-managers-aiming-hold-line-esg-fund-fees-despite-costs#: ~ :text = Money%20managers%20in%20Europe%20said,if%20their%20costs%20have%20increased, accessed on 2 January 2024).
21. Private markets turn down the volume, McKinsey Global Private Markets Review 2023 (2023), https://www.mckinsey.com/ ~ /media/mckinsey/industries/private%20equity%20and%20principal%20investors/our%20insights/mckinseys%20private%20markets%20annual%20review/2023/mckinsey-global-private-markets-review-2023.pdf, (accessed on 2 January 2024).
22. Global Private Equity Responsible Investment Survey, PwC (2023), https://www.pwc.com/gx/en/services/sustainability/publications/private-equity-and-the-responsible-investment-survey.html, (accessed on 2 January 2024).
23. S. Varadharajan, V. Sturgis & J. Lamszus, *Integrating Transfer Pricing and ESG: Practical Considerations*, The Tax Adviser (2023).

be required from 2025, with reference to fiscal year 2024, to disclose information on what they consider as the risks and opportunities arising from social and environmental issues as well as the impact of their activities on people and the environment. It is obvious that the information in the corporate sustainability reporting must be aligned with what is included in the TP package (country file and master file) in order to avoid potential challenges.

Proper governance of the tax strategy and correct reporting go beyond TP and generally impact all of the aspects of uncertainty generated by taxation. The search for certainty is becoming more important every day, and tools such as advance rulings are now used by a significant number of multinational groups to the extent that certain authorities are now requesting a fee for accessing ruling procedures.

Governance is also key for EU taxonomy regulation.[24] The EU Taxonomy Regulation specifies that if an activity supports even one of the environmental objectives and follows the 'no significant harm' principle, it cannot qualify as environmentally or socially sustainable unless the company also follows good governance principles. 'In other words, the EU framework is not E and S and G, but EG and SG.'[25]

4.2 Governing TP Risks[26]

TP is a prominent tax aspect causing significant apprehension for tax directors,[27] and MNEs will consequently have to approach it in a strategic manner to comply with ESG

24. 'The EU taxonomy is a cornerstone of the EU's sustainable finance framework and an important market transparency tool. It helps direct investments to the economic activities most needed for the transition, in line with the European Green Deal objectives. The taxonomy is a classification system that defines criteria for economic activities that are aligned with a net zero trajectory by 2050 and the broader environmental goals other than climate' (extracted from 'EU taxonomy for sustainable activities', available at https://finance.ec.europa.eu/sustainable-finance/tools-and-standards/eu-taxonomy-sustainable-activities_en#legislation).
25. *See 'ESG Taxonomies. Will One Standard Emerge?'*, KPMG Insights, available at https://kpmg.com/xx/en/home/insights/2021/10/esg-taxonomies.html.
26. Also due to the increased attention toward ESG items, in recent years, there has been a shift of the approach by the tax authorities and governments to tax controls from controversies (ex-post) to cooperative compliance tools (*ex ante*).
27. According to a survey performed by EY in 2024, 84% of respondents (tax professionals of multinational groups) stated that they face a moderate or significant risk of double taxation in a post BEPS 2.0 world. (Survey available at https://www.ey.com/en_gl/tax/international-tax-and-transfer-pricing-survey, (accessed on 2 January 2024)). PwC has reached the same conclusion in its report titled 'Tax transparency and Sustainability reporting in 2023' (report available at https://www.pwc.com/gx/en/tax/pdf/tax-transparency-and-sustainability-reporting-in-2023.pdf, (accessed on 10 January 2024)), where it is stated that 'Transfer pricing is at the top of multinational companies' tax risk management agenda. The reason for this is not just the financial consequences of incorrect transfer prices, but also the high level of transparency affecting transfer pricing. Many countries have implemented rules obliging companies to file transfer pricing documentation with the corresponding tax authorities. Furthermore, the EU public CbCR Directive will require multinational groups from the 22nd of June 2024 to publish data that is central to transfer pricing. This trend of increased transparency is expected to be followed by other tax jurisdictions around the world. The CbCR data is also an integral part of a sustainability report prepared in accordance with the GRI standard 207. This transparency and the output of financial data that follows make it important for companies to prepare a narrative to put the data in context.'

purposes. Companies that can include in their tax reports that they are a part of the procedures to mitigate TP risks will be in a more advantageous position compared to competitors who have not collaboratively engaged with tax authorities.

The most relevant procedures to proactively mitigate TP risks are APAs that involve an arrangement between a taxpayer and one or more tax jurisdictions to define in advance methods and criteria for specific intercompany transactions over a fixed period. The taxpayer can initiate unilateral, bilateral, or multilateral APAs depending on the number of tax authorities involved. The decision to include additional authorities beyond the taxpayer's residence country requires a case-by-case analysis considering factors such as the nature of intercompany transactions, the development of the APA programme in that country, and the tax risks of foreign jurisdictions.

While unilateral procedures may require less effort to agree upon since they involve only the taxpayer and one tax administration, it is essential to note that only bilateral and multilateral APAs ensure that arrangements reduce the risk of double taxation and are fair to all tax administrations and taxpayers involved. This provides greater certainty to the concerned taxpayers.

Even minor adjustments in TP can significantly affect taxpayers, particularly when challenges span across all open fiscal years. In this context, proactive risk management before controversies arise becomes essential, and an APA emerges as a tangible strategic tool for MNEs. It stands out as the most suitable instrument capable of providing clarity amid the complexities of TP.

The benefits of APAs are then evident as they offer legal certainty, reduce or eliminate the likelihood of double taxation, and proactively prevent future tax disputes through close interaction between the taxpayer and the authority during negotiations. Resources that would typically be dedicated to resolving tax controversies can then be directed towards investments that are more profitable.

Another tool available to MNEs that intend to begin a cooperative compliance programme on TP matters with the tax authorities where they operate is the International Compliance Assurance Programme (ICAP),[28] which is a voluntary risk assessment and assurance programme by the OECD to facilitate open and cooperative multilateral engagements between companies and authorities which has continued to grow following initial pilot programs in 2018. It covers TP issues, permanent establishments (PEs), and other types of international tax risk. The programme is aimed at

28. On 29 January 2024, the OECD published the aggregated statistics from the Forum on Tax on ICAP. Twenty ICAP cases were completed by October 2023 with more currently in progress.
The average time taken from the initiation of an ICAP process to issuing risk assessment outcomes to an MNE was sixty-one weeks, which is higher than the maximum target timeframe of fifty-two weeks described in the ICAP handbook, in part due to the impact of COVID-19 on the second pilot.
For 40% of MNE groups, all of the main covered TP risk areas were considered low risk by all tax administrations that included them in the scope of the risk assessment.
The risk area that received the highest proportion of low-risk outcomes was PEs (considered low risk in 95% of instances where the topic was included in the scope of a tax administration's risk assessment), followed by tangible property (90%), intra-group services (88%), financing (76%), and intangible property (75%).

providing an efficient and effective approach to achieving tax certainty by analysing CbCRs, TP documentation packages, and all the relevant tax information.

All of these tools allow MNEs to achieve the 'G' goal when implementing ESG programmes.

5 TP AND S OF SOCIAL

As better described previously when dealing with TP and the 'G' of governance, the EU CSRD entered into force on 5 January 2023. This new directive modernizes and strengthens the rules concerning the social and environmental information that companies must report on sustainability. The standards adopted are tools to underpin the EU's sustainable finance agenda. They cover the full ambit of ESG issues, including climate change, biodiversity, and human rights. Companies subject to the CSRD will be required to prepare reports according to European Sustainability Reporting Standards (ESRS). The latter were developed by the European Financial Reporting Advisory Group (EFRAG),[29] which is an independent body bringing together various stakeholders. Concerning the letter 'S' of the ESG, reference might be made to ESRS S1, ESRS S2 and ESRS S3, named respectively 'own workforce', 'workers in the value chain', and 'affected communities'. The objective of these standards is for multinationals to specify their disclosure requirements in order to understand the material impacts on the workforce (own workforce and the value chain workers) and communities living in proximity to the company's operating sites, factories, etc. This encompasses aspects related to the company's operations, value chain, and business relationships with a focus on disclosing pertinent risks and opportunities. As reported in paragraphs 2 and 3, the release of the above information is aimed at a wider audience, i.e., not only to governments and tax authorities, and prejudicial tax conduct might break stakeholders' trust.

5.1 TP Implications of Social Aspects: Revision of the Supply Chain

Examples of implementing an ESG strategy focusing on the letter 'S' include reshoring manufacturing activities from countries that violate human rights or the complete revision of the supply chain to exclude from the list of suppliers those companies with low transparency on labour conditions or those that do not adhere to specific regulations on equipment safety or also that do not have any policy in place regarding gender equality and diversity. Referring to the latter, even if the decision to revise the supply chain impacts the business relations with third parties, there can be significant effects also on the intercompany transactions and the remuneration of controlled entities performing comparable functions to those of the external suppliers.

Consider, for example, a multinational group operating in the luxury sector whose suppliers are related companies already embracing ESG pillars in their operations and third-party manufacturers and performing comparable contract

29. Previously known as the European Financial Reporting Advisory Group.

manufacturing/tolling activities. To identify prices at arm's length, the group relies on an internal comparison based on the cost-plus mechanism.

During one of the regular, thorough due diligence procedures on third-party suppliers to monitor the nature of the cost bases of third parties for the appropriateness of the internal comparison, the group discovers instances of employing underage workers. The MNE then decides to withdraw from existing agreements and find alternative contractors that self-certified the full compliance with ESG principles.[30] These companies apply higher markups than the previous suppliers. Consequently, the group reassesses the TP policy to adjust the markups charged by the affiliated companies. If the group is unable to pass the additional costs on to the end customers, the principal of the transaction (i.e., who made the decision to implement the ESG policy) will be responsible for covering the increased expenses.[31]

The same conclusion is applicable to ethical sourcing; when a multinational group places a strong emphasis on ethically sourced materials or engages in fair trade practices, it may influence the pricing of inputs in intercompany transactions. In these cases, TP impacts are both quantitative and qualitative in nature: qualitative in terms of a comparability analysis, which then generates a quantitative impact in terms of additional costs caused by implementing the ESG-compliant strategy. When implementing ESG policies, MNEs must always perform a proper comparability analysis, and the most appropriate TP method needs to be selected.[32]

Additionally, impacts on business restructurings must be carefully considered, as explained in detail in the following sections.

6 TP AND E OF ENVIRONMENT

The journey is now concluded for understanding the points of contact between TP and ESG, focusing on the first letter 'E' (environment). MNEs that are embracing ESG strategies might face (or are already facing) a number of issues connected to sustainability that request a comprehensive revision of their TP policies.

Adopting environmentally sustainable practices or investing in green technologies can impact MNEs and the value of products or services exchanged between the group entities. This can generate disruptive changes in the business models and supply

30. In the absence of specific requirements for reporting ESG compliance, except for some companies operating in Europe from 2025, there is uncertainty about the actual implementation of ESG strategies by third-party companies. For comparability purposes, MNEs might seek self-certification from third parties regarding the adherence to ESG principles when conducting internal comparisons. However, when performing external benchmarks using commercial databases that rely on publicly available information, there is a risk of including non-comparable entities in the final set with significant differences in their cost bases compared to the tested party.
31. For the sake of simplicity, in the present chapter, the term 'principal' is synonymous with 'parent company'. Thus, when mentioning the former, it also means the parent company for ease of understanding and vice versa.
32. As mentioned, embracing ESG factors may result in higher costs (that also justify higher resale prices when selecting the RPM or the TNMM) but also in higher profit margins due to adopting sustainable or more efficient practices.

chains, including a change of locations for companies of the group; developing new products, processes, or intangibles; improving the brand awareness; or creating new intangibles as well as a change in the cost base (e.g., potential additional costs deriving from a more complex operating model or, on the contrary, potential savings not otherwise reachable).

6.1 TP Implications of Environmental Aspects: the Business Restructurings[33]

The transition of an MNE- to an ESG-driven business generally implies a 'business restructuring' potentially leading also to exit tax risks that should be carefully evaluated. Lacking specific guidance on the ESG in the OECD TPG, reference should be made to its Chapter IX that addresses business restructurings.

According to the OECD TPG and the UN Practical Manual on TP for developing countries (2021), there is no universally accepted concept of 'business restructurings'. These refer to cross-border redeployment of functions performed, assets used, and risks assumed by related parties in a multinational group. They may often involve centralizing intangibles, risks, or functions with the profit potential attached to them.[34]

The most common forms of centralization and decentralization may result in the following scenarios:

- converting full-fledged manufacturers into contract or toll manufacturers;
- adopting limited-risk distribution or commissionaire structures;
- transferring/allocating intangibles to companies located abroad; and
- rationalizing specific operations, including downsizing or closing operations and the concentration functions in a regional or central entity.

33. As mentioned, the concept is also applicable to the cases mentioned in paragraph 'TP and S of Social'.
34. OECD *Transfer Pricing Guidelines for Multinational Enterprises and Tax Administrations*, para. 9.1, Paris (2022). According to para. 9.13 of the OECD TPG, 'the application of the arm's length principle to a business restructuring must start, as for any controlled transaction, with the identification of the commercial or financial relations between the associated enterprises involved in the business restructuring and the conditions and economically relevant circumstances attaching to those relations so that the controlled transactions comprising the business restructuring are accurately delineated. In this regard, the general guidance in Section D.1 of Chapter I is applicable. This guidance requires the examination of the economically relevant characteristics of the commercial or financial relations between the associated enterprises, and in particular the contractual terms of the business restructuring (Section D.1.1); the functions performed by each party to the restructuring, before and after the restructuring, taking into account assets used and risks assumed (Section D.1.2); the economic circumstances of the parties (Section D.1.4) and business strategies (Section D.1.5). In addition, the analysis should be informed by a review of the business reasons for and the expected benefits from the restructuring, including the role of synergies, and the options realistically available to the parties'. The process for setting or testing the ALP in a business restructuring is depicted in para. 8.1.3 of the UN Practical Manual on Transfer Pricing for developing countries (2021).

Some of the reasons reported by businesses for restructuring include the objective of maximizing synergies and economies of scale, streamlining the management of business lines, and improving the efficiency of the supply chain.

An important element of attention relates to those business restructurings that are carried out to achieve a benefit at a group level rather than for each entity of the multinational group. According to the ALP, the arrangement must be beneficial for all of the single entities of the group; therefore, the options realistically available to the parties must be duly analysed together with any compensation payments due for the restructuring:[35]

> To determine whether a business restructuring at arm's length would give rise to a form of compensation, it is then crucial to understand the restructuring. This includes the changes that have taken place, how they have affected the functional analysis of the parties, what the business reasons for and the anticipated benefits from the restructuring are, and what options would have been realistically available to the parties at arm's length.[36]

The existence of a business restructuring and that 'something of value' has been transferred (i.e., functions assets, and/or risks to which a profit potential may be attached and a third party would be willing to pay for) must be demonstrated with an accurate delineation of the transaction. The most accurate valuation methodology should subsequently be identified to compensate the entity affected by the restructuring when it loses a right or asset in relation to the group's business activity.[37]

Finally, the analysis must identify who should bear the costs attached to an indemnification payment.

Indeed, the main difference in the treatment of a business restructuring transaction vs other transaction types is the analysis for profit (or loss) potential. If the transfer of activities, functions, risks, assets and, in general, any object of value is not accompanied by a transfer of profit (loss), the transaction is not a business restructuring. The ALP does not require compensation for a mere decrease in the expectation of an entity's future profits.

---

35. OECD *Transfer Pricing Guidelines for Multinational Enterprises and Tax Administrations*, para. 9.37, Paris (2022).
36. In this respect, the following potential issues should be considered from an exit tax perspective:
    - potential transfer of ongoing concern;
    - potential transfer of specific assets;
    - indemnification for termination or amendment of intercompany agreements; and
    - indemnification for any restructuring costs incurred by the local entity because of the restructuring.
37. Different types of valuation approaches could be ascertained in the literature including but not limited to:
    - cost approaches;
    - flow approaches (e.g., discounted cash flow);
    - mixed approaches (e.g., excess earnings); and
    - market approaches (e.g., multiple, similar transactions).

In a second step, remuneration for the post-restructuring transaction should be identified at market conditions.

When applying the ALP to business restructurings, the question is if the transfer of 'something of value' should be characterized as:

- a standalone asset; or
- computed in the goodwill value (i.e., under the latter circumstances, a transfer of ongoing concern would take place since goodwill cannot be transferred in isolation from the asset to which it is attached).

Over the years, an increased number of restructurings have been driven by sustainability due to the emerging awareness of the need for change.[38] Local regulations (and also incentives) are encouraging ESG investments and developments. Governments often use tax policy to incentivize certain environmentally friendly behaviours such as investment in solar and or wind power or other green technologies. Conversely, governments use tax policy to disincentivize activities that are harmful to the environment, for example, by instituting a carbon tax or a tax on plastics.[39]

An example of a potential business restructuring for environmental purposes (supply chain reorganization) might refer to the change of location of manufacturing units, grouping procurement functions, or the decentralization of logistic hubs, all with the aim to reduce the group's carbon footprint or the consumption of natural resources.

6.2 The Accurate Delineation of the Transaction Concept Is Also Applicable When Dealing with ESG Concepts

Properly applying the ALP requires the 'substance' of the intra-group transactions. Indeed, it is required to examine the actual behaviour of the parties rather than simply pricing a written agreement that might divert from their actual contributions to ensure that MNEs pay a fair amount of taxes where value is actually created. With the accurate delineation concept and the related changes that occurred to the OECD TPG to Chapter I under the Base Erosion and Profit Shifting (BEPS) Project (and also reflected in the UN Practical Manual on TP for developing countries), it is possible to: (i) determine whether a controlled transaction has economic substance through the in-depth steps of the functional and risk analysis referred to as 'accurate delineation of the transaction', and (ii) to disregard transactions lacking economic rationality (keeping in mind, however, that the lack of comparable conditions observable in the free market cannot per se be the reason to disregard transactions as structured).[40]

38. The definition of sustainable development is 'development that meets the needs of the present, without compromising the capacity of future generations'. This definition is included in the World Commission on Environment and Development's 1987 Brundtland report '*Our Common Future*'.
39. J. Coleman, et al., *Transfer Pricing and ESG, Part 1: Public Tax Strategies and Tax Transparency*, 109 Tax Notes International (2023).
40. OECD *Transfer Pricing Guidelines for Multinational Enterprises and Tax Administrations*, para. 9.36, Paris (2022).

The performance of the five-step approach to determine the comparability factors to be identified in the commercial or financial relations between associated enterprises remains the first assessment. When this analysis shows that functions and risks do not adhere to those established in legal agreements, risks and the connected returns should be reallocated to those entities who control and can bear them (i.e., finding the substance of the transaction) to determine the arm's length price.

Figure 6.1 was prepared by HMRC in their Operational Guidance for TP[41] and is of help to illustrate the entire process of accurately delineating the actual transaction to be priced.

Figure 6.1 Flowchart Explaining Accurate Delineation of the Actual Transaction

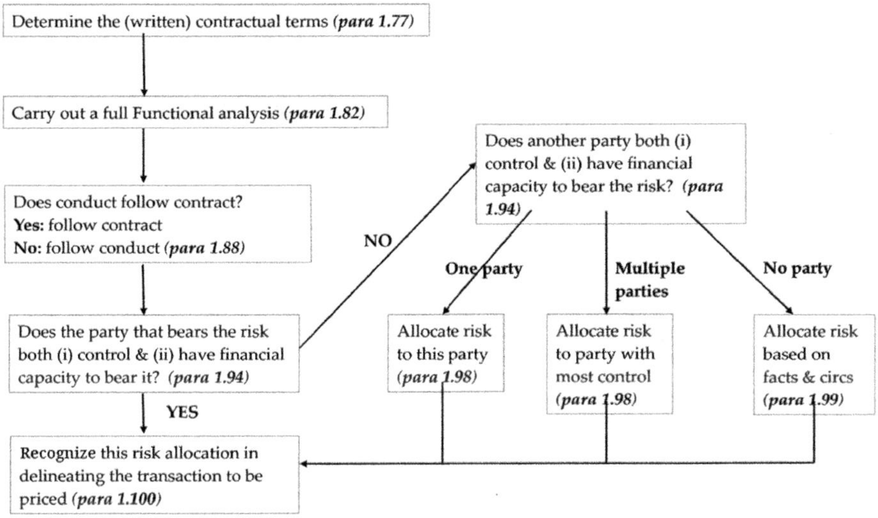

When referring to the concept of 'value creation', it should in fact be considered that functions alone do not determine whether a value has been created; however, the risk-related functional activity (particularly decision-making) for the allocation of profits within the group must be considered.[42] The greater the risk, the greater the remuneration to be expected for an activity. Risk has thus become a central element for the TP analysis, and the OECD TPG, paragraph 1.71 provides a definition that is applicable for authorities and MNEs, i.e., 'the effect of uncertainty on the objectives of the business'. The same definition is reported in paragraph 3.4.4.22 of the UN Practical Manual on TP for developing countries.

41. HMRC, *Transfer Pricing Operational Guidance: Accurate delineation of the actual transaction, Full process* (2024) – HMRC Internal Manual, INTM485024, https://www.gov.uk/hmrc-internal-manuals/international-manual/intm485024.
42. R.S. Collier & I.F. Dykes, *The Virus in the ALP: Critique of the Transfer Pricing Guidance on Risk and Capital in the Light of the COVID-19 Pandemic*, 74 Bull. Intl. Taxn. 12, s. 2.2.1. (2020), Journal Articles & Opinion Pieces IBFD https://doi.org/10.59403/5ec69y.

See paragraph 7 below for further details on the analysis provided by the OECD for contractual risk reallocation and the alignment with economic reality in the ESG context.

7 COMMON TP CONSIDERATIONS WHEN INCORPORATING ESG INITIATIVES

When implementing ESG initiatives in an MNE, the first discussions that arise relate to the allocation of costs, entailing the decision of which is the entity allowed to bear the added expenses and how these should be split based on the ALP. The decision-making process involves conducting an analysis of the effects on each entity's performance and overall operational effectiveness.

In addition, realizing cost savings linked to locations where the multinational group decides to invest because of ESG initiatives can influence the distribution of profits across the value chain in different regions and instigate potential controversies.

Additional impacts on TP policies refer to developing assets (e.g., patents, know-how, brand awareness, or trademarks) tied to sustainable technologies or practices that can complicate the valuation process and require careful assessment of their contribution to the group's overall profitability. Similarly, managing incentives, such as tax breaks or subsidies for green investments, need to be handled to prevent any distortions in TP agreements.

Finally, the way risks are handled within sustainability objectives can impact decisions on TP and necessitate changes.

7.1 Allocation of ESG Costs

The most relevant items when referring to the allocation of costs pursuant to implementing ESG strategies include business restructurings, government incentives, location savings, and managing governance costs.

- The allocation of costs and the exit charges in the case of ESG business restructurings

According to Chapter IX of the OECD TPG, when a change of the business model driven by the achievement of sustainable goals occurs, the allocation of costs among the multinational group entities shall always have to follow functions, risks, and assets used by the group entities.

The ALP requires that profits (and losses) are allocated within MNEs in accordance with the value creation. ESG metrics then require to:

(1) accurately allocate the contribution of the associated enterprises in the value chain; and
(2) select the most appropriate TP method[43] using the correct comparables.[44]

43. Selecting a TP method should be aimed at finding the most appropriate method for a particular case taking into account the respective strengths and weaknesses of the OECD recognized

When a MNE designs an ESG strategy, these are some of the steps it generally takes:

(i) an analysis of the current business model;
(ii) an analysis of local ESG regulations when sustainability or tax transparency is mandatory;
(iii) defining goals based on the above criteria;
(iv) designing the new ESG strategy and definition of the entities to be involved; and
(v) inclusion of ESG criteria in the day-by-day business (from design to actual implementation).

ESG initiatives cannot be evaluated in isolation, but it is required to contextualize the initiatives within the business model and the value drivers. This also applies to the proper allocation of new ESG-driven costs within the group.

In accordance with paragraph 9.13 of the OECD TPG, an accurate functional analysis for a restructuring should comprise a description of the business reasons for – and the expected benefits from – the restructuring.

With reference to points from (i) to (iv), the analysis of the current business model of local regulations and the design of a new ESG strategy should theoretically be managed centrally by the HQ/principal. This is a strategic investment that, in the end, can also generate shareholder profits. The allocation of costs is, by definition, a key element for complying with the ALP. According to the ALP, costs must be sustained by those who are able to control them. As a consequence, if the decision to establish an ESG strategy is driven by shareholders, local operating entities in a typical principal structure should not be impacted by such costs. Even if the benefit of being ESG compliant embraces all of the entities, the limited-risk entities of the group might not have started a transition to ESG compliance and sustained similar costs if not required to do so by the local laws. In this type of business model, potential economic benefits (when available) deriving from implementing ESG policies are generally achieved by the principal only, while local entities always register routine returns. Costs should be

methods. In this respect, the OECD TPG refers to the 'traditional transaction methods' (i.e., comparable uncontrolled price method, resale price method, and cost-plus method) and to the 'transactional profit methods' (i.e., TNMM and transactional profit split method). In addition, *see* Ch. 4 of the UN Practical manual on Transfer Pricing for an explanation of TP methods and the selection of a suitable method.

44. Identifying the correct comparables impacts the efficacy of external benchmarking studies, particularly when an internal comparison is impractical. When conducting benchmarking studies to assess the arm's length price or margin achieved by a tested party obligated to incur costs for ESG compliance, a comprehensive analysis must consider that the pool of potential comparable companies may include entities with lower cost structures due to the non-adoption of ESG policies. Transactions that might have been deemed comparable under different circumstances may now be deemed non-comparable because one transaction involves ESG investments while the other does not. Adjustments to profitability at the tested party or comparable level may consequently be necessary.

allocated to the party that actually took the decision that effectuated the costs, assuming contractual or factual risks.[45]

ESG costs related to strategy, training, and restructurings but also related to point (v) above may be pushed down to local entities only if it is possible to demonstrate that the latter received tangible benefits. For example, when compliance with ESG standards derives from local regulations, local entities should be requested to sustain part of the costs in the first step. Indeed, in terms of options realistically available to the parties, the following scenarios might be considered:

- taking no actions and refusing to sustain the costs; or
- sustaining the necessary ESG costs, i.e., the part of the overall costs borne by the group to adapt the business model that is compliant with the ESG.

Scenario 1 does not seem to be workable as the entity could face potential litigation costs from local regulatory bodies due to non-compliance with local environmental standards. In addition, the group might decide to exclude the entity from intra-group transactions if it does not comply with local regulations. In such a situation, whether the multinational group should relocate the local entity to another state incites the argument that the loss of profit potential for and the consequent exit charge to the company's residence state is approximately zero.

This non-compliance might also lead to negative impacts on the entity's reputation and a loss of competitive position in the market. This is particularly true when direct competitors have already initiated an ESG transition, taking into account the heightened awareness of ESG aspects by final customers in the country or in the specific market where it operates.

When local entities face extraordinary costs that cannot be passed on to customers, and they incur a loss, the key consideration for MNEs is how to justify and support it, especially when the local entity is characterized as 'routine' and 'low risk'. While routine companies are generally not expected to sustain losses over an extended period, a thorough case-by-case analysis is necessary.[46] Comparisons with the practices of independent entities in the open market are essential; however, in the free market, it would typically refrain from continual loss-generating activities unless reasonable expectations of future profits exist. However, in the context of an ESG transition, it becomes plausible for the routine entity to incur a loss, particularly when options realistically available indicate that the local entity stands to benefit from the restructuring, making it a justifiable outcome. Its intra-group remuneration should then not be adjusted accordingly.[47]

45. I. Burgstaller, *ESG Transformation and Transfer Pricing Implications*, International Transfer Pricing Journal, IBFD (2022) https://doi.org/10.59403/sf1x26.
46. OECD *Transfer Pricing Guidelines for Multinational Enterprises and Tax Administrations*, para. 3.64, Paris (2022).
47. Another case might relate to the decision taken by the principal to increase the salaries of workers of manufacturing entities across the group in a comprehensive strategy aimed at investing more in people and the workforce. If the TP policy of the group provides that manufacturing entities are remunerated according to a cost-plus mechanism, nothing happens in terms of remuneration for the routine companies. This is because the additional costs for

Figure 6.2 provides an example of the allocation of costs within a multinational group embracing a change in the business model and implementing ESG strategies.

Figure 6.2 ESG and Government Incentives

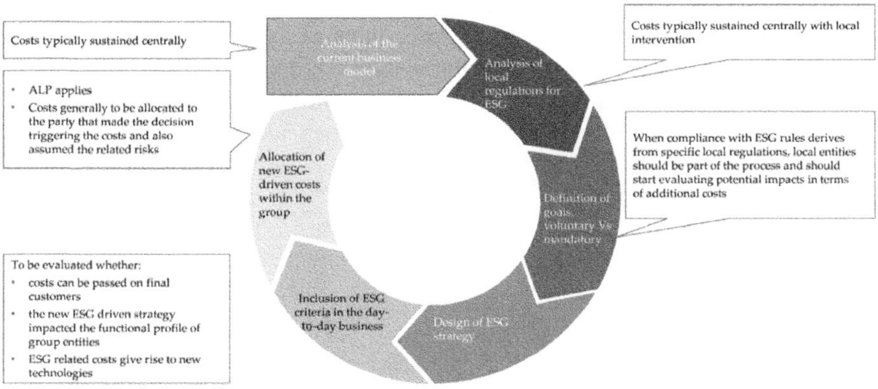

Given states' attention to ESG aspects, it can happen that local entities receive grants and incentives (tax relief, loan guarantees, etc.) from the government for their ESG transition. In this case, MNEs will be requested to analyse the specific characteristics of government assistance and if this can have a material impact on the accurately delineated controlled transaction. Such grants and incentives should theoretically not be transferred to other group companies and should remain with the company actually receiving the benefit, especially in cases when the local entities sustain the costs of implementing an ESG strategy.[48]

– Location Savings

International transfer (mis)prices might theoretically be used to reduce the share of profits allocated to local partners or the legal or contractual share of profit to workers; it might also reduce the rewards to local managers. Therefore, multinational groups should carefully consider the adoption of a proper policy that acknowledges social impacts.[49]

salaries will be included in the cost base subject to recharge (plus the markup) to the principal which will ultimately sustain the additional costs (extra profit reduces). On the contrary, should the decision to increase the salary be taken by the local entity (which also sustains the related risks), a more detailed analysis of the group TP policy is advisable with a potential revision to be done in order to reflect the decision taken by the manufacturing company that will likely sustain the extra costs without recharging them to the principal.

48. A parallelism on this can be done reading the OECD, *Guidance on the Transfer Pricing Implications of the COVID-19 Pandemic*, Paris (2020).

49. On this topic, *see* R. Paz-Vega, *Subsidiary Social Performance and Viability: The Role of International Transfer Pricing*, 16 Proceedings of the International Association for Business and Society (2005) and L. Knowles & I. Mathur, *International Transfer Pricing Objectives*, 11 Managerial Finance (1985) https://doi.org/10.1108/eb013546.

This is particularly true when multinationals operate with their subsidiaries in developing countries where, contrary to countries where CSR has led to improved standards in labour, environmental practices, and human rights, there is an apparent reduction of CSR in improving corporate conduct in the absence of effective and extensive government regulations.[50]

A company embracing ESG principles should consider the TP impacts deriving from the redistribution of wealth in countries where it operates, especially in those cases in which it is actually present in non-developed countries. It is quite common for multinationals to have operations in emerging countries; the presence of controlled entities there might have impacts on what is known as 'location savings'.

The TPG do not provide a formal definition of location savings. However, they focus on two different types:

(1) location savings arising from cost savings due to the difference in the costs of operations (e.g., access to a labour market with lower costs) if compared to a high-cost jurisdiction; and
(2) other features of the local markets, such as the access to a market that may allow the application of a premium price to goods sold (e.g., limited degree of competition, growth of the economy, increased demand for products, etc.) or access to growing markets that allows gaining a competitive advantage.

Only the net location savings can give rise to 'extra profit' that might derive from the relocation of certain activities in the value chain from a high-cost jurisdiction to a low-cost jurisdiction. However, the TPG do not offer instructions on how to split this profit when there are no comparable companies available (on the contrary, when comparable companies are available, reference should be made to what occurs in the free market for properly compensating parties). The TPG state that location savings are not intangibles but primarily a comparability adjustment issue. Indeed, the split of location savings among group companies under the ALP should always consider functions, risks, and assets.

However, multinationals operating in developing countries and benefitting from low-cost skilled manpower or raw materials might even decide to enhance an ESG strategy focusing on the letter 'S' to gain the economic benefit for the developing countries, thus sustaining costs as if it was operating in a high-cost jurisdiction.[51]

50. S.A. Asongu, J.I. Uduji & E.N. Okolo-Obasi, *Transfer Pricing and Corporate Social Responsibility: Arguments, Views and Agenda* (2019).
51. However, it is important to mention that companies should consider how this might impact the risk of double taxation in the event that the tax authority of the developed country challenges the attribution of the entire location saving to the developing country. In this regard, further developments and inputs at the OECD and the UN level would be welcomed. Additionally, local tax authorities might evaluate the appropriateness of identifying certain comparability adjustments to reflect the economic effect of implementing ESG strategies, e.g., during APA negotiations or in the case of tax audits.

Social reporting may imply that multinationals must review and amend their TP policy in order to make it ESG compliant, especially for those groups operating in developing countries.

– Governance costs

Meeting reporting obligations and participating in cooperative compliance programs entail associated costs to be borne. From a TP perspective, the question concerns how (and if) such costs should be recharged to the MNE's various entities.

Some examples of reporting activities that generate costs for the group are preparing detailed ESG information and key performance indicators (KPIs) for funding purposes (e.g., bank financing, etc.), stakeholder communication regarding the ESG, ESG branding projects and communication measures, preparing (public) CbCR, etc.

The OECD TPG do not address ESG items. Therefore, the sole reference available and to which there should be adherence is the ALP. Only after having analysed the functions performed, risks assumed, and assets employed by the parties involved and the results of the benefits test for the services are the proper instruments available to decide whether an allocation of costs is appropriate under the ALP. It might be investigated whether the reporting activities provide a benefit or an expected benefit to all of the group members (that would be willing to pay for it if they were independent enterprises) or only to the parent company that performs the activity solely because of its ownership interest in one or more other group members. The question is if costs can be passed on to the controlling entities or, on the contrary, if they fall within the definition of 'shareholder activity', i.e., activities that cannot be considered to be an intra-group service?[52]

At the same time, does the involvement in compliance programmes, such as an APA, yield benefits for all participating companies that extend beyond just their shareholders? In this context, it seems logical that costs associated with participating in such programs are to be borne locally by the involved companies. The certainty established through an APA also extends to the members of the company's board of directors. By adhering to such compliance programs, they can avoid penalties (in certain countries also criminal) in the event of tax adjustments.

– Intercompany Recharge of ESG Costs: a 'safe harbour' proposal

Taking a holistic view, as previously discussed, the outcome of implementing ESG-driven strategies tends to generally result in additional costs and burdens for multinationals rather than immediate profit returns. They are requested to incur significant costs that can potentially pose tax deduction risks, especially in those cases when costs are genuinely distributed among local entities within the group. This is especially pertinent when the parent company provides 'management services' in the ESG field to controlled entities. Under the general rules regarding intra-group services, determining whether an intra-group service has been provided (i.e., it creates a benefit for the recipient and, thus, it is tax deductible) involves assessing if the activity adds economic

52. OECD *Transfer Pricing Guidelines for Multinational Enterprises and Tax Administrations*, para. 7.9, Paris (2022).

or commercial value to a group member's business position.[53] This evaluation considers whether an independent company in similar circumstances would pay for such a service if provided by another independent entity or would handle the task internally. If the activity is not of this nature, it typically does not qualify as an intra-group service under the ALP.

Given the investment-intensive nature of ESG initiatives, it cannot be assumed that similar services meet the 'benefits test' required by the ALP. As discussed in earlier sections, establishing an ESG-focused strategy involves a long-term perspective that is often set by the parent company and may not always align with the tax priorities of subsidiaries. The advantages of implementing ESG principles may materialize over years with immediate benefits not readily measurable. In such scenarios, a 'safe harbour' concept should be implemented to govern the amount and types of ESG expenses immediately eligible for tax deductions. It is crucial that authentic ESG-related costs are always identifiable and allocable within this framework. This may provide adequate assurance both in the parent company's state and that of the subsidiaries. If there is no safe harbour:

- local tax offices of the parent company state might argue that costs should have been recharged; while
- local tax offices of the subsidiaries' state might contend that costs recharged by the parent company are not deductible.

7.2 ESG and the Potential Creation of New Intangibles: The TP Treatment

An ESG transition may lead to the emergence of new intra-group transactions or alterations in the existing TP model. Assuming a local entity performed investments such as automatization or creating new technologies or intellectual properties (IPs) that generally generated a more efficient manufacturing process that reflects in a lower cost of products, potential future extra profit should remain with this local entity. For example, in the event that a routine manufacturer develops a modern new technology that effectively addresses environmental challenges and might become precious and usable for other group entities, the new intangible good (e.g., a patent, know-how, etc.) must be remunerated separately.

Considering how MNEs are generally structured (especially those adopting a principal model), this can be seen as an extreme scenario that might be seen in future years. ESG investments can indeed have implications on the functional profile of group companies, and new transactions might emerge. The word 'intangible' is intended to address something that is not a physical or a financial asset that is capable of being owned or controlled for use in commercial activities and whose use or transfer would be compensated had it occurred in a transaction between independent parties in

53. OECD, *Transfer Pricing Guidelines for Multinational Enterprises and Tax Administrations*, para. 7.6, Paris (2022).

comparable circumstances.[54] The actual focus of the definition contained within the OECD and UN Guidelines thus seems to be on the circumstance that it is possible to identify an agreed remuneration between independent parties in similar situations.

An ESG transition can then reveal scenarios wherein a multinational group, particularly when one of its routine entities has developed, enhanced, maintained, protected, and exploited (DEMPE) a new ESG-related intangible, will have to revise the intra-group remuneration structure. This reassessment might involve a shift from a one-sided method (cost-plus mechanism or resale price margin method or, in case of using net margins, a transactional net margin method (TNMM)) to a two-sided method (profit split) or to another mechanism such as concluding new royalty intercompany agreements,[55] setting cost contribution arrangements, and similar measures.

Another question that might arise is if an ESG per se can be considered an intangible asset and, in this case, how this – and its economic benefit, if any – should be allocated among the group companies, i.e., would the parent company be the legal owner or, rather, would all group companies that participated in the development of the ESG strategies be entitled to retain a quota of that IP?

Implementing ESG-driven policies by an MNE is reflected in the economic circumstance and is to be considered when performing the comparability analysis.

Unlike traditional intangible assets that can be bought, sold, or licensed independently, ESG practices are deeply ingrained within the fabric of a group's operations. Consequently, the value derived from ESG initiatives is not easily separated from the overall business operations and does not possess standalone value for external entities in the same way as patents, trademarks, or brands. Thus, the ESG hardly qualifies as an intangible. In contrast to tangible or easily identifiable intangibles, the value derived from ESG initiatives lies more in their integration within the business model and their contribution to long-term sustainability rather than their transferability as standalone assets.

Moreover, the OECD has a clear vision of what constitutes an intangible and has included among this category (not an exhaustive list) patents, know-how, trademarks, brands and trade names, licenses and similar, goodwill, etc., therefore, excluding group synergies, market-specific characteristics, etc.[56]

Nonetheless, the development of ESG policies within the multinational group might be treated as 'group synergies'. These refer to the phenomenon where interaction or cooperation among entities produces a combined effect greater than the sum of their separate effects. By definition, synergies generally exist within multinational groups, while the application of the ALP requires treating companies of the same group

54. OECD *Transfer Pricing Guidelines for Multinational Enterprises and Tax Administrations*, para. 6.6, Paris (2022) & *Practical Manual on Transfer Pricing*, Ch. 6, para. 6.2 (2021).
55. It has yet to be defined how these know-how/new patents can be actually remunerated in practice because, in a typical royalty model, usual comparable contracts obtained from databases are generally outdated and, of course, do not reflect the changes in the business.
56. According to what is reported in the UN Practical Handbook on Transfer Pricing (2021), 'intangibles are assets that have no physical existence, but whose value depends on the legal rights of the owner. Examples of intangibles are intellectual property such as patents, copyrights and trademarks'.

as operating separately and independently from each other. Consequently, identifying an arm's length remuneration for synergies appears difficult. As mentioned by L. Angiolilli, who cites G. Marozzi,[57] '[t]he irony is that although the arm's length principle standard was designed to establish the tax base of multinational groups, multinational groups were created to act outside the arm's length standard and benefit from economies of scales and synergies'.[58]

The OECD TPG approach the group synergies in Chapter I, subchapter D.8. and distinguish between: (i) those giving rise to incidental benefits attributable solely to the fact that an enterprise is part of a larger MNE group in the absence of deliberate concerted actions or transactions leading to that benefit, and (ii) synergistic benefits that may arise because of deliberate concerted group actions 'giving an MNE group a material, clearly identifiable structural advantage or disadvantage in the marketplace over market participants that are not part of an MNE group and that are involved in comparable transactions'.[59] In general, such benefits should be shared among group companies in proportion to the efforts and contributions of each company. As previously mentioned, also Chapter VI of the OECD TPG ('Special considerations for intangibles') briefly discusses the concept of group synergies within the broader concept of intangibles, and paragraph 6.30 specifies that 'as they are not owned or controlled by an enterprise, they are not intangibles within the meaning of Section A.1'.

As previously described when detailing the allocation of costs among the group companies, also the distribution of any extra profit that is exploited from implementing ESG strategies must take into account the contribution of the parties in developing the new policies. Any passive associations (e.g., if implementing ESG policies derives from activities carried out by the parent company alone with no local intervention) do not generate specific compensation for local group companies. On the contrary, synergetic efforts consequent to deliberated group actions that generate a surplus in profits should be divided according to the actual contributions of each party; in general terms, the comparable uncontrolled method[60] (CUP) or a two-sided methodology (profit split) appear to be the most appropriate methods.

---

57. R. Marozzi Gregorio, *Presos de transferencia: Arm's length e praticabilitade*, IBDT/Editoria Quartier Latin 51 (2011).
58. L. Angiolilli, *Limiting Base Erosion by Improving Transfer Pricing Rules on Group Synergies for Multinational Enterprises, in Limiting Base Erosion, Series on Intl. Tax* 467 (E. Pinetz & E. Schaffner eds., Linde, 2017), cited by S. Maury, *Applying the Arm's Length Principle to Group Synergies*, International Transfer Pricing Journal, IBFD (July/August 2020) https://doi.org/10.59403/1t2ds35.
59. OECD *Transfer Pricing Guidelines for Multinational Enterprises and Tax Administrations*, para. 1.179, Paris (2022). The UN Practical Manual on Transfer Pricing (2021), in Ch. 2, explains that 'MNE groups are able to minimize their costs through their integration economies, which are not available to domestic firms. Such group synergies can arise, for example, as a result of streamlined management, elimination of costly duplication of effort, economies of scale, integrated systems, purchasing or borrowing power.'
60. Given the nature of the group synergies that is typical of multinational groups, availability of appropriate comparables might be difficult.

7.3 ESG Restructurings and the Control over Risks

The path to an ESG transition for multinational groups additionally shows *new risks* that must be carefully evaluated in the group value chain that imply a revision of the historic functions, risk and asset allocation for applying the TP methods, and related remuneration.[61]

As mentioned in paragraph 6.2, Actions 8-10 of the BEPS Project, then converged with the TPG (*see* paragraphs 1.71-1.106), incorporated further guidance for examining risks that is an essential component of a comparability analysis. As the premise is that increased risk should be compensated by a rise in anticipated returns, it is crucial to identify the risks undertaken, the functions associated with assuming or being affected by them, and the specific party or parties assuming them. Risk assumption is defined as 'taking on the upside and downside consequences of the risk with the result that the party assuming the risk will bear the financial and other consequences if the risk materializes'.[62] The detailed guidance on risks does not imply that they become more important than functions and assets, but it was prepared given the practical difficulties introduced by them. The guidelines provide a six-step framework for analysing risks, specifically:

(1) identifying economically significant risks with specificity;
(2) determining contractual assumption of the specific risks;
(3) performing a functional analysis in relation to risks (which enterprise or enterprises perform control functions and risk mitigation functions, which of them encounter upside or downside consequences of risk outcomes, and which of them have the financial capacity to assume the risk);
(4) determining whether the contractual assumption of risk aligns with the conduct of the parties and other facts;
(5) allocating the risk; and
(6) pricing the accurately delineated transaction, taking into account the financial and other consequences of risk assumption and appropriately compensating risk management functions.

As seen for the costs, group companies that bear significant risks pursuant to changes in the value chain due to implementing an ESG policy, having control over them, and having the financial capacity to sustain them might be remunerated accordingly. This can also imply revising the previous TP policy and selecting different methodologies in order to comply with the ALP.

61. I. Burgstaller, *ESG Transformation and Transfer Pricing Implications*, International Transfer Pricing Journal, IBFD (2022) https://doi.org/10.59403/sf1x26.
62. OECD *Transfer Pricing Guidelines for Multinational Enterprises and Tax Administrations*, para. 1.63, Paris (2022).

8 CONCLUSIONS AND TAKEAWAYS

The ESG and TP are actually more interconnected than expected. Notwithstanding that they follow different paths and have different approaches, they intersect at some point, and the impacts of ESG strategies must be taken into account when MNEs define their TP policies.

In conclusion:

- The ESG is not a new phenomenon, but it encapsulates a collection of longstanding ethical and sustainable business practices. Ethical codes often encompass principles such as fair labour practices, anti-corruption measures, and community engagement initiatives. By leveraging existing tools while expanding the scope to incorporate ethical considerations, MNEs can ensure that their TP practices not only comply with regulatory requirements but also uphold their commitment to sustainability and ethical business conduct. Not being a new phenomenon, each area of the ESG policies can be handled from a TP perspective based on traditional tools and concepts.
- Since tax authorities or international bodies (e.g., OECD, UN) have not addressed how ESG pillars have influenced TP operations thus far, companies are encouraged to rely on existing tools to evaluate the qualitative and quantitative effects of ESG factors on TP. The integration is vital as it can promote sustainability, socially responsible business practices, risk management, enhanced reputation, improved financial performance, regulatory compliance, and contribute to a more sustainable world.
- The impact of the ESG on TP can be far-reaching, affecting corporate structures, supply chain choices, and profit allocation. Most of the times, especially when pursuing environmental and social goals, it may lead to business restructurings that need to be analysed relying on the ALP. However, ensuring a fair application of TP rules might be difficult. Specific ESG TP adjustments will then be requested, and this will be one of the challenges MNEs and tax authorities across the globe will have to face in the coming years.
- In adopting ESG-driven strategies, multinationals often encounter increased expenses and operational complexities rather than immediate financial gains. Allocation of costs is one of the most relevant issues in an ESG TP analysis. In accordance with the ALP, costs for establishing or complying with ESG requirements should always be borne by entities who control them, who made the decision effectuating the costs, and who assumed the related risks. Nevertheless, when thinking about ESG fee recharges across group companies, MNEs might face tax deductibility risks that necessitate thorough assessments when lacking any dedicated 'safe harbour' rule. Such a proposed framework would ensure that genuine ESG-related expenditures are consistently considered for allocation, even in cases when the immediate benefits for the paying entity are not readily apparent.
- The integration of ESG strategies can influence merger and acquisition (M&A) transactions in both the case of 'business restructurings' within the same

corporate group and also when they occur with external entities. ESG considerations could potentially lead to a higher price in a deal, although the independent assessment of such an impact can be challenging. Consequently, it would be difficult to use this value as a potential comparable for TP purposes. It is indeed anticipated that the acquisition price already reflects any additional value derived from ESG factors, thus making it complex to quantify and compare them separately.

- The ESG cannot be included within the concept of intangibles as defined by the OECD TPG but rather impacts the economic conditions when performing a comparability analysis in accordance with the ALP. The development of ESG policies within the multinational group might be treated as 'group synergies', which, in the case of deliberate concerted group actions, imply sharing the benefit - if existing and measurable - among the group companies that actively participated in enhancing the new policies.

CHAPTER 7

Transfer Pricing and New Technologies

Niklas Schwemin & Alexandra Jaszczuk

1 INTRODUCTION

Phrases like 'Data is the new oil'[1] or 'the world's most valuable resource is no longer oil, but data'[2] have been used extensively over the past years and indicate data's value in the twenty-first century. An important expansion to the first statement above is that 'like oil, data is valuable, but if unrefined it cannot really be used'.[3] In-house transfer pricing (TP) professionals of multinational enterprises (MNEs) are struggling to aggregate the significant amount of data that is derived during companies' daily routines that are indispensable for fulfilling their job objectives or are considering some technology solutions to facilitate these goals.

Two of the most important decisions that must be made in the field of operational TP relate to transfer price setting in advance of a fiscal year (FY) and transfer price adjustments during the same, respectively. The goal is to generate arm's length results that are properly documented and that can easily be defended during tax audits around the world. Data that are typically needed include revenue and cost information – from both planning and actual perspectives and generally segmented by transaction.[4] Additional data that is essential for the TP function include information on internal comparables, product revenue shares, ownership structures, employees, and more.

Table 7.1 provides a non-exhaustive overview of typical *TP data* required for various documentation purposes and selected TP controlling or audit needs.[5]

Table 7.1 Transfer Pricing Data Overview[6]

Documents Using Data	*Data Name*	*Reference*
Country-by-country reporting (CbCR)	Revenues per entity (as defined by CbCR guidelines)	section 3.4
	Tax paid on cash basis (as defined by CbCR guidelines)	section 3.4
	Income Tax Accrued – Current Year (as defined by CbCR guidelines)	section 3.4

1. C. Humby (British mathematician), University of Sheffield (2006), https://www.sheffield.ac.uk/dcs/people/academic-visitors/clive-humby (last accessed 3 June 2024).
2. The Economist, Leaders, Regulating the internet giants (6 May 2017), https://www.economist.com/leaders/2017/05/06/the-worlds-most-valuable-resource-is-no-longer-oil-but-data (last accessed 3 June 2024).
3. M. Palmer, *ANA Marketing Maestros* (3 November 2006).
4. OECD (2022), *OECD Transfer Pricing Guidelines for multinational enterprises and Tax Administrations*, Ch. 3, Art. 3.1-3.9, 152.
5. References in the table indicate the section in this article where the handling of the data is discussed in detail.
6. The data mentioned are referring to the requirements typically observed during TP audits when respective documents are scrutinized. Embedding these data into the documents right from the beginning can be helpful for supporting the defence line during the TP audit.

Documents Using Data	*Data Name*	*Reference*
CbCR + Master File	Consolidated Financial Statements – numeric data	
	Consolidated Financial Statements – notes to embed into CbCR	section 3.4
Local File + Master File + CbCR	Detailed address data, ownership, and shareholding data	
	Functional profiles as defined in Table 2 of CbCR	section 3.3
	Number of employees (as defined by CbCR guidelines)	section 3.4
Master File	Group financing sources – external loans per entity (including interest rates, currencies, and maturity)	
	Group intercompany financing – identification of any member of the MNE group financing other MNE entities and respective financing arrangements	
	Business sector analysis – competitors, key players, CAGR, etc., versus group performance (ideally compliant with the group consolidated financial statement and auditors report)	section 3.2
	Aggregated values of transaction types – per entity, per total in group	section 2.1
	TP policy – table overview of implemented intercompany TP policy versus realized profitability per transaction type (based on actual numbers)	
	Group intangibles with values aggregated per transaction type and owner	
Local File	Transactional data reconciled with statutory generally accepted accounting principles (GAAP), general ledger account entries in local currency and the business partner currency, and ideally reconciled with the MNE group GAAP (based on which CbCR is prepared)	section 2.1
	Internal comparables (i.e., uncontrolled sales or purchase transactions with respective profitability analysis)	
	Profit-/Loss (P&L) segmentation, including the aggregated values per intercompany transaction type	section 2.1
	Benchmark studies' results	section 2.4
TP Audit + Local File	Overview of the benchmark studies' results versus realized profit level indicators (PLIs)	section 2.3

Documents Using Data	*Data Name*	*Reference*
TP Controlling	Forecasted transactional values per entity, including P&L segmentation	
	Tax impact per country/ entity based on actual figures or forecasted data	
	Non-deductible costs per entity	
	Year-end adjustments calculation per transaction type and entity	

Source: greenfield finance.

The potential that lies in such data is certainly not being fully achieved. Raw data is seldom used for TP due to the inability to pull the required information from one reliable source. TP information is often spread throughout the entire group, various enterprise resource planning (ERP), or IT-systems, and its collection is very time-consuming. The fact that a multitude of sources is required to provide all required data comes at the expense of additional time needed for reconciling it. Often, manual cleaning and structuring tasks are required to enable TP teams to utilize the data and thus achieve their goal of arm's length results.

Figure 7.1 indicates the difficult data streams that must be managed by TP practitioners, including examples of commonly seen ERP or IT-systems.

Figure 7.1 Transfer Pricing Data Streams

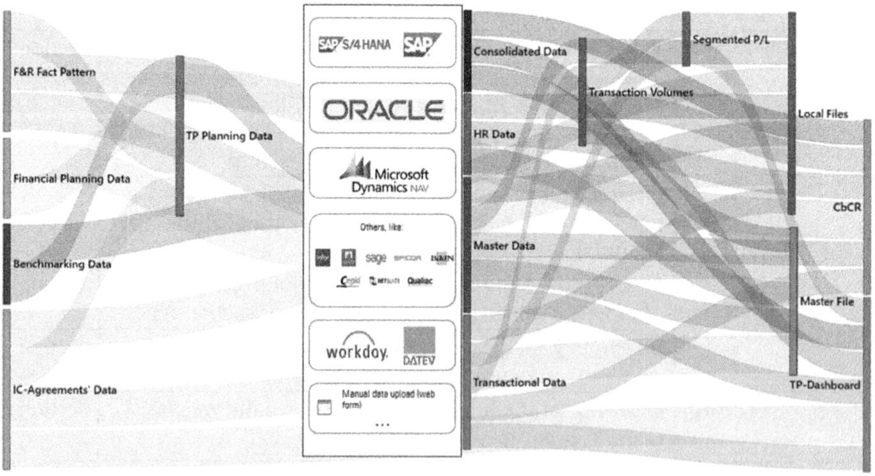

While there are many software tools available to support, e.g., preparing the local file, the CbCR or operational TP challenges, the critical aspects always entail the availability and quality of the data needed by the tools and the connectivity of the different data sources to them. If these are given, internal and external solutions can provide reliable support for the typical TP tasks within an MNE.

In principle, the tools available in the market can be split into three categories (*see* Table 7.2).

Table 7.2 Selected Examples of Automated Solutions Providing Crucial TP Functionalities

Data Consumer	*Data Provider*	*Data Calculator*
TP Documentation tools, such as	**TP Benchmarking tools, such as**	**Tools supporting Operational TP, such as**
Aibidia	Zanders Group	exa OTP
Tpdoc	tpbenchmark	Optravis
WTS TP manager	ai arm's length	Aibidia
Exactera	Smart Zebra	Longview

This chapter provides examples of tools, technologies, and viable tricks that can be implemented to address various challenges related to daily TP in-house work. It shows what standardizations and simplifications are possible when using meaningful data. By doing this, the chapter describes bits and pieces that can help to construct an end-to-end approach for TP tasks. In the end, impetus is given to future potentials in TP.

2 TP OPERATION

2.1 TP Matrix

The cornerstone of TP data is identifying the intercompany transactions to be documented. Taking the viewpoint of one single MNE group company, this includes evaluating transaction partners for the reporting period and determining the type of transactions (transaction type) concluded with them. The questions that must be answered are: 'with whom?', 'what kind?', and 'how much?'. The answers can be provided in the form of a 'transaction matrix' (*see* Table 7.3).

Table 7.3 Transaction Matrix for MNE Group Company

Transaction Type	*Partner A (EUR)*	*Partner B (EUR)*	*Partner C (EUR)*	*Partner D (EUR)*	*Partner E (EUR)*	*Total (EUR)*
Contract R&D	-5,000,000	-7,500,000				**-12,500,000**
Product Sales			50,000,000	35,000,000	30,000,000	**115,000,000**

Transaction Type	*Partner A (EUR)*	*Partner B (EUR)*	*Partner C (EUR)*	*Partner D (EUR)*	*Partner E (EUR)*	*Total (EUR)*
Services	350,000	400,000	700,000	600,000	550,000	**2,600,000**

Source: greenfield finance.

The importance of the transaction matrix – and thereby of the data required to compose it – is evident. Not only does it serve as the core of the TP documentation but it also summarizes the values that will need to be further explained and validated against the arm's length principle (ALP). It will also be used by auditors to identify significant transactions. Tax authorities increasingly demand access to the full set of accounting data and apply analytic tools themselves to identify focus topics for their audits. Thus, it becomes increasingly important to ensure that the TP documentation does not omit transactions or that it shows incomplete transaction volumes. Another benefit of the data-based transaction matrix is the MNE group's ability to align transaction volumes between the transaction partners and, in doing so, increase the quality and reliability of the TP documentation (i.e., the local files, master files, and CbCRs).

A prerequisite for a correct transaction matrix is the structured and uniform handling of data. MNE groups create numerous transaction data,[7] and the challenge is to identify the data sets that answer the previously mentioned three questions.

ERP data is made available in the form of data tables. To answer the three questions above, it is therefore necessary to know what tables and what data fields in the respective tables display the relevant information. These depend on the individual setup of the MNE group's ERP architecture and must thus be evaluated on a case-by-case basis. A basic problem in this regard is that the information is often dispersed over several tables. Consequently, it is necessary to link the details of the tables in a way that dataset 1 can be enriched with information from dataset 2, as only the combination of both will provide the answer that is sought. For instance, transaction data[8] includes information about the trading partner by referring to the partner company code.[9] It also includes information about the account[10] that is used when making an accounting entry. The partner company code and the account, however, are referred to as numbers within the transaction data. Thus, to determine the name of the transaction partner or of the account used, it is necessary to link this information to tables[11] other than the transaction data itself.

7. Transaction data is understood to represent the actual business activities capturing the specific details of an operation versus master data that provides stable, foundational data.
8. In SAP, transaction data is included in the table 'Belegsegment' – technical name 'BSEG'; or in SAP S/4HANA in the 'Universal Journal' – technical name 'ACDOCA'.
9. SAP technical name 'VBUND'.
10. SAP technical name 'HKONT'.
11. Table 'T880' includes the global company data; table 'SKA1' includes the general ledger account master.

To build an automated transaction matrix, it is therefore necessary to link all relevant tables that contain required data with each other. This data model will always be an individual combination of the ERP tables for each MNE group. Figure 7.2 provides an example of a data model for a transaction matrix.

Figure 7.2 Example Data Model

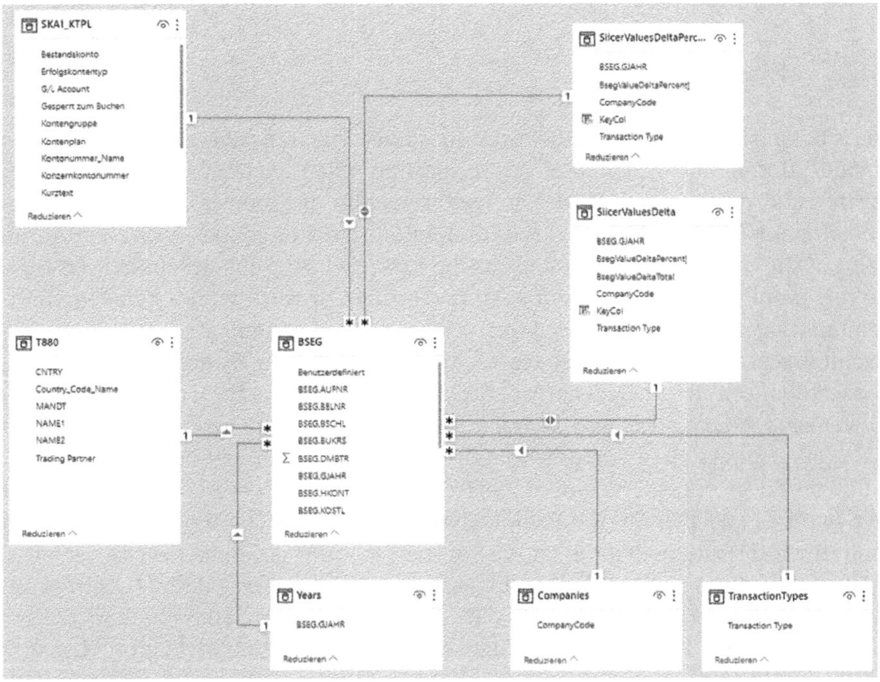

Source: greenfield finance.

The individual data model must be composed in a way that the data linked with each other provide answers to the three questions. Hence, the first step is ascertaining what data points contain the information required.

2.1.1 With Whom?

Ideally, the reporting MNE group company records transaction data in a manner that provides the partner company code for each relevant accounting entry. That code is generally used for consolidation purposes to identify the intercompany transactions and the partners involved. It serves as a tag for these accounting entries. Thus, concerning the transaction matrix, further data analyses can be limited to such entries that refer to a partner company code as these are related to intercompany transactions.

An alternative but more complex way to identify the intercompany transaction partners is to search for specific and known MNE group debtors/creditors in the data that are in countries other than that of the reporting entity. This is an enormous challenge for MNE groups with hundreds of group companies, and the risk remains that some of them are overlooked. To reduce risks related to identifying transactions and the partners involved, it is therefore important for TP managers to become involved in ERP projects and to frame their own demands (i.e., the mandatory use of the partner company code) that will help simplify and improve TP practices.[12]

2.1.2 What Kind?

This is the most difficult out of the three questions. The transaction data itself does not provide information on whether an accounting entry relates to, e.g., the contract research and development (R&D) activity, the sales of products, or certain types of intercompany services; thus, helpful information must be found elsewhere. An indication of the transaction concerned can be extracted from the accounts used for the entry. It would be desirable from a TP perspective to work with a detailed chart of accounts that assigns a dedicated account to each intercompany transaction of the MNE group. If an account is used for an entry, it will then be distinct what transaction is concerned. Unfortunately, charts of accounts that have the level of detail that would be necessary to provide these benefits for TP purposes are rarely seen in practice. Charts of accounts often comprise hundreds of them, even without consideration of additional TP accounts. The aim of the accounting department is, therefore, to reduce their number and thereby the complexity of the daily accounting operations. As a result, the information about what type of transaction was conducted can usually not be taken from the accounts alone, and additional tags are needed. Cost centres, profit centres, work breakdown structure (WBS) elements,[13] or material numbers are some examples of these. They must be defined individually for each MNE group because it depends on the disposed use-concept for these elements. Alignment between the TP and controlling departments is indispensable.

In SAP, there is another possibility to mark transactions for the purpose of TP. It allows using a customized two-digit field as a 'tax tag'. Users can apply this function for TP and define their own nomenclature that provides a specific two-digit code for each group transaction. This is very similar to the tax codes used for value-added tax (VAT) purposes.

Different solutions for creating and identifying data bearing information about what types of transactions a certain accounting entry belongs to are available. An alignment between TP, accounting, and controlling is necessary to build an individual concept that is harmonized with the needs of all stakeholders. Section 6, 'Impulses and

12. Currently, many MNE groups are initiating projects to move their ERP system to the new SAP S/4HANA. This opportunity should not be missed by TP departments for becoming involved from the early beginning.
13. A WBS element is a cost objective in SAP that collects expenses and revenues related to a project.

Conclusion', examines another idea for identifying intercompany transactions considering the current discussions around 'Value-added tax in the Digital Age' (ViDA).

2.1.3 *How Much?*

Identifying the volume of a transaction is rather uncritical. The transaction data in the ERP system provide the amount concerned for every entry. The reporting solution for the transaction matrix sums up the amounts by transaction type and by partner. It is usually also possible to report the volumes in different currencies if the ERP system allows it.

2.1.4 *Automated Transaction Matrix*

If the data model is set up and filled with data, a reporting and analysis tool can be built. Figure 7.3 provides an example of a Microsoft (MS) Power business intelligence (BI) solution for an automated transaction matrix. There are, however, multiple ways to set up something similar.[14]

Figure 7.3 Example Transaction Matrix

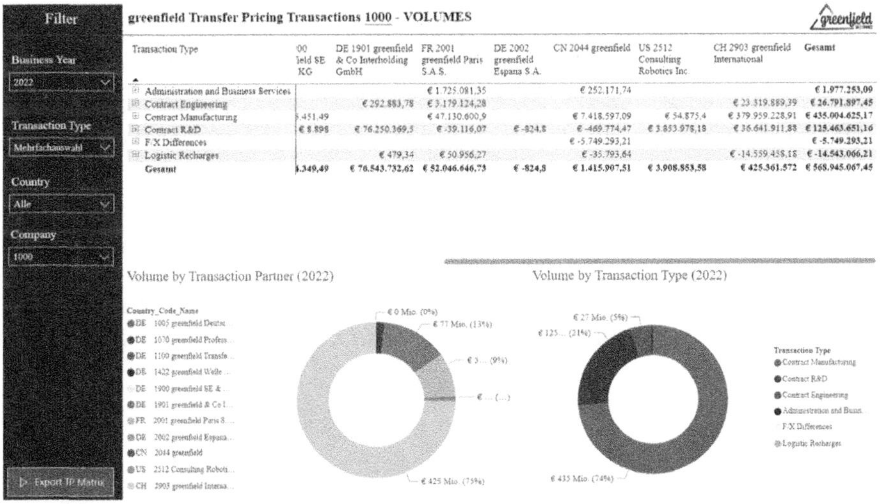

Source: greenfield finance.

14. A similar type of reporting can also be set up directly in SAP using SAP SAC (SAP Analytics Cloud). This allows real-time reporting whereas external reporting tools may require data uploads that only provide information at the given time of the data download from the ERP system.

The sample matrix allows users to identify transaction volumes of a chosen MNE group entity with its transaction partners by transaction type. The data can be filtered by business year, transaction type, country, and reporting company. Doughnut charts visualize the numbers provided in the matrix, and the filtered results can be exported, for instance, into an MS Excel table. From there, the results can be incorporated into the TP documentation. This workflow ensures that the raw ERP transaction data finds its way into the final documentation and reporting for TP purposes.

The transaction matrix should be a standard tool for TP managers as it allows additional compliance management tasks.

Figure 7.4 New Transactions/Volumes

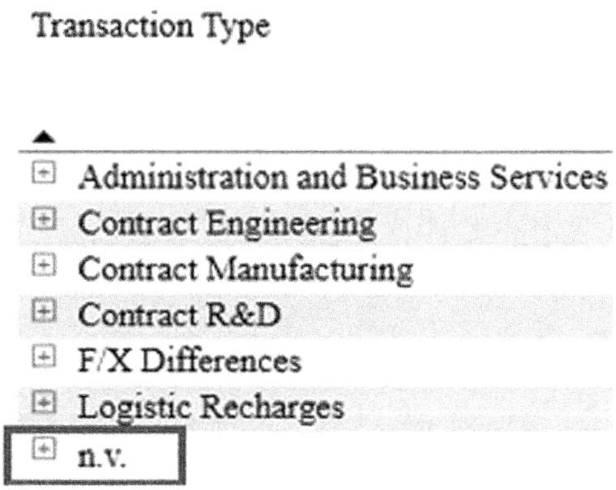

Source: greenfield finance.

Accounting entries relating to intercompany transactions that are not yet considered in the reporting solution are shown in a separate line ('no value'). This helps to identify new transactions that TP managers might not yet be aware of and that are missing in the TP documentation. It also ensures a frequent update of the matrix, as all entries using new tags for existing transactions can also be identified immediately (*see* Figure 7.4).

Figure 7.5 Mouseover Pop-Ups

Transaction Type	DE 1900 greenfield SE & Co. KG	DE 1901 greenfield & Co Interholding GmbH	DE 1908 Bonn Bank GmbH & C
Administration and Business Services			
Contract Engineering		€ 292.883,78	
Contract Manufacturing	€ 5.451,49		
Contract R&D	€ 8.898		
F/X Differences			
Logistic Recharges			
n.v.	€ -890.999,21		
Gesamt	**€ -876.649,72**		

Transaction Type	Neg	Pos
Contract Manufacturing	-544,67 €	5.996,16 €

Transaction Type	Value previous Year	Deviation in %
Contract Manufacturing	€ 6.000,16	-9,14 %

Source: greenfield finance.

What are known as 'mouseover pop-ups' provide details about the transaction volumes, such as credit or debit shares (*see* Figure 7.5). Erroneous entries can be identified, e.g., if it is known that a transaction is only provided but never received. Variances (absolute and %) to previous year volumes provide an immediate impression of significant changes. Those that are significant between two reporting years can also be highlighted with warning signs (*see* Figure 7.6).

Figure 7.6 Warning Signs

Differences in % (2022 versus 2021)

Country_Code_Name	Transaction Type	Difference (%)
FR 2001 greenfield Paris S.A.S.	Contract Engineering	-0.12 ●
FR 2001 greenfield Paris S.A.S.	Contract Manufacturing	-0.07 ●
FR 2001 greenfield Paris S.A.S.	Contract R&D	0.01 ●
FR 2001 greenfield Paris S.A.S.	Logistic Recharges	1.21 ●

Source: greenfield finance.

The above functionalities are only examples of possibilities that data analyses allow. The reporting structures and functionalities can be customized according to the specific users' needs. In any case, they provide an immense improvement under TP risk assessment and compliance aspects. It is a precondition, though, to set up a structured data model in advance. Once again, this requires the close collaboration of the TP, accounting, and controlling departments.

2.1.5 Real-Time Data and Artificial Intelligence

ERP systems, such as SAP S/4HANA, enable the creation of solutions such as the automated transaction matrix within embedded applications. These ERP-embedded solutions directly integrate with the existing system data and ensure real-time functionality. This eliminates the need for time-consuming download and upload tasks, guaranteeing that all insights derived from the solution are based on the most up-to-date information.

Simultaneously, ERP systems are incorporating artificial intelligence (AI) components into their applications. In contrast, the automated transaction matrix in MS Power BI requires users to manually apply filters and settings. With an embedded AI component utilizing natural language processing, users can articulate their queries in everyday language. The system then 'translates' these queries into the necessary filters and settings that offer users a more intuitive experience. This approach eliminates the need for users to possess in-depth knowledge of the solution's design to manually apply filters and settings.

The synergy of real-time data and natural language processing presents a potent and user-friendly support system for TP practitioners.

2.2 Segmentation and Operational TP

Setting up automated preparation of the transaction matrix simplifies the documentation process and reduces the risks of false reports. Yet, the ultimate target of ensuring that MNE group companies' results fall within the arm's length ranges (ALR) determined in advance is not supported by an automated transaction matrix. What is needed to provide this support is a reliable real-time segmentation of the reporting entity's P/L (i.e., all costs attributable to the activity to be analysed in a selected P/L segment). A respective report allows the TP manager to frequently review the outcome of the applied TP parameters (such as intercompany discounts on products' list prices). In the event that results fall outside the predetermined target range, countermeasures can be taken. This is specifically helpful in the case of product sales transactions for which year-end adjustments are not suitable due to their effects on VAT and customs declarations. A real-time segmentation report that allows for countermeasures during the year reduces the need for such adjustments.

The challenge in building a segmentation report is the allocation of costs to the different segments. The transaction matrix can serve as a starting point as the transaction volumes can be considered revenues[15] or (part of the) costs[16] for a

15. In the case that the reporting entity is the provider of the goods or services.
16. In the case that the reporting entity is the recipient of the goods or services.

specific segment. Nevertheless, the whole P/L of the reporting entity must be split into segments. This allows for a reconciliation between the segments for TP purposes and the accounting data. Consequently, segmentation and reporting down to the level of operating profit is preferable even for a function for which an underlying transaction is based on a gross margin (e.g., product sales according to resale minus method), and the arm's length testing is based on the same gross margin. A reconciliation with the accounting data will be possible only if all segments provide the view from net sales to operating profit.

Thus, like the tags needed to build the automated transaction matrix (*see* section 2.1), identifiers are also required to separate the costs into different segments. Direct allocations to specific segments are possible (e.g., costs for internally purchased goods by a sales and service entity) for certain cost categories. Others cannot be allocated directly but need to be split between the segments using appropriate allocation keys (e.g., labour costs of employees involved in activities of more than one segment).

In practice, segmentation work is often done manually in MS Excel. The results may be as appropriate as in any reporting solution. However, the time needed can be immense, and many different versions of the allocation sheets are often produced until the result is available. This makes proper documentation difficult and is a deficiency in terms of processes and compliance. In addition, often only a few people are involved in the segmentation work, and their knowledge is key for appropriate results. If these people leave, a uniform continuation of the segmentation is at risk. An automated solution in the form of a segmentation report is therefore beneficial as it reduces the deficiencies mentioned (*see* Figure 7.7).

Figure 7.7 Segmentation Report

Source: greenfield finance.

Segmentation reports based on the MNE's data model will always be unique to some extent. Segmentation logic must be customized to individual MNE's TP policies and highly depends on the quality and availability of the necessary data. When the required level of detail cannot be found in the ERP data, the reporting solution can work with assumptions and fixed rules regarding the mapping of financial data to the relevant segments. These rules and assumptions must be well documented once agreed with the responsible TP manager.

A custom-built segmentation report is advantageous to companies whose segmentation is built on many assumptions and allocation rules. The conditions for segmenting the financial data are built into the reporting solution and thus cannot be affected by human mistakes. This improves consistency over the entities in scope and over the reporting years. The example in Figure 7.7 is a high-level segmentation of the chosen reporting entity's profit and loss statement (P&L). Information about the revenues, total costs, and earnings before interest and taxes (EBIT) per segment is provided, as well as the resulting key performance indicator (KPI) for the segments. A check is performed to ensure that the sum of the segments matches the total value of the financial statement and warns (e.g., using signal lights) about problems or inconsistencies. The example could be complemented by information on the target benchmarking ranges and details on actual margin deviations from these targets. Risks for potential tax adjustments will be visible and calculable in this case. In the end, a comprehensive 'TP dashboard' can be constructed that provides TP managers with all relevant information at a glance (*see* further aspects in section 2.3).

2.3 TP Dashboard

The transaction matrix and the segmentation report are two important solutions for operational TP managers. Yet, their responsibilities often cover more and demand a continual provision of reports, summaries, and data to multiple stakeholders, including MNE group management, local finance officers, controlling, and tax authorities. The data preparation poses a time-consuming and challenging task, especially when data are irregularly gathered or inadequately structured. In the realm of TP, a lack of control over intercompany operations results in penalties for non-compliance and inadequate or poor documentation but also hinders tax planning and steering possibilities.

In this context, a beneficial tool can be a dashboard that informs about:

- adherence of intercompany transactions to the ALRs and the materiality within non-adjustable periods;
- timely preparation and submission of all three-tier TP documentation elements required by regulations (ensuring compliance);
- forecasted data for budgeting purposes;
- tax impacts at a local level; and
- existence or lack of intercompany contracts in force and their expiry dates (*see also* section 4.2.1).

The following figures present examples of TP dashboard views.

Table 7.4 Arm's Length Check

Co Code	*Transaction Type*									
	Contract Manufacturing	*Sales (LRD)*	*Project – Building Large Public Infrastructure*	*Fully Fledged Production (Complex)*	*R&D Contracted Services*	*Product IP Licensor*	*IC Loan*	*Licensed Production (Project –Automotive)*	*Logistics and Transport Services*	*IC Guarantees*
IN1	arm's length									
FR1		arm's length								
DE1			arm's length							
AT1				arm's length						
US1					adjustment required					
IT1						adjustment required				arm's length
UK1							adjustment required			
NO1								adjustment required		
PL1									0	

Source: greenfield finance.

As mentioned before, the possibility of seeing segmented financial real-time data allows further analyses, such as the identification of transactions that fall outside the targeted ALR. Table 7.4 provides a simplified view of the status of the transactional segmented profit and loss statement per MNE group companies (CO Code) and a reference to the realized PLI (inside/outside the ALR).

Figure 7.8 Risk Radar

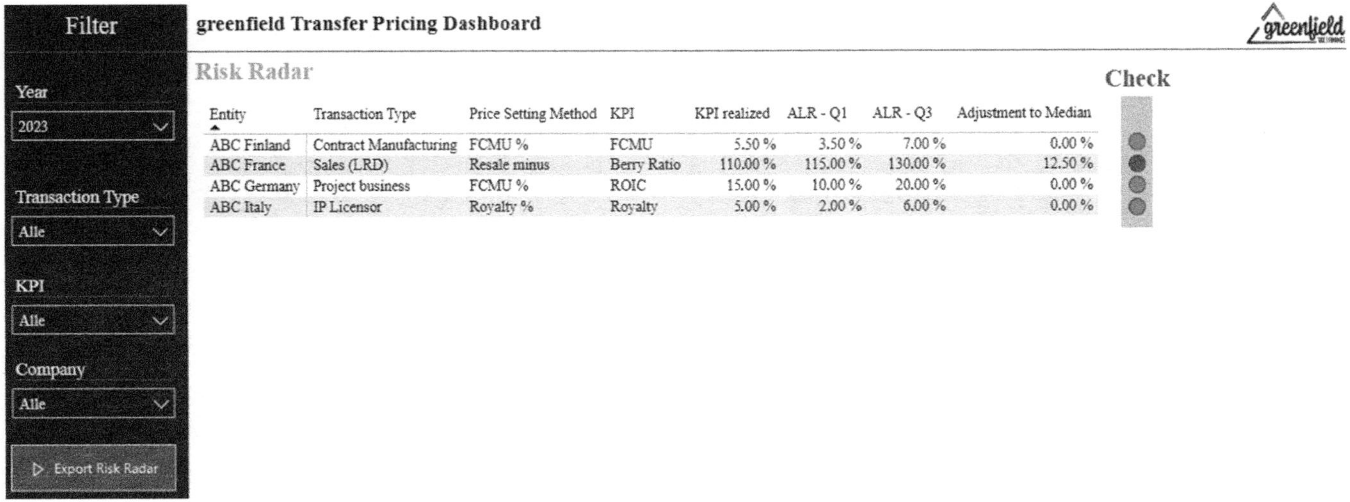

Source: greenfield finance.

Figure 7.8 shows a more detailed *risk radar* that also indicates transactions per entity and their alignment with the ALR. In addition, imminent risks and the level of potential adjustments (in % or as absolute value) can be seen immediately.

Figure 7.9 presents additional examples of TP dashboard items comprising the following charts:

- Local Files status: the chart provides an overview of the local files' preparation status in percentages (dots in the chart) combined with a control system (grey bars indicating days left until the preparation deadline; red bars indicating days the preparations are overdue). The local file status chart requires implementing reporting channels to provide the necessary data.
- Year on Year (YOY) Bridge between Management Service Charge: the chart provides insights regarding the total change (increase or decrease in nominal amounts) of a management service charge year-to-year. This graph is particularly useful when explaining the intercompany charges to the management, local finance responsible, and controlling or tax authorities and can be built upon the data included in the management fee calculation files.
- ALR versus PLI realized: the bars in the chart display the arm's length interquartile ranges for selected transactions. The dots represent realized PLIs per transaction in the selected period. The chart summarizes important information that can be used to monitor the compliance of the actual transaction conduct with the targeted arm's length results. It thereby enables quickly identifying the outliers and performing necessary adjustments when applicable. Implementing a respective report is challenging as it requires robust data including internal and external comparables, profitability data (PLIs realized in the intercompany transactions and unrelated partners), or forecasted data if used for budgeting purposes.
- Cash pool status: the report provides an overview of average daily cash positions in the cash pool. This information is often used for local documentation purposes but also to identify cases for which long term positive or negative positions should be converted into a loan.
- Potential materiality risk from TP audit and number of entities under TP audit - the chart's inner ring shows the number of ongoing tax audits in the MNE group, while the outer ring presents the maximum risk of materiality that may materialize from these TP audits. The information can be used for evaluating tax provisions or reporting to the group management. It requires implementing reporting channels to provide the necessary data.

Figure 7.9 Example of TP Dashboard

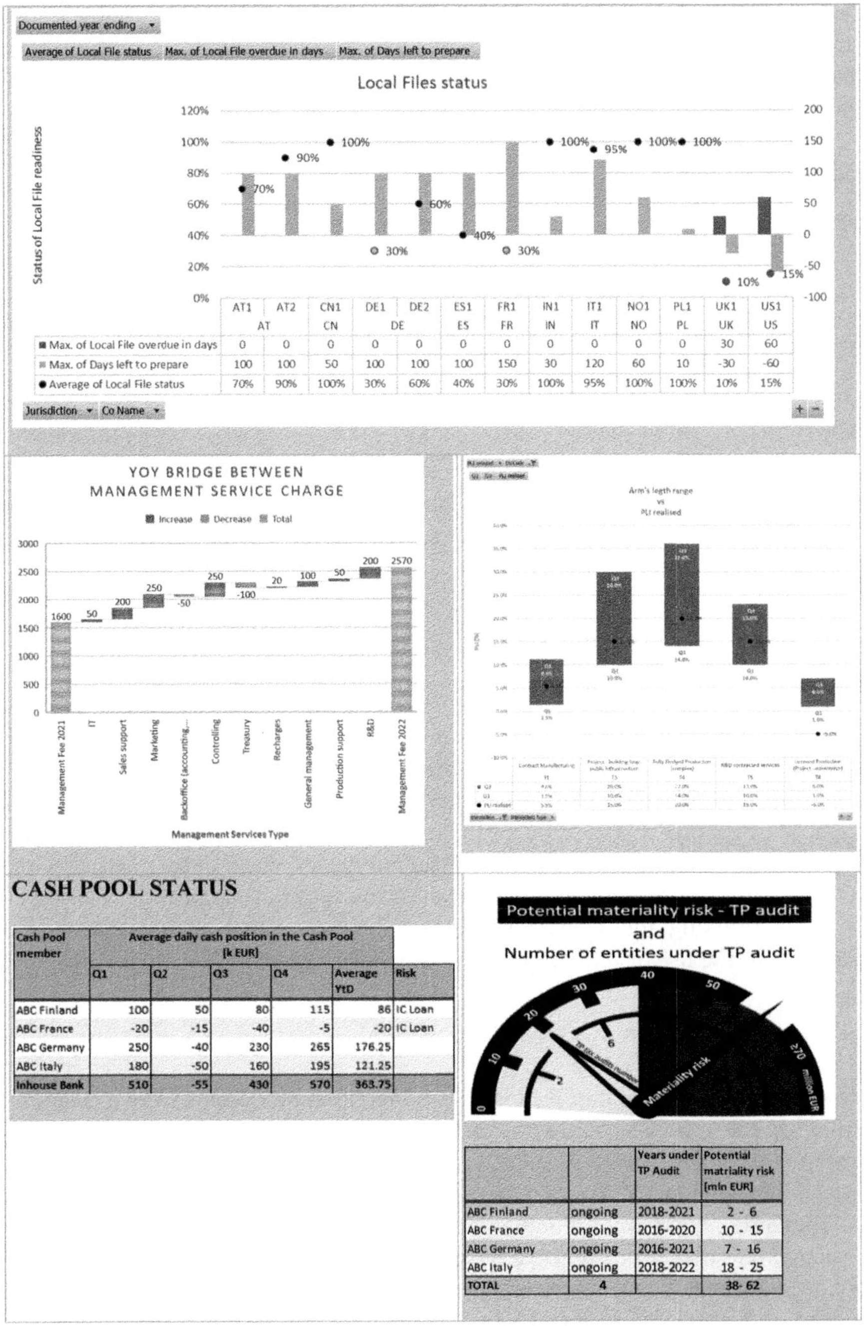

Source: greenfield finance.

It is imperative to note that the examples necessitate the systematic collection of data, ensuring regular or real-time gathering and potential automation or semi-automation via standardized reporting formats within the tax data warehouse. These collected datasets are subject to further analyses through a diverse array of market-available tools or custom BI dashboard solutions responding to the needs of TP managers.

However, each chosen solution warrants a meticulous consideration of its advantages and limitations, including aspects such as:

- capability to archive past period results or overviews;
- user-friendliness for TP personnel;
- flexibility for incorporating, removing, or constructing new overviews;
- additional costs incurred for establishing connections to the data warehouse; and
- contingency plans in the event of service provider disruptions, service lags, or potential data breaches, among other considerations.

Professionals observe a prevalent trend among large MNEs favouring tailored BI solutions, whereas smaller multinational groups often opt for pre-existing solutions in the market, albeit with some compromises regarding deliverables compared to bespoke solutions.

2.4 Benchmarking and AI

Next to the operative challenges effectuated by the need to prepare transaction matrices and segmented P&Ls, a rather simple but time-consuming task is preparing robust benchmarking analyses. Benchmarking results are commonly used to define target results for the routine entities/activities during the financial and TP planning process. They also serve as a scale for the margin controls during the FY. Finally, they are used to document that the outcome of an entity/activity is in accordance with the ALP. Thus, they are an eminent part of the TP routines during an FY.

When thinking about benchmarking analyses, the first decision that must be taken is about the use of internal or external comparable data.

2.4.1 External Data

Preparing external benchmarking analyses is incremental. Coming from a clear understanding of the reporting entity's functional and risk profile and the quantitative database search, the crucial element for a robust study is the qualitative search for comparable companies. The qualitative steps of the analysis include a detailed review of the (potential) comparable companies' functions and risks. Those potential comparable companies that, for instance, are engaged in different functions than the reporting entity, bear another level of risks than the reporting entity, or must be considered to be a part of a group must be excluded from this set of comparable companies. This review process has been manually completed for decades based on publicly available information from mostly the companies' websites. For preparing only one single benchmarking analysis, often hundreds of websites need to be reviewed and scanned for helpful information that allows a judgment on comparability. Websites in different languages must be translated in advance if they are not already published in English. In addition, to compile proper documentation of the comparable companies' selection process, screenshots of their websites must be made and documented. This all means a significant amount of manual 'copy and paste' for the reviewer. Accordingly, preparing a benchmarking analysis usually requires three to five working days.

With its rather simple and repetitive form of work, preparing the benchmarking analysis is an ideal task to be taken over by automating solutions and AI. There are already several providers on the market for respective solutions. All of them focus on reducing the manual repetitive work, especially in the qualitative search steps, by using, e.g., data mining, web scraping, or natural language processing. Comparability factors that can be considered by these technologies include number-based information such as the year of incorporation, financial information, or headcounts. In addition, descriptive texts such as a company's overview, its business description, or market information can be processed. The manual review process gets reduced to verifying the results produced by the software solution. Current use cases show that today's technology-solutions[17] already provide accurate enough results to be adopted as new standards for the way benchmarking analyses are prepared.

2.4.2 Internal Data

While internal data will often provide results that are more robust due to higher comparability, such data must be made available in the first step. This can include agreements with external suppliers and customers, budgets, price calculations, invoices, etc. Such data requires a precise search process, and it cannot be found in one source; thus, TP managers depend on support from other departments. AI can support the identification of potentially useful internal data and, once this occurs, can help sort out the data that can be considered comparable. For example, optical character recognition (OCR) can help in screening invoices for specific article numbers or words. In the same way, agreements can be scanned and searched for certain text passages or concrete clauses.[18] However, using AI when searching for internal comparable data seems to be more advanced than using it for identifying external data. A considerable aspect in this regard is that the standards (acceptance criteria) for internal comparable data seem to be higher than for external ones.

17. Examples of solution providers around automated benchmarking analyses are tpbenchmark from TAXMODEL, solutions from TP Qube, Transfer Pricing Benchmarking Database from Intra Pricing Solutions, Automated Benchmarking by Exactera, Benchmarking Studies from arm'slength.ai, etc.
18. The SAP also provides multiple opportunities (i.e., fields ready to use) to later automatically pull out contractual terms helping to identify internal comparables for the TP analysis such as payment terms, volume-based discounts, market, etc.

3 TP DOCUMENTATION

3.1 Documentation Tool

For numerous years, TP documentation primarily served compliance purposes. However, the amalgamation of AI advancements with electronic data reporting and extensive storage capabilities has transformed the landscape and empowers both tax authorities and taxpayers to effectively manage the shared information.

This transformation significantly impacts the realm of TP in which data reported through the three-tiered documentation package (specifically the CbCR, master file, and local files) can now be not only compared but also subjected to detailed analyses. Tax authorities have begun using AI tools to identify inconsistencies or conflicting information, thereby potentially unveiling an inaccurate portrayal of intercompany arrangements and misleading disclosures.

Therefore, it is highly advisable to integrate reconciliations and checks into standardized TP internal audit procedures. This proactive approach aims to prevent potential consequences and facilitates applying corrective measures if deemed necessary in advance.

Table 7.5 illustrates specific information and data that can already undergo comparison based on the three-tiered TP documentation package. They aim to identify the crucial data elements requiring careful consideration and/or potential automation during the preparation of the documentation package to ensure an aligned presentation of the information.

Table 7.5 Three-Tiered Documentation

OECD CbCR			*Information also Stated in Master File*	*Information also Stated in Local File*
Table 2. List of all the Constituent Entities of the MNE group included in each aggregation per tax jurisdiction	Name of the MNE group:		☒	☒
	FY concerned:		☒	☒
	Tax Jurisdiction			
	Constituent Entities Resident in the Tax Jurisdiction		☒	☒
	Tax jurisdiction of organization or incorporation if different from tax jurisdiction of residence			☒ PEs
	Local TIN (tax identification number)			☒
	Postcode			☒
	City			☒
	Main Business Activity(ies)	Research and Development	☒	☒
		Holding or Managing Intellectual Property	☒	☒
		Purchasing or Procurement	☒	☒
		Manufacturing or Production	☒	☒
		Sales, Marketing or Distribution	☒	☒
		Administrative, Management or Support Services	☒	☒
		Provision of Services to Unrelated Parties	☒	☒
		Internal Group Finance	☒	☒
		Regulated Financial Services		☒
		Insurance		☒
		Holding Shares or Other Equity Instruments		☒
		Dormant		☒
		Other		☒
Table 3. Additional Information	Name of the MNE group:			
	FY concerned:			
	Tax Jurisdiction			
	Constituent Entities Resident in the Tax Jurisdiction			
	Additional Information		☒	☒ PEs, restructurings

OECD CbCR			*Information also Stated in Master File*	*Information also Stated in Local File*
Table 1. Overview of allocation of income, taxes, and business activities by tax jurisdiction	Tax Jurisdiction		☒	☒
	Revenues	Unrelated Party		☒
		Related Party		☒
		Total		☒
	Profit (Loss) before Income Tax			
	Income Tax Paid (on Cash Basis)			
	Income Tax Accrued – Current Year			
	Stated Capital			
	Accumulated Earnings			
	Number of Employees			☒
	Tangible Assets other than Cash and Cash Equivalents			

Source: greenfield finance.

OECD Master File		*Information also Stated in CbCR*	*Information also Stated in Local File*
Organizational structure	Chart illustrating the MNE's legal and ownership structure and geographical location of operating entities.	☒	☒
Description of MNE's business(es)	General written description of the MNE's business, including:		☒
	Important drivers of business profit		☒
	A description of the **supply chain** for the group's largest products or service offerings by turnover plus any other products and/or services amounting to **more than 5% of the group turnover**. The required description could take the form of a chart or diagram;		
	A description of the **main geographic markets for the group's products and services** that are referred to in § 2.b;		☒

OECD Master File		*Information also Stated in CbCR*	*Information also Stated in Local File*
	A list and brief description of **important service arrangements between members of MNE group,** other than research and development (R&D) services, **including description of the capabilities of principal locations providing important services and TP policies for allocating services costs and determining prices to be paid for intra-group services;**		☒
	A brief written **functional analysis describing the principal contributions to the value creation by individual entities within the group**, i.e. key functions performed, important risks assumed, and important assets used;	☒	☒
	A description of **important business restructuring transactions**, acquisitions and divestitures occurring during the FY.	☒	☒
MNE's intangibles (as defined in Chapter VI)	A general description of the MNE's **overall strategy for the development, ownership, and exploitation of intangibles, including location of principal R&D facilities and location of R&D management**.		☒
	A **list of intangibles** or **groups of intangibles** of the MNE group that are important for TP purposes and **which entities legally own them.**		☒
	A list of **important agreements** among identified associated enterprises **related to intangibles**, including **cost contribution arrangements**, principal **research service arrangements** and **licence agreements**.		☒
	A general description of the **group's TP policies related to R&D and intangibles**.		☒
	A general description of any **important transfers of interests in intangibles among associated enterprises** during the FY concerned, including the entities, countries, and compensation involved.	☒	☒

OECD Master File		*Information also Stated in CbCR*	*Information also Stated in Local File*
MNE's intercompany financial activities	A general **description of how the group is financed,** including important financing arrangements with unrelated lenders.		
	The identification of any **members of the MNE group that provide a central financing function for the group**, including the country under whose laws the entity is organized and the place of effective management of such entities.		
	A general description of the MNE's **general TP policies related to financing arrangements** between associated enterprises.		☒
MNE's financial and tax positions	The MNE's **annual consolidated financial statement** for the FY concerned if otherwise prepared for financial reporting, regulatory, internal management, tax, or other purposes.	☒	
	A list and **brief description of** the MNE's **existing unilateral advance pricing agreements (APAs)** and **other tax rulings related to the allocation of income among countries**.		☒

Source: greenfield finance.

OECD Local File			*Information also Stated in CbCR*	*Information also Stated in Master File*	*Information also Stated in Benchmark*
Local entity	Capital structure and legal ownership structure of the local business			☒	
	A description of:	the management structure of the local entity,			
		a local organization chart, and			

OECD Local File			*Information also Stated in CbCR*	*Information also Stated in Master File*	*Information also Stated in Benchmark*
		a description of the individuals to whom local management reports and the country(ies) in which such individuals maintain their principal offices.			
	A detailed description of the business:			☒	
		and business strategy pursued by the local entity, including:			
		an indication whether the local entity has been involved in or affected by **business restructurings or intangibles transfers** in the present or immediately past year and an explanation of those aspects of such transactions affecting the local entity.	☒	☒	
	Key competitors				
Controlled transactions	For each material category of controlled transactions in which the entity is involved, provide the following information:				
		A description of the material, controlled transactions (e.g. procurement of manufacturing services, purchase of goods, provision of services, loans, financial and performance guarantees, licences of intangibles, etc.) and the context in which such transactions take place	☒	☒	☒

OECD Local File			*Information also Stated in CbCR*	*Information also Stated in Master File*	*Information also Stated in Benchmark*
		The amount of intra-group payments and receipts for each category of controlled transactions involving the local entity (i.e. payments and receipts for products, services, royalties, interest, etc.) broken down by tax jurisdiction of the foreign payor or recipient.	☒	☒ if presented on aggregated level in MF	
		An indication of associated enterprises involved in each category of controlled transactions and the relationship among them.			
		Copies of all material intercompany agreements concluded by the local entity.		☒	
		A detailed comparability and functional analysis of the taxpayer and relevant associated enterprises with respect to each documented category of controlled transactions, including any changes compared to prior years.[1]	☒	☒	☒ functional profile of the tested party
		An indication of the most appropriate TP method regarding the category of transaction and the reasons for selecting that method.			☒

OECD Local File			*Information also Stated in CbCR*	*Information also Stated in Master File*	*Information also Stated in Benchmark*
		An indication of which associated enterprise is selected as the tested party, if applicable, and an explanation of the reasons for this selection.			☒
		A summary of the important assumptions made in applying the TP methodology.			☒
		If relevant, an explanation of the reasons for performing a multi-year analysis.			☒
		A list and description of selected comparable uncontrolled transactions (internal or external), if any, and information on relevant financial indicators for independent enterprises relied on in the TP analysis, including a description of the comparable search methodology and the source of such information.			☒
		A description of any comparability adjustments performed and an indication of whether adjustments have been made to the results of the tested party, the comparable uncontrolled transactions, or both.			☒

OECD Local File			*Information also Stated in CbCR*	*Information also Stated in Master File*	*Information also Stated in Benchmark*
		A description of the reasons for concluding that relevant transactions were priced on an arm's length basis based on the application of the selected TP method			
		A summary of financial information used in applying the TP methodology.			
		A copy of existing unilateral and bilateral/multilateral APAs and other tax rulings to which the local tax jurisdiction is not a party, and which are related to controlled transactions described above.			
Financial information	Annual local entity financial accounts for the FY concerned. If audited statements exist, they should be supplied, and if not, existing unaudited statements should be supplied.				
	Information and allocation schedules showing how the financial data used in applying the TP method may be tied to the annual financial statements.				
	Summary schedules of relevant financial data for comparables used in the analysis and the sources from which that data was obtained.			☒ if TP Policy comprising benchmark results is presented	☒ P&L segmentation

Source: greenfield finance.

Within the market, numerous solutions facilitate the digitalization and/or automation of the three-tiered TP documentation. Yet, to effectively reconcile, compare, or detect inconsistencies within the three-tiered TP documentation package, it is crucial to assess whether these readily available solutions support critical requirements[19] (such as but not limited to):

- reconciling the aggregated transactional data reported in the CbCR with the master file and local files (requiring multiple entries for a single transaction, i.e., statutory transaction value in local currency and group GAAP transaction value in group currency);
- preparing the local file for a fiscal period different than the group reporting period (and respective multiple transactional entries to be further able to reconcile these transactional data with the group documentation or intercompany local counterpart);
- possibility to present numerical data supporting the functional profile of the local entity (e.g., percentage of intercompany sales versus sales realized from external customers and percentage of intercompany costs versus costs of purchases made from external suppliers – both depicting to what extent the local entity is affected by the intercompany arrangements);
- verifying inconsistencies stated in the functional profiles in the CbCR, master file and local files or between local files of different parties to the same transaction;
- control over appendices (e.g., lack of intercompany agreements or benchmark appended, effective dates in the intercompany agreement);
- possibility to use AI for descriptive parts of the documentation (e.g., industry analysis, summary of the benchmark studies, etc.) or for analytical aspects (e.g., functional profile, conclusions over arm's length character of a transaction based on the transactional data, i.e., PLI realized and benchmarked range);
- possibility to create comparability studies using internal comparables and respective TP adjustments (requiring a connection to management reporting tools or alternatively warehousing all data – not only intercompany-related data);
- flexibility in the presentation manner (e.g., building tables, graphs, or process flows in the descriptive parts);
- reconciliation or automated graphical presentation of the intercompany supply chain of the group;
- value chain analysis presentation, i.e., attributing respective value chain parts to functional profiles of the local entities; and
- possibility to more broadly use CbCR and other TP data, e.g., Pillar Two.

19. The list represents an idealized collection of requirements that would help bring operational TP to a next level.

AI tools such as ChatGPT revolutionize the possibilities to automate (descriptive) parts of the documentation and are genuinely an added value when automatically embedded into a tool employed to prepare comprehensive TP documentation. However, expanding existing documentation tools or connecting them to multiple AI tools is often not possible or enabled.

Hence, it is crucial to acknowledge that tailored, customized reports and dashboards can fulfil most of these requirements by utilizing standard technologies/approaches commonly employed by most MNEs such as business intelligence, MS Power BI, ChatGPT, or MS Sharepoint (enabling, for example, intercompany contracts reconciliation and management)[20] and comprehensive data warehouses.

3.2 Industry Analysis

The industry analysis is a standard component of the TP documentation. It critically examines the conditions under which an MNE is conducting its business by evaluating general economic circumstances, the specific market situation, the competitive environment, main customers or industries, general trends, etc. A comprehensive industry analysis establishes the framework for the economic analysis of the transfer prices. Up to now, it has been created manually for a certain year – often further developing existing information included in respective annual reports.

New technology solutions, such as large language models, change the way industry analyses will be prepared in the future. Solutions like Perplexity AI or ChatGPT provide opportunities to create this part of the TP documentation automatically. Publicly available sources can be incorporated into the results as the solutions are able to reference up-to-date information from the internet.[21]

Results can be improved when available solutions are enriched with dedicated background information and training material such as a template structuring or already known industry information, e.g., from the group's annual report. With that, large language models will not only provide sound starting points when writing industry analyses but will also be able to provide almost complete results. Yet, sources and statements must always be checked for credibility and accuracy, and the result should be consistent with annual statutory local management reports and the group consolidated financial statements that often include multiple comments or statements regarding the business sector and the market or industry.

Including this technology in available TP documentation tools will be the next step to further enhance best practice automated documentation solutions.[22]

20. For more details, please refer to s. 5.2.
21. As mentioned in s. 3, alignment of data and information is incredibly important. Public information on general economics used by AI tools should therefore be reconciled with other information provided, e.g., in the annual reports.
22. Please also refer to s. 3.1.

3.3 Functional and Risk Analysis

The functional and risk analysis (FAR) forms the heart of the TP documentation. It analyses the functions, risks, and assets of an MNE group's different companies and thus provides the basis for determining the entity characterization.

A FAR is included in all TP documentation (master file and local file) and should, therefore, be carried out/verified on an annual basis. It can be observed in practice that a solid FAR is performed only once when the TP documentation concept is set up. Primarily in the years after, the description of the functions, risks, and assets remains unchanged in the documentation. Performing a solid FAR or verifying that its results are still appropriate requires a detailed debate with the stakeholders of the activities along the value chain. Automation can help shorten and simplify this task.

A possible starting point can be a high-level determination of the reporting company's functions based on its financial information. An analysis of the accounts used for postings allows first conclusions.

Table 7.6 FAR Pattern

Entity	*Country*	*R&D*	*Manufacturing*	*Marketing*	*Sales*	*Service*	*Administration*
ABC GER	Germany	X	X	X	X	X	X
ABC FRA	France				X	X	X
ABC ITA	Italy				X	X	X
ABC FIN	Finland	X	X			X	X
ABC SGP	Singapore				X	X	X
ABC CN	China				X	X	X
ABC UK	UK				X	X	X
ABC USA	USA	X		X	X	X	X
ABC SVE	Sweden				X	X	X

Source: greenfield finance.

Table 7.6 shows a high-level FAR pattern. It can be used as the basis for a more detailed FAR. If extensive interviews with the stakeholders were conducted in year one and, thus, a detailed understanding of the functions, risks, and assets is reached, verification of the FAR status can be achieved by sharing questionnaires that seek confirmation about the most critical aspects. This can be supported by tools that are often already available for companies, such as MS Forms.

Results should be gathered, e.g., as MS Excel data, that would thus allow further analysis and easy comparison to previous years.

Figure 7.10 FAR Questionnaire

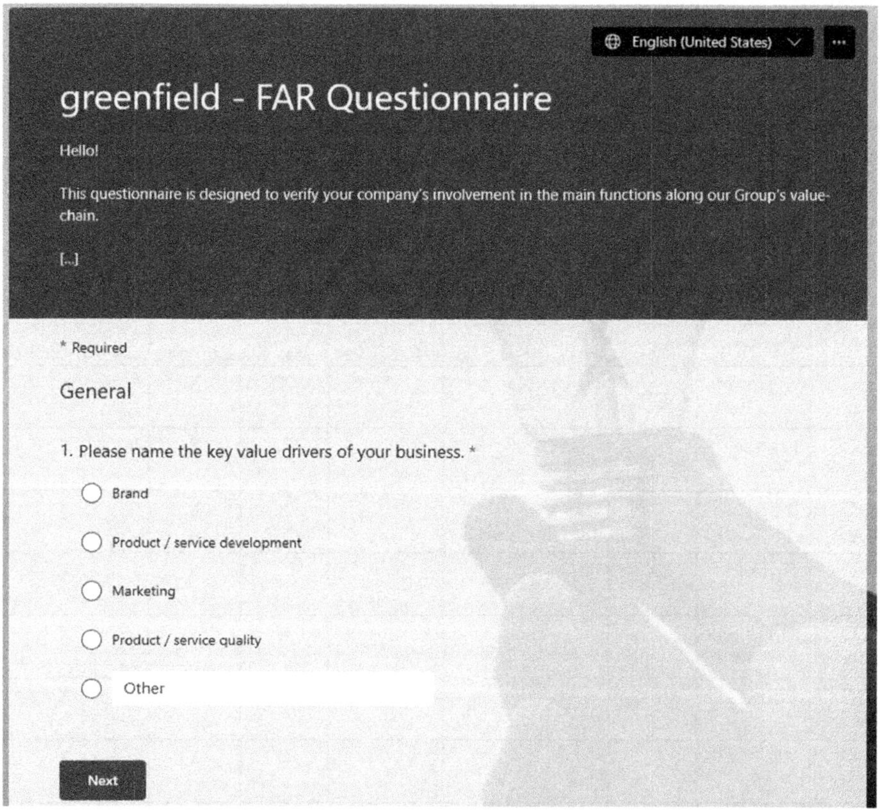

Source: greenfield finance.

Figure 7.10 shows a sample question of a questionnaire built in MS Forms that should be customized for each MNE group. Answers can be given as yes/no, as pre-formulated, as free text, as a ranking (three out of five stars), or even as a date. In addition, it can be decided for each question whether it is a mandatory question or not.

Depending on the type of question (allowing a distinct answer only or being an open question), the results of the questionnaire can be transformed into a written FAR. A distinct answer can be allocated to a specific predefined text. The complete FAR documentation will be built by the sequence of the texts. This solution provides very standardized FAR documentation that does not allow for individual details; however, it consequently ensures that it is written consistently for the entire group.

Alternatively, in the case of open questions, the given answers could be connected to a trained large language model. ChatGPT, for example, allows training for specific use cases. For the FAR documentation, training material could contain existing FAR documentation, literature explaining the relevant aspects, etc. This solution depends significantly on the quality of the given answers but provides the potential for automated but still very individual and detailed FAR documentation.

Certain information gathered with the questionnaire can even allow weighting of a function/asset/risk. For instance, if the MNE group uses a grading system to rank its employees, a question could be to name the highest grade involved in a function. Comparing the grades between different companies involved allows a conclusion about decision making and ultimate responsibilities. Obviously, a critical review will remain necessary in any case.

Nevertheless, the frequent verification of the FAR (by using automated questionnaires) will increase the reliability of the TP documentation and enhance the quality of the MNE group's tax compliance management.

3.4 Country-by-Country Reporting

The Organization for Economic Co-operation and Development (OECD) introduced the CbCR as part of its Base Erosion and Profit Shifting (BEPS) Action Plan. The requirement for it was first established in 2015 as part of Action 13 of the BEPS Project. It aimed to enhance transparency by providing tax authorities with detailed information about the global allocation of income, economic activity, and taxes paid by multinational companies in each jurisdiction where they operate.

As of 2023, MNEs have become well-versed in the CbCR standard. However, due to numerous practical complexities and diverse interpretations related to its practical application, the OECD has augmented the standard with additional guidance through several iterations of the Guidance on the Implementation of CbC Reporting (issued in 2017, 2018, 2019, and 2022)[23] together with clarifications over common errors made by MNEs in preparing them.[24]

In 2023, MNEs encountered novel challenges posed by new regulations, notably the most recent updates released in October 2023 regarding the Minimum Tax Implementation Handbook (Pillar Two).[25] It serves as a nexus between the CbCR and global minimum tax and demands heightened consistency in the locally reported tax

23. OECD, *Guidance on the Implementation of CbC Reporting*, https://www.oecd.org/tax/beps/guidance-on-country-by-country-reporting-beps-action-13.htm (last accessed 3 June 2024).
24. OECD, *Common Errors Made by MNEs in Preparing Country-by-Country Reports*, https://www.oecd.org/tax/beps/common-errors-mnes-cbc-reports.pdf (last accessed 3 June 2024).
25. OECD, *Minimum Tax Implementation Handbook (Pillar Two)*, https://t4.oecd.org/tax/beps/minimum-tax-implementation-handbook-pillar-two.htm (last accessed 3 June 2024).

data of entities within MNEs. Consequently, it necessitates enhanced approaches within corporate tax departments to ensure swift and accurate data collection from their local entities.

Despite the need posed by the Minimum Tax Implementation Handbook (Pillar Two)[26] to automate tax data collection, the majority of central MNE units responsible for preparing the CbCR have not yet implemented automated processes for this purpose.

In the following section, prevalent challenges are outlined that were encountered within MNEs concerning Table 2 of the CbCR: Overview of allocation of income, taxes, and business activities by tax jurisdictions (*see* Table 7.7). They underscore the urgent need for the swift adoption of centralized, automated tax data systems. Additionally, pertinent comments or recommendations concerning tax technology or potential automation opportunities are given.[27]

Table 7.7 Overview of Allocation of Income, Taxes, and Business Activities by Tax Jurisdiction

<table>
<tr><th colspan="2">Table 2 of CbC Report Fields</th><th>Comments</th></tr>
<tr><td colspan="2">Company name</td><td></td></tr>
<tr><td colspan="2">Tax Jurisdiction long</td><td></td></tr>
<tr><td colspan="2">Tax Jurisdiction</td><td></td></tr>
<tr><td rowspan="3">Revenues (CbCR)</td><td>Unrelated Party</td><td rowspan="3">The CbCR guidelines prescribe that revenues encompass all income, inclusive of other operating and financial incomes (contrary to IFRS). Hence, a crucial query emerges concerning the appropriate level of aggregation for this data. This consideration is paramount, given the subsequent need for a detailed breakdown into third-party and intercompany transactions. Ideally, comprehensive identification of revenue or revenue-reducing transactions at every account and business partner level is necessary to precisely fulfil this requirement.
However, practical constraints often arise, particularly when utilizing consolidated data that lack the required granularity of information. Additionally, local entities operating on different ERP systems from the centralized</td></tr>
<tr><td>Related Party</td></tr>
<tr><td>Total</td></tr>
</table>

26. OECD, *Minimum Tax Implementation Handbook (Pillar Two)*, https://t4.oecd.org/tax/beps/minimum-tax-implementation-handbook-pillar-two.htm (last accessed 3 June 2024).
27. Please note that comments were directed solely towards specific data required in Table 2, aiming at the most typical challenges based on the detailed 'Guidance on the Implementation of Country-by-Country Reporting: BEPS Action 13 updated October 2022'.

Table 2 of CbC Report Fields		*Comments*
Revenues (IFRS)	Unrelated Party	one may not furnish such detailed data. Consequently, tax professionals frequently encounter the need to compromise on the granularity and accuracy of reported data, opting to present them at an available aggregation level – such as per primary P&L item per business partner – while omitting the specifics of individual transactions. Interestingly, while the Guidance on the Implementation of CbC Reporting lacks explicit specifications regarding the required aggregation level, tax professionals engaged in digitalization and automation of tax operations recognize the significance of this information. They acknowledge its importance not only for CbCR purposes but also as a critical step forward in Pillar Two reporting and subsequent tax calculations.
	Related Party	
	Total	
	Dividends received	The calculation of profit (loss) before tax necessitates that dividends from constituent entities are excluded from this figure. Therefore, the collection of tax data regarding dividends received becomes imperative to accurately deduct these amounts from the reported profit (loss) before tax. While this step typically follows a routine procedure, its omission could lead to inaccuracies in the reported profit (loss) before tax for CbCR and consequentially affect Pillar Two calculations.
Profit (Loss) before Income Tax		
Income Tax Paid (on Cash Basis)		Another critical piece of information, causing challenges in the absence of granular data (e.g., included in a tax data hub),[28] pertains to income tax paid (on cash basis), often requiring manual collection or additional information from local entities within a multinational group. Why this position in the CbCR is so problematic is explained in the aforementioned guidelines published in 2022, which emphasize that the tax paid during the fiscal period should normally 'include not only advanced payments fulfilling the relevant FY's tax obligation but also payments fulfilling the previous year(s)' tax obligation (e.g., payment of the unpaid balance of corporate income tax accrued in relation to the previous year(s), including payments related to reassessments of previous years), regardless of whether those taxes have been paid under protest. The amount of income tax accrued-current year and income tax paid (on cash basis) should be reported independently'.
Current liabilities for income taxes	+A	
Withholding tax payable	+B	
Income tax receivables	-C	

Table 2 of CbC Report Fields		*Comments*
Withholding tax receivable	-D	The latter means that without transactional data, the professional centrally responsible for the tax reporting is not capable of fulfilling the legal obligations required by CbCR if not supported by additional information from the local entities. Presently, businesses utilizing specific integrated systems can streamline the collection of this tax data by implementing AI solutions or integrating tax coding into dedicated fields. Moreover, local tax returns submitted by entities, combined with AI tools, offer a means to cross-reference and compare the collected tax data with the information reported locally to tax authorities.
Manual correction (if required)	+E	
Income Tax Accrued - Current Year		
Stated Capital		
Accumulated Earnings		
Number of Employees		Another crucial element posing challenges due to the lack of a structured approach, yet not explicitly defined in the aforementioned guidelines, revolves around the inclusion of temporary or intern staff in the count of employees. Additionally, uncertainties arise regarding whether hired personnel should be indicated in terms of headcount or full-time equivalents. Additionally, 'where the financial data of an affiliated entity is reported on a pro-rata basis, the number of employees of the constituent entity should also be reported on a pro-rata basis'.[29] A consistent approach and methodology should be explicitly stated in the comments provided in Table 3 of the CbCR. Regardless of the above stated, again, this information must be readily available (in the tax data hub) otherwise posing uncertainties or necessity to request additional information from the affiliated entities.
Tangible Assets other than Cash and Cash Equivalents		
Assets		
Intangible Assets		
Cash and cash equivalents		
Income Tax IFRS (Pillar Two)		Please note this field creates a bridge towards Pillar Two report

Source: greenfield finance.

28. Please *see* s. 5.1 for more details.

All of the information requiring additional comments to be provided in Table 3 of the CbCR can also be automated based on specific criteria defined in the Guidance on the Implementation of Country-by-Country Reporting: BEPS Action 13, updated October 2022.[29] The considerations concerning the CbCR encapsulate specific issues extensively addressed in the guidance. These concerns tend to amplify in complexity when examined alongside the Minimum Tax Implementation Handbook (Pillar Two),[30] thereby necessitating an evaluation of CbCR fields that become a pivotal factor in the simplified approach and final calculation of the top-up tax.

In addition to the challenges inherent in CbCR reporting, tax professionals continually grapple with monitoring dynamically evolving legal statutory definitions and deadlines associated with CbCR notifications.

4 TP DECLARATIONS

While the transaction matrix, segmentation, documentation, or CbCR are on everyone's radar when thinking about TP, declarations are of limited consideration. Declarations in the sense of this section mean specific forms with TP information that must be provided together with the annual tax declarations in some countries (for the purpose of this article, countries considered are China, Finland, France, India, and Poland). Such TP declarations increase the time pressure for TP managers to gain a comprehensive overview of the TP facts, figures, and circumstances regarding the lapsed FY. Evaluating the transaction volumes, segmenting a company's P&L, or identifying new transactions become urgent tasks after the year-end. TP declarations require TP managers to have a reliable view of these elements that should be harmonized within the entire group so that declared data match each other.

Through TP declarations, tax authorities possess relevant TP data shortly after year-end and way ahead of tax audits. This is advantageous for them when preparing for audits. Cross-checks between the data included in the TP declarations and other transactional data become possible. A key role in this regard is seen in the current developments around ViDA. If tax authorities, like in Italy, receive real-time transactional data (reference is made to e-invoicing), they could be aware of considerable transactions even before the taxpayers' TP managers are. From quantity and quality perspectives (information and data requested), TP declarations are very heterogeneous.

In France, TP information must be provided on the form '2257-SD'. In addition to general information about the taxpayer (such as address, business activities, business year, fiscal agents or customs agents), a description of the general TP policy, the transaction volumes per type, the respective transaction partners' countries, and the underlying TP method must be specified. In Finland (form 78), specific questions about

29. OECD, *Guidance on the Implementation of Country-by-Country Reporting*, https://web-archive.oecd.org/2022-10-17/407167-guidance-on-the-implementation-of-country-by-country-reporting-beps-action-13.pdf (last accessed 3 June 2024).
30. OECD, *The Pillar 2 Rules in a Nutshell*, https://www.oecd.org/tax/beps/pillar-two-model-rules-in-a-nutshell.pdf (last accessed 3 June 2024).

the existence of minimum profitability levels, cost contribution agreements, or transfers of business activities must be provided. 'Form 3CEB' addresses similar questions in India. Information about the internal organization, including names, headcounts, and responsibilities, as well as segmented financial data, must be stated in related party transaction forms (RPT forms) in China, where a total of twenty-two RPT forms must be considered by MNEs.

In Poland, form 'TPR-C' demands detailed information about the taxpayer's intercompany situation, including various financial ratios. Table 7.8 illustrates how its mandatory information already covers most of the information contained in the local file. Thus, Polish tax authorities already have all relevant TP information by the eleventh month after an FY ends when the tax declaration deadline is exhausted.

Table 7.8 TP Information in Declaration (Poland)

OECD Local File		*TPR-C (Poland)*
Local entity management structure and organizational chart		General information
Description of the business and business strategy		Financial indications of the taxpayer
Key competitors		
Description and context of controlled transactions	< -------- >	Type of transactions
Value of payments and receipts of controlled transactions	< -------- >	Value of transactions
Identification of related entities		
Intercompany agreements		
Comparability and FAR	< -------- >	Functional profile of the counterparty
TP method selection	< -------- >	TP method
Tested party selection		
Selected comparables	< -------- >	Summary of benchmarking analysis
	< -------- >	Arm's length price/ profit-level-indicator
Comparability adjustments		
Financial information for TP method	< -------- >	Actual price/ profit-level-indicator
APAs and tax rulings		
Annual financial accounts of the local entity		Information about performed year-end adjustments

Source: greenfield finance.

The increasing amount of information itself that must be filed with tight deadlines after the FY ends is a challenge for MNEs, and tax authorities implementing data analytical technologies increase the likelihood of exposures and TP investigations. Consequently, TP managers' needs for reliable and harmonized real-time data become obvious.[31] Key to addressing the challenges resulting from increasing transparency requirements is improved data quality and availability that can be achieved with a 'single-source-of-truth' concept ('tax data hub') as explained in section 5.1.

5 TP DATA MANAGEMENT

5.1 Tax Data Hub

The previous sections highlighted what is already (and will become even more) important to TP management, which is the standardization and centralization of TP data. Reporting obligations such as transaction volumes, segmented P&Ls, CbC information or even information about functions/risks/assets cover different data points. Yet, they must all fit together. MNEs using different ERP systems face the challenge of identifying these various data points, accessing the information by setting up individual interfaces per ERP system and harmonizing the information. Thus, in any application that works with the information from the ERP systems, a considerable number of interfaces must be established which increases the time and costs for implementing each single application.

A tax data hub is a centralized platform that consolidates and manages diverse TP-related data. It serves as a repository for the information needed to prepare all mandatory reports ('single-source-of-truth'). Figure 7.11 provides an overview of the general architecture of a tax data hub.

31. Rödl, Gu/Zhu, *Watch Out: Related Party Transaction in China* (13 July 2022), https://www.roedl.com/insights/china-transactions-related-party-transfer-pricing (last accessed 3 June 2024).

Figure 7.11 Tax Data Hub Architecture

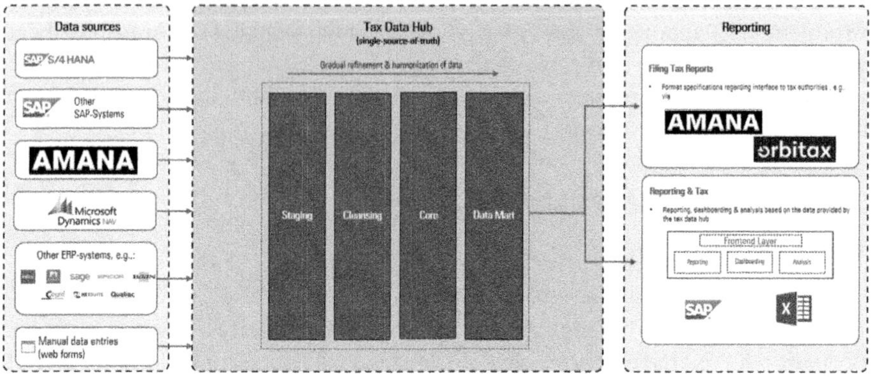

Source: greenfield finance.

While different data sources can be linked to the data hub (data entry), and even a manual upload of information is possible, e.g., via web forms, the data hub itself refines and harmonizes the data being uploaded. This happens in four steps:

(1) Staging
The staging step ensures that all relevant data is available by storing the information from the source systems in an unmodified form. Accordingly, the data hub documents the unmodified raw data and thereby allows backtracking of the reporting information to its starting point.

(2) Cleansing
The raw data made accessible in the staging step is modified in the cleansing step. Modifications include correcting errors, plausibility checks, and transforming the data into the data model needed for the different reporting solutions that are linked to the data hub (data exit).

(3) Core
The data hub core stores all data objects and attributes. This includes the history of the data and its harmonization (what was the starting data, when was this data uploaded, from where was the data uploaded, what changes were made and when, and what is the final data). Within the core, also comprehensive computations can be applied.

(4) Data mart
Data marts can be defined for the different use cases of the data hub, i.e., the different reporting applications that will use the data from the hub (e.g., transaction matrix, CbCR, Pillar Two, etc.). Each data mart selects the data from the core that is relevant for its purposes. This data is then edited according to the respective topic and made available for the reporting solution linked to the 'data exit' of the data hub.

Reporting applications that use the data of the data hub can comprise third-party software providers that support the MNE in complying with its declaration obligations. The data can also be used to simplify and streamline internal reporting, such as the TP dashboard (*see* section 2.3), or to provide data that needs to be reflected in other internal processes. An obvious but complex example is Pillar Two for which its calculations require extensive information from all MNE groups' entities. The required data will likely be found in a bundle of different source systems and will only be available if substantial steps of the year-end closing were already made. The Pillar Two calculations themselves could be done in the data hub but will probably be run by an external software solution and can be pushed back into the data hub. As the results of these calculations (especially qualified domestic minimum top-up taxes) must be reflected in the year-end accounts before their finalization, the data hub can serve as an information source even for this internal process.

The architecture of a data hub can be described as a layer concept (*see* Figure 7.12). It is not required to identify and define all use cases for the data hub before setting it up. Instead, once the technical infrastructure of the data hub is available, it can be filled with case-by-case data.

Figure 7.12 Tax Data Hub – Layer Concept

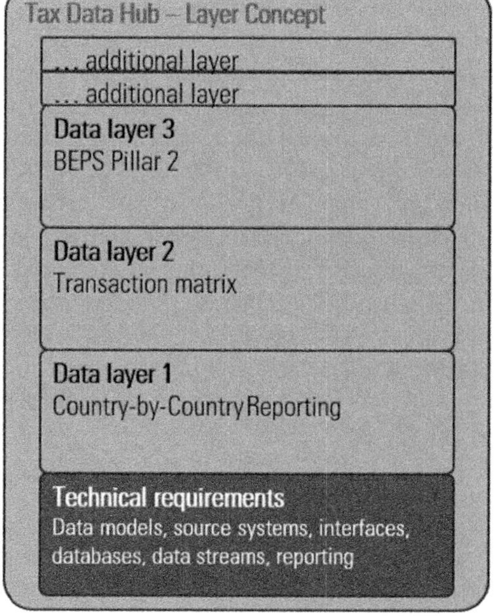

Source: greenfield finance.

The layer concept allows a flexible and scalable use of the data hub. It is a powerful tool in the evolving tax and TP landscape and supports transparency and efficiency.

In section 2.1.5, the combination of real-time data and AI in the form of natural language processing was explained. Applying this combination to relevant TP data from one data hub will increase the benefits even further.

5.2 Intercompany Contract Management

Next to the operational aspects illustrated in the previous sections, intercompany contracts also require appropriate treatment. As part of the three-tiered documentation approach formulated by the OECD, they must be integrated into the local file.[32] Thus, there is a need for having intercompany agreements aligning the contractually agreed terms with the operational behaviours and ensuring an appropriate document management system. The latter will become especially important in the event that the contracts are demanded by tax authorities.

32. OECD (2022), *OECD Transfer Pricing Guidelines for multinational enterprises and Tax Administrations*, Annex II to Ch. V, 546.

Setting up intercompany agreements that support the conduct of intercompany transactions (instead of jeopardizing their own position) requires the consideration of third-party agreements as templates, as well as corporate law and TP expertise.[33] Ideally, MNEs have a dedicated person who manages this task. Templates should be developed for specific transactions that are 'waterproof' in terms of corporate law and their impact on operational TP. In practice, it is often observed that intercompany agreements are written manually in MS Word by copying certain clauses and phrases back and forth from existing or other 'best-practice' documents. Transactions that are similar in nature and operation may, therefore, be based on differently stipulated contracts. In addition, there is often no central document management system, and consequently, intercompany agreements can be found at various places in the MNE group (e.g., legal department, TP department, operational department(s) involved in the transaction).

At the same time, companies are often not aware that they already possess technologies to streamline and simplify handling intercompany agreements. As an example, using metadata in MS Sharepoint is described below.

5.2.1 Intercompany Agreements' Library

Filing documents has been done in customized folder structures for a long time (and it still is for most companies). A TP manager searching for an intercompany agreement must navigate through a path to find the relevant document. For big MNE groups, these have become too long and nested to provide a user-friendly solution. They even bear the risk that documents of the same kind (like intercompany agreements) are saved in more than one folder or that one, and the same document is saved in different folders, depending on its owner or creator. Moreover, to distinguish between similar but not identical documents, proper and comprehensible naming of each individual document is necessary, which is also highly dependent on its creator and not necessarily reasonable for other users.

A possible simplification of this situation (that is also likewise applied by common document management solutions) can be achieved when using the documents' metadata. MS Sharepoint allows establishing libraries and saving documents in them with customized metadata.

33. Exactera, *Intercompany Agreements: What Every Tax Executive Should Know* (11 December 2023) https://exactera.com/resources/intercompany-agreements-what-every-tax-executive-should-know/ (last accessed 3 June 2024).

Figure 7.13 Intercompany Agreements' Library

Name	Changed	Changed by	Business Unit	Contract Type	Status	Signature Date	Expiration Date	ID
Dokument.docx	11.12.2023	Niklas Schwemin	BU ONE	Manufacturing	Template	20.12.2023	30.12.2023	1
Dokument1.docx	08.12.2023	Niklas Schwemin	BU THREE	Service	Signed	14.12.2023	31.12.2023	4
Dokument2.docx	12.12.2023	Niklas Schwemin	BU TWO	Sales	Draft			3
Dokument3.docx	11.12.2023	Niklas Schwemin	BU ONE	Manufacturing	Template	20.12.2023	30.12.2023	5

Source: greenfield finance.

Figure 7.13 illustrates an example of an intercompany agreements' library with categories of metadata for the date the document was changed, the person who made it, the business unit it applies to, the contract type, its status of implementation, its signature date, its expiration date, or its agreement ID. Even though the documents do not have self-explanatory names, the metadata allows the user to identify the agreement that is wanted. The categories mentioned are just examples and can be customized individually according to the users' needs and preferences. It shows, however, that a document management system for intercompany agreements can be built relatively easily. Even if there are hundreds of agreements in the library, a filter function supports identifying the correct one with just a few mouse-clicks. However, as with the raw data for the transaction matrix or the segmentation report, users must develop their individual system and logic to come up with usable tags (categories of metadata) in advance – again, a sound data model is key.

Once the tags are defined and the library is filled with the documents and metadata, it is also possible to create respective reports using these data by, for instance, building a report that highlights the contracts' expiration dates (if this metadata is set up and administered). To support the reporting function, metadata fields can be set as 'mandatory' so that the documents' creators will be asked to provide the respective information.

5.2.2 Intercompany Templates

A second advantage of using MS Sharepoint for managing intercompany agreements is a template function that can be embedded. Intercompany agreements can be created dynamically, making use of the given metadata that can be inserted into a predefined template, e.g., of an intercompany contract manufacturing agreement. This will ensure that each of them that is created contains the same wording as the template. Only the metadata (such as the contracting party, the date of execution, or maybe even the rate of the mark-up to be applied) can be changed by the creator.

Figure 7.14 Example of Metadata Used in Intercompany Agreement

Source: greenfield finance.

Changes of the meta data can either be done in the new document by choosing the relevant entry (*see* Figure 7.14). Another way is to administer this directly in MS Sharepoint. The meta data will be transferred into the document automatically.

Using MS Sharepoint metadata is an easy way to ensure that standard contract templates are used when creating new intercompany agreements. It also supports a user-friendly document management function that even tracks the different versions as well as the changes that are made and by whom. Thus, it is also beneficial from a compliance perspective compared to document management in a folder structure.

6 IMPULSES AND CONCLUSIONS

6.1 ViDA[34] and Transaction Reconciliation

Section 2.1 discussed the benefits of an automated transaction matrix and the ways to identify the data required for this solution. Different approaches using standard functions of ERP systems were mentioned. ERP data must provide answers to the questions 'with whom', 'what kind', and 'how much'. Ultimately, the transaction matrix meets the need of TP managers to be able to reconcile all intercompany invoices with the transaction volumes reported in the TP documentation. The line of reasoning is that each intercompany service exchange is reflected in an intercompany invoice, of which each one is respectively reflected in an accounting entry. The latter creates datasets that can be used to fill the automated transaction matrix. The solution statement is found in the accounting entries that need to be enriched with sufficient information to answer the three questions. In doing so, the information required must be collected from different sources, i.e., various data tables and data fields. These must be linked to each other as only their combination provides the complete and correct answers. Building a data model including these links is a complex task, involves different departments of a company, and the result is responsive to later changes, e.g., concerning the tags used to identify the type of transaction to which a certain entry belongs. Such changes require immediate adoption of the solution/reporting concept for TP. In the case that the changes are not communicated or are communicated too late between all stakeholders, reports will provide erroneous results; thus, alternative approaches are welcome.

In the end, all details needed to compile the transaction matrix are included in the intercompany invoice.[35] This document includes the service recipient (= transaction partner), details about the quantity/scope and kind of the service (= kind of transaction), and the price/fee for the service (= transaction volume).[36] The current discussion surrounding the ViDA initiative permits further considerations as to whether the intercompany invoice could be used as the only source of information for the transaction matrix.

34. Value-added tax in the digital age.
35. Considerations in this section focus on outbound invoicing.
36. Invoices contain more information that can be useful for further analyses.

Even though ViDA is only a European-wide initiative, its discussions and conclusions will certainly also influence behaviours in other countries. One discussion point is the introduction of common standardized digital reporting requirements (DRR) along with electronic invoicing (e-invoice) for intra-community transactions. The DRR encompasses data points that must be filled with information to produce a valid e-invoice. Like the customized data fields in the SAP for tax tags, the DRR allows for additional, individual data points regarding the e-invoice format. Assuming a given 'TP-nomenclature' and using the possibility of additional data points, each invoice could carry a TP tag that indicates that the invoice is TP relevant (i.e., that it is an intercompany invoice) and potentially even what kind of transaction it belongs to.

To serve as an immediate approach, the 'TP-nomenclature' could be set up by each MNE group individually. A wider approach would include an EU-wide/global TP-nomenclature. This becomes specifically interesting because implementing an e-invoice can be connected to the reporting obligation towards tax authorities. For instance, in Italy, a real-time reporting obligation for B2B and B2C invoices was implemented on 1 January 2019, for which the invoices that are issued must be pre-approved by the competent tax authority, and only then can they be sent to the recipient.[37] Therefore, the Italian tax authority possesses all information included in the invoice at the moment of the transaction. It is a logical consequence that this data will be used in tax audits in the future. The alignment between data included on and collected from invoices with the data reported in tax declarations, TP documentation, and elsewhere becomes requisite.

Even now, certain intersections should be verified. The CbCR includes information about revenues with related and unrelated parties. Information provided in it should, therefore, correspond with that reported in the transaction matrix/TP documentation and with other information available for tax authorities – such as the information from e-invoices in Italy.

The critical point regarding the use of the e-invoice as a single source of information for the transaction matrix is the question of how it can be ensured that the invoice carries the correct 'TP-nomenclature' referring to the type of intercompany transaction, i.e., a mechanism is needed that ensures that the correct reference is included on the invoice. To move away from the complex identification of a transaction type within the ERP system itself,[38] a tax engine could be a plausible solution. Usually, tax engines are used in the field of VAT to determine the tax code for a transaction based on the given facts of the case. The evaluation of the tax code happens outside the ERP system. The tax engine determines the conditions of the transaction and, as a result, provides the ERP system with the respective tax code. The tax code itself is bound to a certain tax consequence in the ERP system that enables it to apply the correct VAT rates and texts on the invoice. This can theoretically also be applied to identifying the transaction type.

37. Taxback International, https://taxbackinternational.com/country-vat-guides/europe-vat-guides/italy-vat-guide/ (last accessed 3 June 2024).
38. Please *see* s. 2.1 for more details.

As a result, the entire process of identifying transaction partners and TP-relevant transactions, as well as grouping them into the existing transaction types, would be shifted from happening within the ERP system to happening outside it. In addition, the alignment between the TP data with the intercompany invoices and, thereby, with the information that tax authorities will increasingly gather in the future anyway provides another benefit. Should a harmonized 'TP-nomenclature' exist, improvements could also be reached regarding balancing MNE TP information across the countries.

6.2 Conclusions

TP managers face increasing challenges regarding documentation and reporting obligations. Demands for transparency are growing continuously. To ensure compliance of intercompany transactions with the ALP and to limit risks for MNE group companies, real-time data analyses are indispensable. Data quality and availability become a key factor when attempting to respond to these challenges. For TP managers, this means that additional competences must be added to their profiles. A sound understanding of processes has been a requirement for a long time, but this will now be extended by a technical, data-centric component. Understanding the connections between processes, data creation, and data filing, on the one hand, and how to use the data points created in advanced technology solutions, on the other hand, will be necessary to handle the challenges and make the difference between easily being able to prove compliance or not.

The tools and solutions described in this chapter all require the awareness and proper handling of data as such. If an appropriate data basis is established, it can help in dealing with the increasing demands. It will be interesting to observe how (quickly) tax authorities adopt these technological developments.

Index